BRICK BY RED BRICK

Ravi Matthai and the Making of IIM Ahmedabad

BRICK BY RED BRICK

Ravi Matthai and the Making of IIM Ahmedabad

T T Ram Mohan

RUPA

To Anil Deshpande and Suresh Chandrashekhar
friends in need

Contents

Acknowledgements

I am deeply indebted to Prof. Dwijendra Tripathi, a former faculty member of IIMA, for his help. Prof. Tripathi provided me with facts and anecdotes; pointed to useful reference material; and read the entire manuscript – first, as each chapter was being written, and later, when the entire book was completed. On both the occasions, Prof. Tripathi provided invaluable comments and made corrections.

Prof. Tripathi brought alive for me a personality whom I know only through his writings and the accounts of others. He even re-enacted a few dramatic scenes involving Ravi Matthai for my benefit. Prof. Tripathi's enthusiasm for the book never ceased to surprise me. He explained it very simply, 'I am doing it for Ravi.'

Several others contributed to this book in various ways:

My wife, Jayashree, plodded through the manuscript as it was shaping up. She helped me eliminate sections where the telling flagged and simplify the language in many places. She was a pillar of strength to me during the rough patch I went through while working on the book.

My mother, Padmini Vijayaraghavan, and Bhavana Mehta went through two chapters each of my manuscript and confirmed that they made sense.

Mrs Syloo Matthai provided me with detailed notes on Matthai's family background and childhood. Prof. V L Mote, a former faculty member of IIMA, trudged up to my room on the second floor and spent two hours sharing his reminiscences. Prof. Samuel Paul, a former director of IIMA, was kind enough to share his recollections and impressions. So was Prof. G S Gupta, a former faculty member of IIMA.

Prof. T V Rao, a close associate of Matthai and currently adjunct faculty at IIMA, shared many anecdotes and provided valuable background on the Jawaja project. Mr Ashoke Chatterjee, former director of NID, who was associated with the Jawaja project, went through chapter eight and gave detailed comments. Dr C Rangarajan, chairman of Prime Minister's Economic Advisory Council, spared time for an interview and helped me confirm and correct some of my hypotheses.

The late Prof. C K Prahalad agreed to meet me at a short notice while on a visit to Ahmedabad and also responded to my queries over email. Prof. P N Khandwalla, another former director of IIMA, gave me a brief assessment of Matthai's contribution. The IIMA librarian, Anil Kumar, accessed and placed at my disposal all material that he thought would be useful to me. For me, he has long been one of the most valuable resources in the Institute.

Suchitra Ramani kept egging me on whenever I showed signs of slackening.

V K S Nair and U K Harindran, both officers at IIMA, who grew up in the Institute in Matthai's time, provided valuable information and material. K S Venkitadri, a former secretary to Matthai and now settled in Kerala, shared several interesting anecdotes.

Working with the team at Rupa Publications has been a rewarding experience. Sheila Kumar's editing added value and some of the deft changes she made came as a revelation. Kapish Mehra, the proprietor, was unfailingly courteous, helpful and prompt in responding to my communications. Shikha Dimri saw the book through to the final stage with great consideration and diligence.

To all of them, my heartfelt thanks.

Preface

It's the exposed red brick structure that strikes you when you arrive at the old campus of the Indian Institute of Management, Ahmedabad. The tall *Asopalav* trees that stand like sentinels lined up against the fortress-like formations of the student dormitories are another striking feature. The architecture conveys an impression of solidity, of something built to last.

The founding fathers of IIMA did more than create solid buildings. They laid the foundation for IIMA's enduring success. This book is an account of their stupendous efforts, and in particular, of the role of one man – Ravi Matthai – the Institute's first full-time director. It is not a biography of Matthai; it is a story of institution-building in which Matthai is the leading actor. This is my own endeavour. It is not supported by the Institute in any way, except for the facilities I am entitled to as a faculty member.

I had heard of Ravi Matthai when I joined the Institute in late 1998 but did not know much about him. A few months after I had joined, I attended a function to welcome the new batch of students in the two-year post-graduate programme. In a routine address that lasted just about 15 minutes, the then director invoked Matthai thrice. In the first couple of years, I noticed that many of the important processes or initiatives in the Institute were traced back to Matthai's time.

These early impressions – of a larger-than-life figure – stayed with me. One day, I stumbled upon a collection of Matthai's speeches and writings. Going through the papers, I was struck by the quality of his writings. It was evident that this was a man who had thought through the IIMA experiment with great care.

On the occasion of the forty-eighth anniversary of IIMA, I penned a portrait of Matthai in my column in *The Economic Times*. I was touched by the response it evoked. The article seemed to have struck a chord with many people.

Among those who responded was Shreekant Sambrani, a former faculty member of IIMA. Sambrani proposed that we collaborate on a biography of Matthai. I agreed. Thereafter, I did not hear from him. But the idea of a book on Matthai and IIMA had been planted in my mind.

Sometime in 2009, preparations commenced at the Institute for celebrating its golden jubilee (starting in December 2010). I revisited the idea. The timing was perfect. But I hesitated. Did a mere director of a management institution merit a book?

Also, the documentation at the Institute was patchy. But it had preserved on CDs a set of papers of Sarabhai containing letters and memoranda relating to the formative years. I used these to get started. The first two chapters draw heavily on them.

On Matthai's ideas, there was enough material. But I was stuck when it came to chronicling the events in his tenure. I could put together some important happenings by talking to people, but this was far from adequate.

By a stroke of luck, one day, the minutes of the Faculty Council meetings held in Matthai's time landed on my lap, as it were. The minutes were thorough enough to add up to a chronicle of the period. It was just what I needed. Much of chapters 4 and 5 is based on these minutes.

I had been a student at IIMC. During my stay there and also after I joined IIMA, I had often wondered what gave IIMA its premium rating. The three older IIMs – IIMA, IIMB and IIMC – all have access to the same pool of faculty and student talent. All have been handsomely supported by the government. So what was special about IIMA?

To many of us at IIMA, the answer seems obvious enough: IIMA had the benefit of Matthai's leadership whereas the others did not. It was mainly on account of Matthai's leadership that IIMA quickly established itself as the nation's pre-eminent management institution. And it has stayed at the top ever since. In a milieu in which institutions of higher learning seem almost fated to decline with time, this is a noteworthy achievement. How IIMA has been able to manage that is worth studying.

IIMA's strengths are not obvious to a casual observer. The offices and hostel rooms are utilitarian. The faculty may not seem impressive at first sight. There is a deceptive ordinariness about the place.

IIMA grows on you with time. The peer culture, the system of committees, the habit of periodical review, the balance of power between the director and faculty – these are things that one comes to appreciate only after one has been with the Institute for at least five years.

Some of the frequently used expressions in the Institute are: 'process', 'culture', 'institutional values'. They derive from a substratum of attitudes that Sarabhai and Matthai sought to foster in the initial years. When you have been at IIMA for long enough, you begin to understand that this is what institution-building is all about.

After I had commenced work on this book, I passed through a stormy period on both professional and personal fronts. It was difficult to even think straight, much less do any writing. My project stalled. My friends, Anil Deshpande and Suresh Chandrashekhar, would hear nothing of my giving up the idea. 'You have to put your head down and get it done,' they insisted.

Sometime in February 2010, I went back to my manuscript. Quite miraculously, the inspiration returned. In the months that followed, even as Ahmedabad baked in its worst summer in a century, I wrote furiously. The book became a magnificent obsession. There were days when I could not think or talk about anything else. Jayashree and Nandu indulged my enthusiasm, although at times they had to warn me – 'Another word about Matthai and we leave the room.'

Several former faculty members and staff of the Institute helped with their recollections and by pointing to references or contacts. Useful material popped up from nowhere. It was almost as if an unseen hand was orchestrating everything from behind the scenes. By last August, the book was substantially done; by the end of September, I had the offer from Rupa Publications.

Now that the book is out, I lack a sense of accomplishment. I did not write this book. It came to be written.

Note: *I refer throughout to 'Bombay' and 'Calcutta' (instead of 'Mumbai' and 'Kolkata') because these were the names in vogue during the period covered in the book.*

1

The Grand Design

'Ravi who?'

There was bewilderment in the IIMA community when Vikram Sarabhai announced the appointment of Ravi Matthai as the first full-time director of IIMA. Sarabhai had been honorary director for a little over three years since IIMA was founded in December 1961. In 1964, he felt the time had come for him to step aside in favour of a full-time director. The search committee had finally zeroed in on Matthai in 1965.

Matthai was all of 38 years old at the time; I doubt IIMA would consider a person of that age for the post of director even today. He did not have advanced academic qualifications, he had obtained his BA (Hons) from Oxford. He was a recent entrant to academia, having spent a little over a year at IIM, Calcutta, after a decade's experience in industry.

IIMA had already assembled a small group of academics, some of whom had trained at Harvard Business School (HBS). The lady who was in charge of the academic programme at the time was an academic of some stature, had spent time at HBS and was Sarabhai's first choice for the post.

On the face of it, Matthai did not have much going for him. Why on earth had the Board of Governors picked a young man with no major academic accomplishments to speak of, for the post of director? And yet it was to prove one of the great decisions that Sarabhai and his colleagues on the board took.

Over the next seven years, Matthai would go on to put IIMA firmly on the map of India as a centre of academic excellence. Who was this man and how did he get the job? The answers must wait. First, we must step back and delve a bit into IIMA history.

The fifties were a period of institution-building in India. Most of this happened in the public sector, which Prime Minister Jawaharlal Nehru viewed as the principal agent of change in the country. He famously called the giant public enterprises, in defence, steel, irrigation and other areas, the 'temples' of modern India.

Education, especially institutions of higher learning, also came in for attention. In engineering, the government had made a start with the four IITs that were set up, with foreign collaboration. Management education was awaiting a similar initiative.

As a paper prepared by MIT in connection with its collaboration with IIMC was to note:

> ... in India, as in almost all nations except the United States, the idea of professional management education analogous to professional engineering education, is not widely accepted. Here, 'management education' generally connotes, not education for management, but the education of managers.[1]

India then only had schools of commerce which produced clerical rather than managerial personnel. In 1953, the All India Council of Technical Education (AICTE) advised the Government of India that commerce colleges could not meet the needs of industrialisation. It recommended the establishment of an entirely new set of 'management studies' programmes.

The government then created a permanent Board of Management Studies in the Ministry of Education. In the period between 1953-57, seven universities or technological institutes came up to offer part-time post-graduate evening diploma programmes, duly approved by the board. These programmes led to diplomas rather than degrees. They were part-time in nature, except for one programme offered at IIT, Kharagpur, and lacked qualified staff. Many relied heavily on the involvement of practitioners.

Four of these programmes – at the universities of Bombay, Calcutta, Delhi and Madras – were in Business Administration. The remaining three were in Industrial Organisation and were offered by the Indian Institute of Science, Bangalore, IIT Kharagpur and VJTI in Bombay.

The next move forward came in 1957 when the government set up the Administrative Staff College of India (ASCI). Its first Court of Governors included several business and political leaders and was headed by none other than Dr John Matthai, father of Ravi Matthai. (In this book, I will refer to the father as 'Dr Matthai and the son as 'Matthai'). ASCI was modelled on its counterpart in England and got off to a good start. However, it was not able to attract enough students to become self-supporting and it could not gather an adequate number of permanent faculty.

Then, there was the All-India Management Association. It had been conceived as a national management institute but had ended up as a federation of local associations. Its only educational venture was a top management summer programme in Srinagar. The MIT paper, cited above, noted that none of the initiatives in management education until then had a research orientation and the teaching centred around senior management personnel.

The push for a major initiative in management education came from the then representative of the Ford Foundation in India, Douglas Ensminger. As early as in March 1955, Ensminger discussed with officials of the Indian and American governments, the idea of American assistance for Indian management development.

Why American assistance? The MIT paper, referred to above, made the case succinctly:

> ... the unique contribution to be expected from the United States is our experience in the initial preparation of young men for ultimate business enterprise leadership. There is good evidence that, despite the continuing dissatisfaction with the overall quality of business education in this country, our best post-graduate (i.e., Master's degree) programs are eminently successful and have demonstrated beyond any doubt the validity of the professional management for education concept.

The response from both the Indian and American sides to the Ford Foundation initiative was encouraging. This prompted Ensminger to correspond with C N Vakil, then Head of the Economics department at Bombay University, on the subject of creating an institute of management studies. The vice-chancellor of Bombay University at the time was none other than Dr Matthai. Dr Matthai and Vakil both responded favourably to the idea.

In April 1956, the Ford Foundation requested the dean of the Harvard Business School to recommend a team to work on the proposal. Two professors were nominated by HBS, Richard Meriam and Harold Thurlby. They visited Bombay in early 1957 and, on their return, submitted a report of their findings and recommendations.

They recommended the establishment of an institution modelled on the American business school. However, they were careful to suggest that the institute be independent of the university. Clearly, autonomy was part of the design of the IIMs at the very outset.

Precisely for that reason, the Meriam-Thurlby report does not seem to have gone down well with Bombay University. Dr Matthai, who had been favourably disposed towards the project, retired in 1957. Thereafter, for a year or so, the project appeared to be stalled.

The project then revived in mid-1959, following discussions between Ensminger and the new vice-chancellor of Bombay University. A fresh round of correspondence followed. This resulted in one change. The University of California, Los Angeles (UCLA), replaced HBS as a potential collaborator for the proposed venture. In late 1959, Associate Dean George W Robbins of the UCLA visited India and prepared a report titled, 'Recommendations for an All-India Institute of Management.'

The 28-page report outlined the organisational form for the proposed institute, the goals of the proposed institute, its policies and programmes, facilities required and the costs thereof and a three-year programme for development of faculty.

Its main recommendations were:

▶ An all-India institute should be established with support from industry as well as government (the central as well as state governments).

▶ The location of the institute should be decided after taking into account access to resources, presence of varied businesses and an 'environment favourable to vigorous growth and experimentation.'

▶ The institute should be set up as an autonomous society under the Societies Registration Act. The governing board would have representatives from government, business and education.

> ▸ The institute would offer Master's and doctoral programmes and training programmes for managers, and it would engage in research as well.

The report recommended the creation of only one institute to start with, although it did indicate that two or three institutes could come up later. It insisted, however, that until one institute was established and running, scarce resources should not be dissipated over a multiplicity of institutions.

The report considered three forms of organisation for the proposed institute: i. a department of a university; ii. a new autonomous creature of the state; and iii. an autonomous society under the Societies' Registration Act. It recommended the third form and spelt out its reasons at length:

> As a department of a university, the institute would operate in a community of scholars, drawing strength from the other scholars whose disciplines comprise the university. At the same time, it would present the university with difficult problems of policy and administration because of its innovations, its size, its rate of growth, and its special budgetary needs. The resulting stresses may be very serious for the university and would almost certainly retard, if not forestall, the Institute's development.
>
> The second method, by special Act of Parliament, would have the possible advantage of empowering the institute to grant its own degrees but the process of enactment would likely be too slow and uncertain, while the institutional framework would be quite inflexible in practice.
>
> The third method had ample precedent in India and it permits rapid, independent action based upon appropriate collaboration of business, government and education. While it may restrict the types of degrees to be awarded, this method provides ample compensating factors in freedom and flexibility.[2]

Clearly, being part of a university set-up was ruled out – that would cramp the style of the proposed institution. The choice was between methods (ii) and (iii). As a society, the proposed institute would have maximum flexibility but would not have the power to grant a degree. The founding fathers of the Indian Institute of Management, Ahmedabad (IIMA) opted for the creation of a society to start with but wished to graduate towards an autonomous institute created by an Act of Parliament. In the early seventies, they changed their mind. They chose to keep IIMA as a society for reasons we shall make clear in Chapter 5.

Thus, the idea of autonomy, so dear to the IIMs, was enshrined in the two early proposals for a management institute itself, the Meriam-Thurlby report, as well as the Robbins report. However, Robbins was keen that the governing board should have representatives from the government.

He did not think that autonomy meant that the government should be kept out of the governing boards of the proposed IIM. That is an idea that has emanated from the IIM fraternity in more recent years and contributed to the strained relationship between the IIMs and the government.

The report dwelt on the number of students to be admitted over a ten-year period, the criteria for admissions and the evaluation of student performance. It also made detailed recommendations on faculty development. It proposed several methods: hiring faculty with a teaching, corporate or government background and sending them to a US business school for six to eight months; inviting visiting faculty with short and long-term appointments; hiring graduates as research assistants and sending them abroad for a doctorate after a couple of years of work at the Institute; and sending graduates abroad for Master's and doctoral programmes.

IIMA was to stick to the important recommendations made by Robbins with respect to the scope of activities, the organisational form and the participation of government as well as industry. All the methods of faculty development recommended by Robbins came to be followed over the years; the credit for the basic design of IIMA must, indeed, go to Robbins.

The Robbins report was accepted in principle at a meeting of the Planning Commission in December 1959. The Ford Foundation promised financial support. It had taken five years, 1955-1960, for the basic idea to find acceptance. Thereafter, things moved forward rapidly and several crucial decisions were taken in a five-month period, July-November, 1960. There were two significant departures from the recommendations made by the two reports.

Both reports had urged the creation of one management institute, to start with, so that the limited resources available were not dissipated. However, the Ministry of Scientific Research and Cultural Affairs, headed by Humayun Kabir, decided to go in for two Indian Institutes of Management.

What could have prompted the government to override the recommendations of external experts? Perhaps it was felt that at least one out of two might survive. Perhaps it was believed that competition was essential; indeed, one communication from Kabir to Ensminger spoke of 'healthy rivalry' between the two IIMs.[3]

Whatever the reason, the ministry's decision has turned to be a far-sighted one. Five decades on, even seven IIMs are not adequate for India and there isn't any real competition to the three leading IIMs. Starting off with two IIMs was the right thing to do. It was one of those situations where India's much-maligned political and bureaucratic authority showed themselves capable of better judgement than outside experts.

The second crucial departure from the Robbins report had to do with the choice of location. In the early stages of the project, Bombay had seemed the obvious choice for the lone institute recommended. With two institutes now being envisaged, it appeared initially that the locations would be Bombay and Calcutta but by September 1960, Ahmedabad was elbowing Bombay out.

The proposal for an institute at Ahmedabad, it appears, was first made by G L Mehta, earlier Ambassador to the US, and it won out with surprising ease. Several reasons have been given for Ahmedabad's emerging as the surprise choice.

The Maharashtra government was lukewarm towards the idea of providing land and other facilities reasonably close to the city centre. The University of Bombay was not terribly enthusiastic about an autonomous institution that would function outside its purview.

Then, there was the role played by Sarabhai. When Sarabhai got to know that the project had run into heavy weather in Bombay, he sensed an opportunity to move the project from Bombay to Ahmedabad. He got the enthusiastic support of both the state governments, which promised land, and of local businessmen who promised financial support for the building.

It is hard to judge how much of a difference these factors made. The University of Calcutta, too, was opposed to an autonomous institution outside its purview and there was little enthusiasm amongst the business community in Calcutta but that did not prevent an IIM from coming up there.

There could be a more prosaic explanation. Calcutta and Ahmedabad both had powerful sponsors in Delhi. Kabir, the minister, was a Bengali and M S Thacker, the secretary in his department, was a Gujarati.[4] The Ahmedabad lobby, as I have mentioned, had other influential backers in G L Mehta and Sarabhai.

It is interesting that the Ford Foundation quickly came round to accepting both the departures from the original plan – the idea of two IIMs instead of one and of locations other than Bombay. It is even more interesting to note that in proposing the setting up of an IIM, the Foundation chose to disregard the views of two eminent academics whom it had consulted. (One of them was the celebrated management professor, Herbert Simon of Carnegie Institute of Technology.) The academics were against the very setting up of an IIM; they cautioned that an institute in India modelled on the American business school was 'at best a relatively high-risk venture.'[5]

Just think of it. Two American experts did not want an IIM in the first place. Two reports, again the work of American experts, wanted only one IIM to be created. Yet, the government, with the support of the Ford Foundation, went ahead with the setting up of two IIMs. This does suggest that the creation of institutions cannot always be the result of rigorous reasoning. Like many great acts of creation, it is often guided by a strongly felt intuition. As Ravi Matthai once put it, 'The building of an educational institution is often an act of faith...'[6]

The initiative taken by the Ford Foundation in the setting up of the IIMs is well known to those in the IIM fraternity and has been chronicled, too. What is not as known is the role played by the Department of Company Affairs (then part of the Ministry of Finance) in creating a certain receptivity in the government to the idea of IIMs.[7]

In 1960, the department nominated S K Bhattacharyya, then corporate finance advisor in the department, to a team of management and accounting professionals headed by Minoo Rustomji, finance director of Telco (today's Tata Motors), to study the management and financial practices in the UK, Europe and USA. (Bhattacharyya was later to become one of IIMA's well-known faculty members).

Box 1.1: Institutions are not always planned, they just happen

It is interesting to examine the planning process by which the two IIMs came into being. We have the benefit of a detailed evaluation by four experts, three of whom were actively involved with the projects.[8] The evaluation takes up three questions. How good was the planning? How good was the implementation of the plans? How favourable were the outcomes?

The evaluation identifies 19 aspects of any planning for institution-building. Of these, nine aspects were carefully considered by IIMA and eight by IIMC. Seven aspects at IIMA and eight at IIMC were largely ignored, three were considered but insufficiently. It appears that the planning for the two IIMs was of indifferent quality.

As for implementation, eight aspects were fully implemented at IIMA and five at IIMC. Again, the implementation of plans was not very successful. Taking the two IIMs together, 15 out of a total of 38 outcomes were judged to be favourable. Thus, neither the planning nor the implementation of the IIMs adhered to the management text nor were the outcomes as successful as theorists would like.

How do we reconcile these conclusions with the general perception that the two IIMs got off to a good start? The authors provide the answer. Institution-building is not necessarily a process of following a particular sequence of steps or conforming to a set of pre-conceived outcomes. It is a creative process in which the results can be favourable, provided conditions exist for creativity to flourish.

The two IIMs managed to obtain a degree of freedom from external constraints and they also managed to bring together some creative people. So they achieved a fair degree of success without any meticulous planning or implementation. In institution-building, freedom and creativity are everything.

As part of the tour, the team visited HBS where it became acquainted with the school's case method of teaching. On his return, Bhattacharyya put up a note to the department's secretary, D L Mazumdar, an ICS officer, making a strong case for setting up management institutions in the country, along the lines of those in the US. Since Indian industry was then dominated by the British and British industry itself was run by people from Oxbridge, Bhattacharyya expected his report to gather dust.

He was pleasantly surprised when one day, breaking protocol, Mazumdar invited him for a chat to discuss the report. Mazumdar showed great enthusiasm for the idea of management institutions. He agreed that the department should play a catalyst's role in any such effort. However, he felt that he would not be able to push the idea as his relationship with his minister happened to be strained.

Bhattacharyya was to be surprised a second time. Sometime thereafter, Mazumdar sent word Harry Hansen of HBS and Kamla Chowdhry (later to join IIMA) would be going over to meet him. Bhattacharyya should prepare a position paper and join them.

At the meeting, Hansen did not say much other than to make the point that if support from the government and industry was forthcoming, HBS would be happy to provide academic support to an IIM by way of curriculum development, faculty secondment and training of Indian faculty. Mazumdar assured him of support from his side.

Hansen wanted to know whether Indian industry would be willing to employ products of management institutions and provide financial support. Mazumdar guardedly replied that some developmental work would be required but, ultimately, support from industry would depend on the capabilities of the products of the proposed institutions.

Within the government, there was an understanding by now of what management institutions were all about and how they might contribute to these institutions. This must explain why in late 1960, when the proposal for setting up IIMs was mooted, it moved forward as rapidly as it did.

Once Ahmedabad emerged as one of the two locations for the proposed IIMs, four remarkable personalities collaborated to quickly carry forward the idea: Vikram Sarabhai, Kamla Chowdhry, Kasturbhai Lalbhai and Prakash Tandon.

The central figure undoubtedly was **Vikram Sarabhai**, who served as honorary director of IIMA from 1961 to 1965. Scion of a well-known business family, the Sarabhai Group, he is best known as the father of India's space research programme. While undoubtedly a scientist of high calibre – he was awarded the prestigious S S Bhatnagar medal in 1962 – Sarabhai's bigger contribution to the nation was as an institution-builder.

Sarabhai is best known as the founder of the Indian Space Research Organisation (ISRO) in Thiruvananthapuram. He was also the founder or a central figure in an amazing variety of institutions in Ahmedabad: the Physical Research Laboratory (PRL); the Ahmedabad Textiles Industrial Research Association (ATIRA); IIM Ahmedabad; the Community Science Centre in Ahmedabad (now named after him); the Centre for Environmental Planning and Technology (CEPT); the Blind Men's Association, and the Operations Research Group (ORG). After the death of Homi Bhabha, he became chairman of the Atomic Energy Commission in May, 1966.

Sarabhai took his tripos in natural sciences from Cambridge in 1940, worked on cosmic rays under C V Raman at the Indian Institute of Science, Bangalore and went back to Cambridge for his PhD, which he got in 1947. Returning to India, he set up the PRL when he was just 28. He married Mrinalini, a celebrated dancer, in 1942.

Building people was Sarabhai's forte. He had an unusual ability to connect with people at all levels, a way of making them feel at home. People came away energised from a meeting with him.[9]

Tandon has provided us this charming vignette of Sarabhai:

> Vikram was so much essentially an institution builder that I wondered if he could have been a researcher, unless it was that like many of our real researchers, he too went the way of administration. His interest in research overflowed into building an institution around it to encourage the growth of the subject and the men, rather than a personal contribution to the subject and its knowledge. I do not think he added anything himself to physics, industrial research or management – he had not the time – but he widened the horizons in those areas, and of the men who trained and researched in them. It is significant that in the plethora of institutions we have built in India since Independence, his were among the exceptions that flourished: textiles, management, space. Into whatever he built, he also conveyed his own characteristic refinement and excellence, whether a personal relationship, a building, or its landscaping. You could see his hallmark.[10]

Kamla Chowdhry, Sarabhai's friend and companion for many years, was closely involved in conceiving IIMA and seeing through the implementation of the project in the formative years. She had re-built her life following a tragedy.

Chowdhry was a Punjabi who grew up in Lahore. She studied first at Shantiniketan, Rabindranath Tagore's famed university, and then at Calcutta University. At 20, she married a young ICS officer of her choice. Her husband happened to be posted in what is now Pakistan. Barely three months after the marriage, her husband was shot dead. This was sometime in the early 1940s.

We have two versions of what happened. Tandon tells us that her husband happened to be trying someone in his capacity as district magistrate.[11] The man foolishly thought he could escape the sentence by killing the magistrate. Another version has it that the murderer was a fanatical tribesman whose only motive was to kill a Hindu *kafir*.

According to the second version, Chowdhry and her husband were asleep in their dak bungalow garden. It was Diwali and crackers were being burst all through the night. It was only as the night grew chilly and Chowdhry tried to cover herself and her husband with a blanket that she realised that her husband was dead.

The police had no clue as to the killer or his motive. One day, a man was captured with a gang of tribesmen and questioned. He thought he was being asked about the murder and confessed.

The Lahore High Court assigned the task of defending him to a briefless barrister who had got himself empanelled as defence counsel in appeals against death sentences passed by the Sessions Court. The barrister was none other than the well-known writer, Khushwant Singh, to whom we owe the second version.[12] Singh could not do much by way of mounting a defence. The murderer was duly hanged.

Years later, when Chowdhry moved to Delhi after leaving IIMA, she and Singh served on the board of Delhi Public School. They often dined together but right until her death in January 2006, Singh says he could never bring himself to tell Chowdhry that he had defended her husband's murderer.

After her husband's death, Chowdhry joined Lahore University for a Master's in Psychology, then proceeded to Michigan for her doctorate. She joined ATIRA, one of the many institutions that Sarabhai founded, and the two together thought up the IIMA project.

Theirs was no ordinary professional relationship. Tandon gives us a vivid sense of how they complemented each other:

Vikram and Kamla fitted perfectly, like the tenons and mortises of a dovetail. He spoke freely and was projective; she was slow and had to carefully define her thoughts before she expressed them, and then only hesitatingly, withdrawing from each answer. He could think on his feet while her voice dropped when faced with an audience of more than two. He was always advancing while she was withdrawing. She had to feel wholly at ease, almost at a level of intimacy, before she would project; he was at home anywhere. ... I saw Vikram and Kamla together at conferences, and there appeared always a perfect rapport between them professionally, an aura of deep relationship. ... After each day (at an ATIRA conference), Vikram would go to Kamla on his way back from work, and they would together go over the day's discussions and decisions, and plan the next. In the morning, he would drop in for a coffee before he began his day.[13]

Chowdhry had been a contemporary of Sarabhai's wife, Mrinalini, at Shantiniketan in Calcutta and she was readily accepted into the Sarabhai family when she moved to Ahmedabad. Soon, however, a romantic triangle evolved among Sarabhai, Mrinalini and Chowdhry that was to prove stressful for all of them. Chowdhry's proximity to Sarabhai created its own problems at IIMA as well, in the initial years.

Chowdhry joined IIMA at the very inception. She was sent to HBS for the Advanced Management Program in order to get acquainted with HBS's pedagogy and came back and initiated the well-known 3-tier management programme (3-TP) for IIMA. As we shall see in Chapter 2, Sarabhai would have liked Chowdhry to succeed him at IIMA but this did not come about.

Kasturbhai Lalbhai was one of the prominent businessmen of Ahmedabad. He founded Arvind Mills and was a leader of the textile industry in the undivided state of Bombay. He worked closely with the leaders of the independence movement, including Mahatma Gandhi and Sardar Vallabhbhai Patel and is known to have contributed generously to the Congress Party. Nani Palkhivala, the eminent lawyer, has said of him, 'Kasturbhai was among the small band of men who could be called the builders of nations – not merely builders of business or builders of industries.'[14]

Like Sarabhai, Lalbhai was an avid institution builder. ICICI, ATIRA and the Reserve Bank of India were some of the institutions he was actively associated with and to which he made important contributions. He took great interest in promoting education. He was one of the promoters of the Ahmedabad Education Society, which is still active in the field and today runs a business school just across the street from IIMA.

Lalbhai was that rare businessman with the highest commitment to ethics and integrity in business. Stories about his integrity abound. He once prosecuted a close family member for defrauding a charitable trust. When Sardar Patel was about to be jailed for his role in the Salt Satyagraha, he entrusted the Congress Party funds to Lalbhai. Again, when Gandhi wanted to raise funds from Ahmedabad millowners, he chose Lalbhai as the trustee.

Indeed, as business historian Dwijendra Tripathi has noted, Lalbhai acquired a reputation that was 'disproportionate to his business power ... because of his values and ethics.'[15] It is said that if only he had been a little less scrupulous, his business empire would have been even bigger.

Lalbhai was among the businessmen who responded enthusiastically to the idea of locating a management institute in Ahmedabad and also contributed towards the costs of building in the initial stages. He served on the board of IIMA for many years and is known to have been very particular about safeguarding the academic autonomy of the Institute.

Lalbhai quickly found that there was a price to pay for serving on IIMA's board. His board meetings at his own companies typically ended in fifteen minutes. At IIMA board meetings, he found himself spending two to three hours.[16] IIMA's management development in the old campus is named after him.

Prakash Tandon, the first Indian chairman of Hindustan Lever, was a man of many parts. He was a highly respected manager, of course, but also a first-rate writer whose autobiographical trilogy was long regarded as among the best autobiographies to have come out of India along with those of Gandhi, Nehru and Nirad C. Chaudhuri.

After retiring from HLL, Tandon became a manager in the public sector, heading the State Trading Corporation and Punjab National Bank and the National Council for Applied Economic Research (NCAER). He was also a member of several government committees, including one that evolved norms for working capital for banks.

Tandon was amongst the executives and academics invited to a meeting in Bombay in 1957 when Meriam and Thurlby were working on their report on the creation of an institute of management in India.[17] Later, Sarabhai and Chowdhry got him on to the Board of IIMA soon after it was founded. Tandon took over as chairman in 1964 when Jivraj Mehta stepped down after ceasing to be the chief minister of Gujarat.

HBS itself was receptive to Tandon's association with IIMA as he had attended the Advanced Management Program there in 1958. When Chowdhry was finishing her AMP in 1963, HBS invited Tandon to join the discussions on IIMA. Tandon was somebody who could straddle both the managerial and academic worlds comfortably and it was also left to him to oversee the transition from Sarabhai to a rank outsider, Matthai.

In his last year, even as Matthai was delivering the director's address, Tandon passed a small note to the chief guest. 'In a little way I feel I have achieved something – to have left a young successor first in Hindustan Lever and now in Ahmedabad, both barely forty years of age.'

The chief guest 'smiled knowingly; for she herself was a young prime minister.' If you haven't guessed, the chief guest happened to be Indira Gandhi.[18]

Planning for the institute at Ahmedabad now began to proceed at a rapid pace. The Government of India set up a Planning Committee under the chairmanship of Dr Jivraj Mehta, chief minister of Gujarat. It had six other members including Sarabhai, Lalbhai, Isvaran (chief secretary, Government of Gujarat), and Thacker, secretary, Ministry of Scientific Research and Cultural Affairs (the forerunner of the ministry of HRD).

The Planning Committee first met on 29 July, 1961, and went along with Robbins' recommendation that IIMA would focus on teaching and research. It would offer Master's and doctorate programmes. An advertisement for the post of director would be issued at the earliest. A meeting with Robbins was planned for November when he would be in India. Collaboration with UCLA would be explored and Robbins' help in the selection of a director would be sought.

The society for IIMA was registered on 11 December, 1961. As proposed by Dean Robbins, IIMA came to be promoted jointly by the Central Government, the Government of Gujarat and by local businessmen. The relationship between IIMA and the Central Government is governed by a Memorandum of Association (MOA) and Rules, which also outlines the objectives of the Institute and the powers of the Board of Governors, the executive arm of the IIMA society.

The MOA was drawn up by the Planning Committee in consultation with the Central and state governments and has remained unchanged since. It contains provisions that have, in the recent past, been seen as limiting the autonomy of the IIMs; for instance, the government's approval is required for appointment of the director.

The MOA also gives powers to the Central Government, in consultation with the state government, to take over the Institute if it is not satisfied that the Institute is functioning properly. Sarabhai, Thacker and others worked closely in drawing up the MOA.

Over time, the Central Government became the sole provider of funds and its contributions have dwarfed those of the other two promoters. But, on paper, IIMA is accountable directly to the society and is governed by the Board of Governors in which the Central Government has only two out of a total of 25 members.

The director's post was advertised in October 1961. The advertisement mentioned that the Institute was being set up jointly by the Government of India with the assistance of the Government of Gujarat, the Ford Foundation and industry and commerce, and that it would conduct advanced training and carry out research.

Significantly, there was no mention of the post-graduate programme; that was thought of a little later. There were only 25 responses and the quality of applications was far from impressive, to put it mildly. The applicants included an MA in Economics with four years' experience in private firms, a BSc with about two years of technical experience, an intermediate from Andhra University who had spent 20 years in the tobacco industry, and several people in junior positions in industry and government.

Only one academic, a professor with a university department, applied. Some of the applicants did not even think it necessary to state their educational background or their experience. For all the enthusiasm in government and business circles, the idea of a management institute seems to have been rather poorly regarded by the world at large.

The time had come to firm up an American collaborator for IIMA as envisaged in the Robbins report. This turned out to be less easy than might have been hoped for. On the IIMA side, there was some reluctance to go with UCLA when an institution of higher quality such as Harvard might be available. IIMA began to make overtures to HBS. Thacker, the secretary in the ministry, visited HBS while on a visit to the US in April.

These overtures to HBS did not go down well with the Ford Foundation, which had proceeded with the IIMA project on the assumption that UCLA would be the collaborator. John Coleman of the Ford Foundation in India wrote a sharply worded letter to Sarabhai saying that he was 'disturbed' to learn that the idea of UCLA's involvement was yet to be accepted by IIMA.[19]

Coleman said that the decision to involve UCLA had been taken long before Ahmedabad was chosen as the site for one of the IIMs. The only reason for selecting UCLA was that it was a high quality institution and because other quality institutions had too many things on their hands to be able to get involved in the IIMA project. The tone of Coleman's letter was quite abrasive:

> While it would obviously have been desirable to consult the potential 'users' of the school's product, as you have urged, this was simply not possible in this instance. The final site was unchosen, as you know, until just two months ago. The Foundation felt a need long before this to begin the search for an American counterpart group. There was no intention of thrusting anything down anyone's throat; there was only a desire to line up the resources needed to get the job done.

Where you and I have failed most significantly to see eye-to-eye is on the role which this American counterpart is to play in the Indian Institute. I simply do not see that any of the candidates considered for the counterpart role, with the possible exception of Harvard, is characterised by an educational philosophy which sets it off uniquely by itself. (And even Harvard, I am told, is moving away from its complete commitment to one educational approach, the case method.) The key factor for India regarding any such school should not be its distinctive way of doing things, for that way is American-made and not suitable for export. Rather, the key factor is the school's commitment to high quality and meaningful education and research.[20]

Coleman could not have made his position clearer. Sarabhai then wrote to Lalbhai saying that IIMA was faced with a choice: either choose the best partner or go along with what the Ford Foundation had decided on its own. He asked if they could discuss with US ambassador J K Galbraith (a Harvard man), whether any alternative funding source could be explored if the Foundation remained adamant. He also wrote to Thacker, making his own preference explicit:

Harvard, I am sure, would be interested and does not appear to be overcommitted. Most probably its present responsibility in Turkey will end this year or the next. The strange thing is that the Business School was never explicitly asked by the Ford Foundation.

Most people would not dream of passing over an institution like Harvard.[21]

Nevertheless, in June, Sarabhai visited UCLA to pursue the idea of a collaboration. He must have been relieved to find that UCLA had not made up its mind on the project. During the discussions, an alternative proposed by MIT was discussed, which was that a consortium of institutions in the US should assist with the setting up of both IIMA and IIMC.

On 31 January, 1962, a third and crucial meeting of the Planning Committee of IIMA took place. A status report on IIMA prepared for the meeting mentions a significant change in plans: UCLA had declined to collaborate and Mehta had requested Ensminger to find some other collaborator in the US. Discussions with HBS were promptly renewed; HBS was soon to agree.

It is notable how firm Sarabhai was when it came to the choice of a US collaborator, how he stood his ground in the face of pressures from the Ford Foundation and how he managed to rally his board and the Government of India behind him. The Foundation's financial support was crucial, so there were risks to antagonising it or ignoring its counsel. Nevertheless, Sarabhai would not compromise on a matter of principle: it was for IIMA to decide which US school it should collaborate with.

I have devoted considerable space to IIMA's search for a collaborator. With good reason. The collaboration with HBS was crucial to the early success of the Institute. It is interesting to speculate on whether IIMA would be where it is today if UCLA or some other business school had been its collaborator, instead of HBS.

Following the decision to explore the possibility of a collaboration with IIBS, the Ford Foundation arranged for Harry Hansen, a faculty member at HBS, to visit India in the third week of January. Hansen attended meetings of the Planning Committee held in quick succession on 28 January and 31 January, 1962.

Thanks to the Ford Foundation, Hansen had already had group discussions with about 30 people from trade, industry and government in Ahmedabad and Baroda. Hansen had prepared a detailed note on plans for IIMA, which was discussed at the meeting.

The Institute would have three activities: teaching, research and consulting. Teaching would be on three levels: senior executive, junior executive and graduate. The senior executive programme would be launched in January 1963. In late 1963, a junior executive programme would be offered. In 1964, the graduate programme would commence. No mention was made of a doctoral programme although this had been mentioned in the Robbins report.

A director would be appointed but it was advised that the appointment should not be made in haste. Teams of six to eight faculty members from IIMA would be sent to HBS for training every year, over five years. They would get acquainted with the case method and spend about four months each in the Middle Management Programme and on independent studies in fields of their choice.

On their return, they would spend a year developing materials for the graduate programme and perhaps offering a junior executive programme. While the first team was at Harvard, another set of faculty would be recruited, who would spend a year at Ahmedabad, then proceed to Harvard. HBS would assign a programme advisor for two years, who would advise on faculty matters. Land of around 64 acres would be acquired by the Gujarat government to set up a campus for IIMA.

Consequent to this meeting, Hansen prepared a note for the Ford Foundation which was duly forwarded to Sarabhai. After setting out the aims of the proposed institute, Hansen raised some issues about locating the Institute in Ahmedabad. He said Ahmedabad had two big positives: both local industry and the state government were very keen on a management institute, and labour-management relations in Gujarat were healthy.

On the negative side, Hansen noted, Ahmedabad lacked the diversified trade and industrial base, as well as the cosmopolitan culture and recreational opportunities of Bombay, and suggested that this might come in the way of attracting good faculty to the proposed institute. Faculty would have to carry out their research in other places, notably Bombay, and cultivate the necessary relationships for the purpose.

If Bombay were to have its own management institute at a later date, this might diminish the importance of the institute in Ahmedabad. Furthermore, any management institution located in Bombay would be able to avail of the services of visiting businessmen and government leaders as occasional faculty. So, it was necessary for the proposed IIMA to have a presence in Bombay.

One possible solution was to locate a research branch in Bombay. Hansen did not favour this idea because he felt that businessmen in Bombay were unlikely to be satisfied. They were bound to mount pressure for a third institute in Bombay (after the ones in Calcutta and Ahmedabad) and this would worsen problems of getting faculty for the Ahmedabad Institute. Bombay's expectations needed to be addressed more forcefully, Hansen argued. It would not suffice to have a branch in Bombay. Instead, a separate organisation should be created there, called the Bombay Institute of Business Research.

There would thus be two institutes whose activities would be coordinated by joint board membership, and they would have a common director and common academic staff. In addition, the institute in Bombay would have a director for research. The Bombay business community would be asked to provide resources for the building and equipment for the research institute and cover recurring expenses beyond the amount committed by the Central Government.

Hansen further proposed that, after five or seven years when IIMA was on stream, a system of visiting professors from abroad should be established whereby one or two faculty members would be made available every year. The programme advisor should continue to stay in touch with IIMA. The Ford Foundation would pay for HBS faculty visits to India for five years, Indian faculty visits to HBS, and foreign exchange for procuring books for the library.

The grand design for IIMA was finally in place. It would be sponsored by several parties, not just by the Government of India. It would be constituted as an autonomous society. The objectives for the institute had been spelt out. The choice of collaborator had been made. It was now time for implementation – formalising an agreement with HBS, recruiting faculty, training them and launching various programmes.

2

Laying the Foundation

These days, it is not unusual to see television vans parked outside the Kasturbhai Lalbhai Management Development Complex (KLMDC) of IIMA's old campus ever so often. They are there to cover the meeting of the Board of Governors. Images of board members arriving for or leaving after crucial meetings are flashed on tv screens. Mediapersons thrust their mikes in the chairman's face, seeking sound bytes.

The IIMs, especially IIMA, have been in the news in recent years following differences with the Government of India over various issues: the fee for the PGP; creation of extra capacity to accommodate the OBC quota; and, in 2009, because of the problems that arose with the computerised Common Admission Test (CAT).

However, this is a recent phenomenon. The board, which is the operating arm of the IIMA society, has preferred to stay in the background for most of IIMA's history. Board meetings were uneventful and went unnoticed, as they should. The board has 25 members. The Central Government and the state government have two representatives each; then there are representatives of alumni, industry, members of the IIMA society, etc.

The chairman is appointed by the Government of India and holds office for five years. Among those who have been chairmen are: Prakash Tandon, V Krishnamurthy (former chairman of SAIL), Keshub Mahindra (of the Mahindra group of companies),

A P Venkateswaran (former foreign secretary), I G Patel (who had been director of IIMA earlier for two years) and N R Narayana Murthy (chairman of Infosys Technologies).

The board met for the first time in February 1962. It was chaired by the Gujarat chief minister, Jivraj Mehta. Both IIMA and IIMC had the chief ministers of their respective states as chairman when they started. At IIMA, the chief minister quickly made way for a non-political chairman. This was in the heyday of socialism. Neither the Central nor the state government has insisted on having a politician as the chairman of IIMA, any time since.

Among the invitees to the first board meeting was Douglas Ensminger of the Ford Foundation. Prakash Tandon, S L Kirloskar, B K Birla and Navnitlal Shodhan were co-opted as board members.

The board got down to business quickly. The first order of business was to make sure that the necessary funds were in place. The Central Government agreed to give IIMA a grant of up to ₹1.2 million every year. The Government of Gujarat agreed to pay the cost of 65 acres of land (₹2.7 million) in three installments; 40% immediately and the remaining 60% in two installments spread over a year. It was also suggested that local industry contribute around ₹3 million towards building costs.

This tripartite funding arrangement has often been cited to support IIMA's contention in recent years that the institute cannot be said to be a Central Government entity, that it is something of a public-private partnership. But this was only the pattern of funding proposed at the outset; the building cost escalated significantly and the Central Government had to cover the large increase. Over time, the Central Government became the sole provider of funds.

At its first meeting, the board also took several decisions that were to shape the relationship with HBS as well as the character of IIMA.

HBS asked for a say in the selection of director. This would include the opportunity to interview the final candidates for the post. The board declined, saying that action to select a director had already been initiated.

This does not sound a very convincing reason for not letting HBS participate in the selection of the director. It is more likely that the board wanted to define the limits for the collaboration with HBS. It clearly felt that the choice of director was one area that was out of bounds for the foreign partner.

Ensminger said politely that HBS was only interested in ensuring the right type of person was selected as director by the board and did not press the issue any further. (Later, HBS did make itself heard on the choice of the first full-time director; the board could not stick to its earlier position, and was obliged to take HBS' views into account.) HBS also wanted a say in the selection of faculty to be sent for training to HBS. The board readily agreed to this.

The board took another decision with far-reaching consequences. It agreed to Hansen's suggestion that the research and teaching staff of the Institute as well as the director, be permitted to engage in private consulting work subject to certain restrictions and without being required to share fees with the Institute or any other body. M S Thacker, the government representative, objected, saying the Ministry of Finance did not favour private consultation by faculty.

The board stood its ground. It insisted that allowing consultancy by faculty would not merely improve the quality and value of teaching provided by the Institute but also help in establishing close relations between industry and the Institute. The latter, in turn, would encourage the flow of competent people from industry to the Institute for training.

What was perhaps left unsaid was that consulting would help augment faculty income which was subject to government pay scales.

Looking back, it is doubtful whether IIMA could have attracted and retained quality faculty over the years without the lure of consulting possibilities. It is interesting that the board took a strong line on this issue and it is also interesting that the government went along after recording its objection. IIMA's founding fathers did not hesitate to assert the autonomy of the Institute at the very outset.

The board took other decisions. The IIMA society would be registered as a Trust so that it would be eligible for tax-deductible decisions. The award of a degree would be the ultimate objective of the Institute. The board must 'exercise restraint in any powers it exercised over academic activities.'

The board rejected a key proposal made by Hansen, which was to start a separate organisation in Bombay for carrying out research. It felt that IIMA should have an all-India character in order to gain the support of business from all over the country and that it should not be seen to be favouring any particular location outside Ahmedabad. However, the board felt that research centres could be started in Bombay and other places.

The meeting of the Board of Governors was adjourned so that the selection committee for the post of director could meet. Ensminger and Choksi were invited to attend the meeting. The committee decided that there was no suitable candidate from the list of those who had responded to the advertisement. Sarabhai was asked to coordinate the activities of IIMA in an honorary capacity until a director was found. An IAS officer, G C Baveja, deputy secretary with the Government of Gujarat, was appointed officer on special duty.

Sarabhai and Ensminger both felt that no rigid date should be set for the commencement of the MBA programme. It was more important to ensure that faculty was in place first. As Sarabhai put it, 'The quality of the course should take precedence over the timing of it.'[1]

In February 1962, Sarabhai wrote to a private trust, asking for use of their building in the Shahibaug area of the city. He wanted the use of the building up to June 1963 with scope for extension to December 1963. IIMA operated out of these premises until the first campus buildings came up in 1965.

Following the board meeting, it was decided to recruit eight to ten faculty members who would be sent to Harvard by July 1962. IIMA would also appoint research associates and fellows on five-year contracts. On completion of one year's training at HBS, the faculty member would be designated professor or assistant professor.

Faculty would be sought through advertisement, by directly contacting various government organisations in India and through educational advisors at Indian offices in Washington, Bonn and London. In the US, recruitment could be done by Hansen, Chowdhry and Sarabhai during Sarabhai's visit planned for March and April 1962. An advertisement was to be released in April 1962 and initial offers made in May. Hansen could be present for the selection in India.

We hear a great deal of talk these days about the 'faculty crunch' at the IIMs, how the institutes find it difficult to attract faculty because the pay is so poor, how corporate opportunities are so much more attractive, and so on. In the 1960s, when IIMA was being set up, there wasn't a large pool of faculty that the new institution could tap, the terms were not attractive and IIMA lacked the advantages that go with having a reputation.

And yet, Sarabhai and others found ways to tackle the problem. If highly trained faculty members were not available, then people who had the potential to flower into academics would be selected and sent abroad for training. IIMA would scout around the US and other foreign countries for Indians who might be interested in working in India. Sarabhai and his team had little going for them apart from zeal and determination. It worked. In about two years' time, IIMA was able to put in place a sizeable enough faculty to start the MBA programme.

In May 1962, HBS took a formal decision to collaborate with IIMA. This was an epochal event. There are B-schools and B-schools. The rankings of the top schools tend to fluctuate from one year to the next. In some years and some rankings, HBS may be No 1. In other years and other rankings, it may be ranked lower. But these fluctuations mean little. HBS retains its mystique in the B-school fraternity.

Partly, this has to do with HBS being part of the much bigger Harvard University. When I visited HBS while a student in the US, I was told that the business school does not have the standing within Harvard that it has in the outside world. Harvard values its physics and chemistry departments and its law and medical schools more. (I was shown a row of some six air-conditioners jutting out of the first floor of a building. Every one of those rooms, I was told, housed a Nobel laureate). The B-school is perceived as the university's milch cow, the one that pulls in a lot of money.

HBS celebrated its centenary in April 2008. This meant that, in 1961, when IIMA was founded, HBS had had a head start of over 50 years. In the US itself, HBS has had a substantial lead over other schools and the advantages of an enormous war-chest. HBS' corpus today is $2.1billion.

Funding is crucial to the success of any university or college in the US. More funds means better infrastructure and better paid professorships that can be used to attract high quality talent. The dean in a typical US school has two main functions: fund raising and recruiting faculty.

Box 2.1: Is management a science?

Can management be called a science? The question continues to be debated to this day. At its very inception, IIMA needed the Council for Scientific and Industrial Research (CSIR) to certify that IIMA was engaged in 'scientific research'. Only then would it be eligible for tax deductions on contributions made by individuals or businesses.

CSIR raised two questions. Did management research qualify as 'scientific research'? Secondly, management research was mentioned as only one of several objects in the Memorandum of Articles of Association of IIMA. Since the Institute would be engaged in several other activities, such as teaching, hiring faculty, buying assets, etc., could it claim to be engaged in 'research'?

Sarabhai addressed all these issues.[2] Scientific research for the purpose of income tax meant any activities 'in the field of natural or applied science for the extension of knowledge.' Research to be carried out at IIMA certainly qualified as applied science. Work done in production, marketing, finance, would find application in business and industry, and would be based on scientific methods and tools. For good measure, Sarabhai enclosed a book titled *Contributions to Scientific Research in Management* published by UCLA.

As for IIMA being engaged in several activities other than research, Sarabhai clarified that IIMA would primarily focus on two activities: teaching and research. All other activities, such as holding property, awarding diplomas, hiring faculty, etc., were subsidiary activities meant to promote these two primary activities.

Sarabhai went on to say that of the two activities, teaching and research, he would say the latter was more important because it provided the necessary material and foundation for teaching and training. He also pointed out that at HBS, expenditure on research was high; it was half the expenditure on teaching. Whether IIMA has conformed to Sarabhai's stated order of priorities is another matter.

At HBS, it is said, when a faculty member comes up for tenure (a permanent faculty position), the dean asks simply: Is this guy in the top two or three in his field? If not, what would it take to get somebody who is in the top two or three? The academic game in the US in many ways resembles that of football clubs that lure the best talent by shelling out what it takes.

For IIMA, the appeal of HBS did not lie merely in the latter being an acknowledged leader in the field. The founders of IIMA were keen that the Institute should influence practice. HBS scored in this area because its teaching was built around the 'case' method, in which real-life problems were dissected in the classroom. IIMA has distinguished itself over the years through the use of the 'case' study although its importance at the Institute has somewhat dwindled over the years.

Soon after HBS gave its assent to the collaboration, Sarabhai left for Harvard to work on the details. Before leaving, he wrote to IIMA's chairman saying that he proposed to take advantage of Chowdhry's presence at Harvard as a faculty member.

Sarabhai wrote:

Prof Hansen and I may discuss with Dr Kamla Chowdhry the possibility of her joining the Institute. She would be invaluable in planning out the first Advanced Management Programme for early 1963 and for setting up selection programmes and research programmes for case collection in collaboration with the Harvard faculty. She has, moreover, first-hand experience and contacts with the industrial organisations in western and northern India.[3]

Chowdhry indicated she would be interested if she was offered reasonable terms and gave Sarabhai her CV. She mentioned a remuneration of ₹1,700 plus ₹500 as special allowance. After reaching Harvard, Sarabhai reviewed Chowdhry's background with Hansen and the two decided to recommend to IIMA that Chowdhry join the Institute in July but commence work on behalf of IIMA even while at Harvard. She would be given the title of acting programme director for the purpose of correspondence. (Later, this title was changed to coordinator of programmes, perhaps because the word 'director' seemed to carry more weight than was thought appropriate.)

Sarabhai wrote in his note to the chairman that 'though her appointment may be made in the grade of a senior professor ... she should shoulder the responsibility of putting together the academic and research aspects of the programme of the Institute. Moreover, she should also assist in the selection and training of the faculty of the Institute.' The board approved Chowdhry's appointment. Later, in February 1963, Chowdhry was sent to HBS to take part in the Advanced Management Programme to get a feel for the course contents and the pedagogy of a B-school.

The search for other faculty began in right earnest. An advertisement in late 1962 drew 20 applications for the post of senior professor, 60 for professor, 140 for assistant professor and research associate and 650 for the post of fellow. It doesn't seem a bad response at all – one is not sure IIMA can draw such a response today. It is also interesting that faculty positions at IIMA drew a better response than the post of director advertised a year earlier. Had the idea of IIMA gained some momentum by then?

The process of selecting faculty in the early stages was meticulous. Sarabhai, Chowdhry and Baveja did the first level of selection for each category. The short-listed candidates would then be interviewed by a screening committee. People of stature from industry and elsewhere were associated with the screening committee for the various functional areas.

The screening committee held group and individual interviews and made recommendations to a personnel committee that took the final decision. By February 1963, Sarabhai was able to report that five faculty members had been selected. Amongst them was Samuel Paul, later to become the second director of IIMA.

Among the bright sparks considered for a faculty position was the now famous economist Jagdish Bhagwati. John Fox, director of overseas relations at HBS, wrote to Sarabhai, saying that he and others from IIMA had met 'this fellow' in Delhi and his behaviour then could be described as 'diffident bordering on arrogance'.[4]

Fox thought he would check with his son who was then at Oxford and had Bhagwati as his tutor. Fox's son was lavish in his praise for Bhagwati. He wrote to his father that Bhagwati was regarded as one of the 'brightest men of his age group at Oxford ... a lofty and theoretical species of brilliant economist which India seems to turn out.' He had an 'acute and complete understanding of the Western mind.'

This stellar recommendation spurred IIMA into approaching Bhagwati. Alas, Bhagwati was not interested.

HBS ran an International Teachers Program (ITP). The programme was for nine months. Since its inception, the programme had attracted a total of 153 participants from 32 countries and representing 54 institutions where business administration subjects were taught. HBS wrote to IIMA inviting it to nominate faculty for its 1963-64 sessions.

The ITP had been designed to achieve several objectives: to provide participants with some of the latest thinking in the various areas of business administration; to expose them to some of the latest teaching techniques, especially the case method of instruction; and to enable them to learn more about the problems of research and administration in some of the leading schools of business administration in the US.

Participants were required to take some courses in the MBA programme. Along with the class schedule, participants would have seminars and luncheon meetings with HBS faculty where course development, case writing, teaching techniques, etc., would be discussed. They would also be free to attend seminars at the doctoral level.

The programme included three field trips, one each to New York, Washington and Chicago. There would be visits to government institutions, other business schools and also industrial plants. At the end of the programme, participants would be required to write a report, typically a detailed outline of a syllabus for a business management programme.

The financing of a participant in the programme was either arranged by his or her institution or through a grant by some agency, such as the US Agency for International Development (USAID), a cultural exchange programme or a private foundation. In the case of IIMA, the Ford Foundation picked up the tab.

IIMA decided to send its faculty to the ITP in batches of about six or so. The first batch would leave by September 1962. The tuition fee was $2,000 and living expenses, another $2,500.

Faculty assigned to the programme were required to sign an agreement with the Institute that they would serve IIMA for a period four times the period of training, subject to a minimum of two years and maximum of five years. If they decided to leave before that period, they would be required to pay IIMA the full cost incurred by the Institute and the Ford Foundation on their training, including salary paid in the training period.

The decision to participate in the ITP was among the important ones taken in the formative years of IIMA. Sarabhai and others understood that not all the early recruits to IIMA would have strong academic qualifications. Exposure to the course work and pedagogy at a top school such as HBS would make a big difference.

However, there was a larger institutional purpose to sending faculty to the ITP. If people spent time together in an academic environment, they would develop a shared approach towards building an academic institution and they would also develop a certain understanding amongst themselves.

IIMA did not have many academics with outstanding credentials in the early years and yet its programmes were able to make a mark very quickly. The common approach fostered by the exposure to HBS and the sense of camaraderie amongst faculty who had spent time together contributed in a big way. Herein lies an important lesson in institution-building: you do not need extraordinary people in order to create great institutions; you need ordinary people who are highly motivated and are driven by a shared sense of purpose.

In the first week of January, 1963, a group of five senior HBS professors arrived at IIMA. Their visit was intended to plan for the first PGP batch in 1964. They spent four weeks in India, two weeks in Ahmedabad and one each in Bombay and Delhi.

Their tour was organised around a programme called 'programme of understanding business and government in the Indian environment.' The programme was intended to enable HBS faculty to get a feel of the Indian business environment and judge what sort of curriculum would be appropriate for the proposed two-year programme. It would give HBS faculty the opportunity to explore the potential for developing case materials on Indian business and for doing research. The HBS group would also get a sense of whether IIMA would be able to place its graduates in the initial years, an important requirement for the success of any B-school.

The visit was meticulously planned. About 12-15 visits to organisations were planned in each of the three cities. Each meeting was to last half-a-day. It would start with a half-hour meeting with the CEO and top management, followed by an hour or so with other executives. A group meeting was planned with the executive committee of the local management association and a luncheon meeting with about 30 CEOs. There would also be lectures and group meetings in the evenings at institutions such as the National Productivity Council and the Indian Institute of Public Administration.

The meeting with the group of CEOs itself was planned in some detail. The team leader would give a short introduction to the role of HBS in the US. This would be followed by a talk by another faculty member on business policy that would review current thinking on the subject in the US.

I mention these details to give the reader an idea of the sheer hard work that went into the founding of the Institute. The Institute was new, the MBA programme would also be new, so it was important to get Indian industry on board – as providers of material, as potential recruiters and, hopefully, as contributors of funds.

In March 1962, plans for the campus for IIMA began to take shape. The National Institute for Design (NID) wrote to Sarabhai saying that after discussions with Hansen, preliminary estimates for accommodation for the next three to five years had been drawn up.

These included a teaching, administration and research block, including the library (which was to become the main building later); residential accommodation for participants of the management development programmes and for visiting faculty and their families; residential quarters for faculty and staff; hostels or dormitories for students for the two-year PGP; recreational facilities for faculty and students and sports grounds.

The total cost was estimated at ₹3 million over a period of five to seven years. These plans and the costs kept getting revised. The initial building cost finally ended up at over ₹10 million.

In August 1962, the board took another momentous decision, one that, in its own way, was to define the character of IIMA. It approved the appointment of B V Doshi as the Indian architect and Louis Kahn as the foreign consultant. The two would work directly for IIMA. NID would be paid a fee of 5% of the cost of the building, including interior fittings and decorations, plus the cost of travel and living expenses for Louis Kahn in India.

When Kahn was approached by Sarabhai, he was a well-known professor of architecture at MIT, though he had been associated with the University of Pennsylvania for most of his career. The decision to involve an architect of his repute was a bold one and it showed an ability to think big.

Kahn is regarded as one of the most influential architects of the twentieth century. According to *Time* magazine, he enjoyed a 'near divine status' in the world of architects.[5] Born in 1901, Kahn was a Jew whose family had migrated from the erstwhile Russian empire to the US in the early years of the last century. He graduated from the University of Pennsylvania and thereafter started his career as an architect.

It is said that the distinctive style he developed later in his life was derived from the ruins of ancient buildings in Greece, Italy and Egypt. Among his famous buildings are the Jonas Salk Institute in La Jolla, California, the Kimball Art Museum in Fort Worth, Texas, and the Capital Complex in Dhaka.

Kahn's involvement in the IIMA project was intense and there was much discussion and correspondence on various key elements in the project. One sticking point was a pond that Kahn wanted as a natural barrier between staff quarters and the dorms and academic area.

Sarabhai was reluctant to go along as it would push up the initial investment and also impose significant recurring costs. The design proposed by Kahn required mechanical appliances for cleaning. Sarabhai proposed a lily pond with fish that would prevent mosquitoes breeding. Eventually, the idea seems to have been given up. What IIMA has today is a smallish moat in which one can sometimes spot fish and turtle.

Over the years, IIMA's old campus, designed by Kahn, has become an attraction in itself, drawing busloads of tourists, Indian and foreign, to this day. The highlight of the campus, which appears in most photographs of IIMA in the media, is the main building and classroom complex on two sides of a rectangle, with the library building connecting the two. In the quadrangle between the main building and the classroom complex is an open-air assembly called the Louis Kahn Plaza.

The fourth part of the rectangle is vacant and houses a lawn where many campus events are held. In one corner of the lawn rises the service tower 'which stands like a sentry and symbol of learning.'[6] The rest of the campus consists of dormitories or hostels, residences for academic and administrative staff, a sports complex and an executive development complex.

For those with a taste for architecture, the following passage should give an indication of the great man's thinking:

The spaces created with the classrooms and small-sized seminar rooms give a feeling of closeness essential to encouraging the spirit of exchange of ideas between the teachers and students. A much wider corridor leading to the classrooms is not merely a passage but also a meeting place to provide opportunities for continued discussion and self-learning.[7]

I have walked the corridors of the main building complex for over ten years now. To this day, I cannot step into them without experiencing a sense of immensity, a feeling of elevation.

Kahn worked on the IIMA project from 1962 until his death in 1974. He died of a heart attack in a toilet in Pennsylvania Station in New York City. He had just returned from India, where he was overseeing the ongoing work at IIMA. When Kahn was found dead he could not be identified for three days as he had crossed out the home address on his passport.

I remember two couples from Spain ringing the bell of my house on the campus, one afternoon about four years ago. IIMA had by then added another campus on a piece of land across the street. The men were professors of architecture in Spanish universities. They had done the rounds of the old and the new campus and wanted to see what the residential accommodation designed by Kahn looked like.

I welcomed them gladly and gave them the run of my house. They spent about half-an-hour going from room to room, making sketches and letting out 'oohs' and 'aahs', and thanked me profusely for the privilege. I asked one of the professors how he rated the new campus, which was broadly modelled on the old one.

'On a scale of ten, I would give it five or six.'

And the old campus?

'Ah, that is beyond any scale. It is the work of a maestro.'

By late 1962, the funding pattern for IIMA had been broadly set. The Gujarat government would provide 65 acres of land, industrialists would contribute ₹3 million towards building costs, the Central Government would pay ₹1.2 million towards recurring costs and Ford Foundation would make a grant of $472,000.

The HBS collaboration itself had been firmed up earlier. The first batch of around ten faculty members had been recruited as also the administrative staff. Six of the faculty had left for HBS to join the ITP. Now, preparations for IIMA's academic programmes could begin. The most important was the flagship two-year PGP. An admission policy was formulated and an Admissions Office created. The admissions policy document spelt out the selection procedure in some detail.

The minimum requirement for admission into IIMA would be a Bachelor's degree in Arts, Sciences, Commerce, Engineering or Law. Proficiency in English, performance in Mathematics at the high school level and consistency of high quality performance during the candidate's academic career would be important criteria.

Extra-curricular activities would be used to judge a candidate's leadership, motivation, etc. Work experience was not insisted upon but where a candidate had work experience, it would be critically evaluated; it 'should be of such a nature that it contributed to the personal growth of a candidate and the learning process of the group.'[8]

Candidates would be selected using an overall assessment of the application form, past academic performance, test score and interview. A maximum of four times the number of the batch size would be called for interviews. Interviews were to be held in about a dozen locations.

Minimising travel for candidates was one consideration. The policy document mentions two others: emphasising the all-India character of IIMA and building relationships with local bodies. The test would be for 45 minutes, the group discussion 45 minutes, and the interview 15 minutes. The admissions panel would have three members.

At the very inception, the Institute was clear that nobody should be denied entry for want of funds. The Board of Governors approved a financial aid scheme and IIMA continues to extend financial aid to this day. Sarabhai wrote to various businessmen seeking support for scholarships of ₹2,500 per year to take care of needy students. Over time, IIMA was able to provide scholarships on its own and has stood by its commitment that no candidate who was selected would be denied access for want of funds.

As everybody knows, the biggest strength of the IIMs is the quality of its students. The sheer selectivity of the process – only one in about 500 students makes it to IIMA – is a big factor but the objectivity, fairness and rigour of the selection process also contribute. The first batch had ten applicants for every seat.

There have been some changes to the format over the years but the essence of the approach formulated nearly five decades ago still stands. There was something about the Institute, maybe the sheer excitement of institution-building, maybe a sense of being entrusted with a sacred task, that got people to think through every aspect of an activity and to think far into the future.

IIMA operated on a makeshift basis in the initial years. From 1962 to 1965, faculty and staff were accommodated in a bungalow in Shahibaug not far from the office premises. A floor of another bungalow nearby was rented in order to house the library. For the PGP, one seminar room and two small rooms were rented at ATIRA. Student accommodation was provided at 18 apartments rented at the Housing Board near Paldi.

The first batch, comprising 60 men and women, commenced on July 1, 1964. IIMA had just 14 full-time faculty members at the time but most of them had been to HBS and were familiar with the nitty-gritty of teaching in an MBA programme. The chairman of PGP was Warren Haynes, an HBS appointee.

The PGP was inaugurated by Balwantrai Mehta, chief minister of Gujarat. Sarabhai explained the rationale for the two-year PGP and highlighted the hard work that had gone into the programme, as also what would be needed to sustain its quality:

> We felt that a rigorous programme of this nature was not only required to prepare young managers, but was essential for the internal development of the Institute. We believe that even though Executive Development Programmes are equally important for our initial needs, the very success of these programmes for practitioners depends on a faculty matured through the discipline of research, project work and instruction that lies behind the MBA programme.
>
> ...One of the distinguishing features of this programme is the extent of preparation that has gone into it – work in the selection and training of faculty, in contacts with industry, case research, techniques of selection, the conduct of the courses and the hundred-and-one small details which have been involved in it. The Institute's programmes will indeed be still-born if this activity, which is almost in the nature of a research and development function, does not become an integral part of the Institute's normal operation.[9]

Sarabhai also spoke of the culture that had been created at the Institute:

> I feel proud that we have over the two years, established a new culture in the Institute, a culture which is informal and at the same time, involves major responsibility by the faculty and the

individual teacher. What we are teaching is largely the result of this culture.

The reference to culture was apt. Academic institutions spring up all the time in our country, MBA programmes are a dime-a-dozen. The success of an academic institution is a function of its culture. Sarabhai and his colleagues in the early years had understood this and made every effort to see that the Institute's activities were suffused with this understanding. Later, Matthai was to give greater substance to the culture of the Institute.

Preparations for the other key programme of IIMA, the 3-tier programme (3-TP), had also been proceeding at a brisk pace. (It preceded the PGP). The 3-TP of IIMA is something of an innovation in executive training and one that was well-suited to the Indian market. It still runs successfully.

The idea behind the programme is simple enough. If you wish to bring about change in an organisation, you need to get managers at all levels onto the same wavelength. This is especially true of Indian companies where it is the people at the top who need to be persuaded most about the need for change and about ways to usher in change. Most executive programmes ignore this basic truth. They fail to make an impact on the organisation because they are aimed at managers at a particular level.

Chowdhry was the leading figure in the 3-TP. Her stint at the AMP at HBS had equipped her well for the purpose. The programme was launched in Jaipur in January–February 1964. A target of 40 participating organisations was set and it was largely met. This was no mean achievement considering that IIMA was new and so was the concept itself. No doubt, the well-designed programme brochure and the HBS association helped.

A mix of private and public sector institutions participated. The private sector institutions included Arvind Mills, Tata Chemicals, Tisco, The Times of India group, Mahindra and Mahindra, TVS and Mukand Iron and Steel. The public sector firms included Air India, SBI, LIC and Bank of Baroda. Two MNCs were present: Smith, Kline and French, and Otis Elevator. It is interesting that Hindustan Lever did not figure in the list despite Tandon's association with IIMA.

S K Bhattacharyya was invited to watch the 3-TP and he came away impressed:

> ... I watched with fascination the case discussion relating to the strategic dilemma experienced by a company under the disguised name of International Manufacturing Company ... since its sales had been substantially affected by the lower-priced but more versatile sewing machine from post-war Japan ... should it continue with its existing product lines and marketing strategy or adopt a newer strategy which utilises its distinctive competence design and engineering? ... No clear answers emerged, but at the end of the session, it was clearly evident that the kind of strategic analysis based on an actual case had demonstrated that people trained in strategic analysis would be of great value to industry.[10]

Bhattacharyya was also struck by the programme design:

> The programme content (and the duration) of the three tiers in the programme differed substantially and focused on skill-building, management planning and control, and strategy formulation respectively. The programme was knit together by the common thread of the overall organisation reference point, even though the thrust and content in each tier was different.

Bhattacharyya joined IIMA soon thereafter. After a brief three-month stay in Ahmedabad, he was sent to a 14-week management development programme in HBS instead of the year-long ITP. Partly, this had to do with a sense of dissatisfaction among the two batches of faculty who had attended the ITP; they had ended up feeling that the programme was somewhat unorganised and that they had been pretty much left to fend for themselves.

A high point at this time was the visit to India of Dean Baker of HBS. His visit included a trip to Jaipur when the 3-tier programme was going on. Hansen wrote a memo to Sarabhai outlining the arrangements proposed in detail that would be worthy of a visit by a head of state.

The memo begins on a somewhat pompous note: 'I am personally responsible for the success of Dean Baker's visit.' It then talks about Baker's meetings in various places, the seating arrangements at lunches and dinners, and shopping trips for Mrs Baker. Hansen is particular about the delivery of flowers at each place that Baker visits: in Delhi, he was to be presented flowers with a card from Sarabhai; in Jaipur, with a card from faculty; in Ahmedabad, by faculty and staff; and in Bombay, by the Harvard Club.

The memo drew a rather sharp response from Sarabhai. IIMA's founder was clearly irritated at being dictated to on the minutiae of Baker's visit. But then, Harvard does take its leaders seriously. In one of his books, the economist, J K Galbraith, talks of a phone call from the office of the president of Harvard to the White House. The secretary from Harvard says, 'Is that the White House? The president would like to speak to Mr Truman.'[11]

The fledgling institution required enormous work on the part of all concerned – the director, the board, the faculty and the staff. Sarabhai was an honorary and part-time director. He had numerous other commitments at that time. Yet, the time and energy he devoted to IIMA is incredible. There are three volumes of letters he wrote and received in the initial years. His monitoring of day-to-day activities at IIMA was pretty intense.

Managing faculty, as every academic knows, is a huge challenge. Faculty members have huge egos and do not like to be questioned. They have security of tenure and cannot be easily pushed around. To get them to give of their best requires considerable leadership skills. It is remarkable how hands-on Sarabhai was when it came to dealing with faculty issues.

In the Sarabhai papers is to be found a memo put up by an HBS faculty member, Melvyn Cohen. It runs into two pages and describes at length what Cohen has been up to during his one-and-a-half month stay at IIMA.

Two case studies on production management were nearing completion; Cohen's note gives the gist of each; another study on entrepreneurship and small enterprises, covering 15 small manufacturing firms in the Ahmedabad area, had been initiated, its objectives are described; a similar study on larger firms was being contemplated; yet another project was intended to compare pairs of domestic and foreign firms in similar product lines, in about 15 cities; a research fellow was being groomed to pursue some of these studies.

The note then goes on to describe various administrative and support activities Cohen had been preoccupied with. And all this in one-and-a-half months! One wonders whether many faculty members at IIMA today can match this level of productivity.

Another faculty member, Bharat Dalal, talks of the work he had done in collecting case material in the areas of marketing and sales management. His note lists companies contacted during a one-month stay in Bombay, the persons contacted, the output that would result and ends up seeking sanction for certain expenses incurred. One note lists 117 contacts with companies made by Chowdhry and

B K Hegde in the period of one month in nearly a dozen cities all over India.

A memo from Michael Halse of HBS, outlines progress in work on agricultural enterprises. Yet another memo spells out the case for hiring other faculty to teach a course in management of agricultural enterprises in the second year of PGP, which would be 1965-66. The PGP was to commence in 1964, so there was an urgency to these missives.

Bhattacharyya writes of the difficulties faculty members experienced in making the transition from the lecture method to the case method:

> They (faculty) could not comprehend how any teaching could be properly academic in content when at the end of the session, you did not acquire a set of academic principles or come to a clear-cut solution you could live with.[12]

Coming to grips with case-writing was not easy:

> We started writing cases which – in so far as the initial specimens were concerned – with the benefit of hindsight can best be described as 'lousy'. They were no more than descriptions of a problem experienced by a company and were bereft of any finesse or marshalling of data for developing a coherent perspective, leading to a conclusion that the problem sought to be analysed, discussed and resolved was not very clear.
>
> We still had not learnt such case writing tricks as 'putting the red herring in' so that the person analysing the case was taken up the garden path. We learnt later that the whole objective of such carefully planted red herrings was to ensure that the case analyst could

distinguish between grain and chaff. We conducted case sessions based on our amateurishly written cases which appeared somewhat half-baked ... Never was the adage 'practice makes perfect' better illustrated than at the time of our initial case writing days.[13]

Gradually, faculty mastered the art of writing and teaching cases although faculty members who had come in from academia had greater difficulty in adapting to a pedagogy that did not involve mere lecturing. Initially, cases were required to be sent to HBS for editing and this contributed towards quality control.

The late C K Prahalad is one of the best-known names to have come out of IIMA. He belonged to the first PGP batch, was awarded a gold medal and returned to join the faculty of IIMA after a brief stint in industry. Prahalad told me that he himself wrote some ten cases in the one-and-a-half years he spent at IIMA in his first stint. (He later returned for a second stint after completing his doctorate at HBS). 'The trade-offs were very clear,' Prahalad said, 'you sacrificed consulting income so that you could produce more cases.' Prahalad added with a chuckle, 'I understand people are still using some of those cases; I can't understand why.'

Going through the papers and reminiscences of the early years, one is struck by the energy and dedication of people at all levels. People were busy writing cases, testing it out amongst themselves, in executive programmes, developing courses, discussing and arguing about matters. Sarabhai and the board watched from a distance and were ready to encourage and facilitate. There was a sense that something unique and extraordinary was being attempted and people were determined to give of their best.

Even after the PGP was launched, gaining acceptance for it in the realms of higher education in India was not easy. The Secretary,

All India Board of Technical Studies, forerunner to today's AICTE, questioned IIMA's decision to admit fresh graduates.

The Robbins report had said that 'previous under-graduate work in business is not essential.' The secretary felt that the report was referring to the under-graduate programme in business management, which was widely offered in the US. He underlined that the report had not said prior work experience was not essential.

The secretary advised that IIMA should only admit graduates with prior work experience upto five years. In making the suggestion, the secretary anticipated a debate that has not died down to this day. Does it make sense to provide management education to candidates who have virtually no experience?

IIMA's own defence has been that the acceptability of its 'product' amongst the best institutions in the world is in itself an answer. If Goldman Sachs and McKinsey and others are willing to hire from IIMA, just as they hire from the top B-schools in the US, IIMA's model of admitting students with very little or no work experience stands validated – so runs the argument.

But this has not satisfied everybody, including those within the system. In recent years, IIMA has sought to meet the criticism by launching a one-year executive PGP (PGP-X) which requires five years or more of work experience. But the debate on whether a management programme can add much value to fresh graduates continues.

The syllabus of the PGP came to be questioned. Some institutions which provided part-time instruction had approached the AIBTS, asking for the power to grant degrees, on the ground that they offered courses which were at par with IIMA's courses. The secretary was of the view that IIMA's syllabus was inferior to that of many part-time courses. Separately, it was suggested that the syllabus did not conform to what the board itself had laid down some years before.

The faculty work load also came under the scanner. The secretary wanted to know why faculty had fewer than 18-24 hours of teaching every week; those hours were the norm elsewhere. It took some effort to convince him that the case method involved greater effort both in the writing of cases and in teaching them.

Echoes of the question about faculty work load, raised in the early years of IIMA, can be heard to this day. As recently as in 2008, the report of an IIM Review Committee headed by R C Bhargava, chairman of Maruti Suzuki Ltd, contended that the IIMs had not been able to expand their intake because the faculty was not teaching enough.

One of the important issues the founding fathers had to wrestle with was getting degree-granting status for the PGP. Getting such a status would require the consent of the University Grants Commission and for an Act to be passed by Parliament. Since this would take time, it was decided to launch the PGP first as a diploma in management and then pursue the matter of getting degree-granting status separately.

By mid-1964, a core faculty was in place and the two key programmes of IIMA, the 3-TP and the PGP, had been launched. The academic programmes got off to a flying start. However, there was still one important unfinished business – the appointment of a full-time director who would take over from Sarabhai.

Sarabhai's first choice for the job a year earlier had been Chowdhry; she had all the right credentials. She had a US doctorate, had taught at HBS and had attended the AMP. As coordinator of programmes, she had effectively been No. 2 to Sarabhai. Above all, she enjoyed the confidence of both Sarabhai and Tandon.

However, the choice of Chowdhry ran into opposition from several quarters: HBS, IIMA faculty and the board itself. HBS apparently felt that Chowdhry lacked the necessary administrative abilities, whatever her strengths as an academic. The faculty was divided. The board was reluctant to go along with somebody about whom many faculty members had reservations.

Tandon sums up the situation:

> A problem that loomed large was the appointment of a permanent director in place of Vikram, who was honorary and part-time, and Kamla who deputed for him without the strength of holding it in her own right ... Some thought Kamla could be the permanent director and others opposed this completely. I was surprised at Harvard's opposition to having a woman director in principle. They were quite clear that a woman would not be able to run an organisation that needed not only academic acumen, which they conceded she possessed, but also administrative strength, which they felt she did not possess, nor would probably any other woman. I felt they were prejudiced on this point, although I did concede that Kamla was not outgoing enough and did not have the kind of firmness she would need in plenty to deal with a young and ambitious faculty, some hundreds of very lively students, industry and donors, especially the Ahmedabad group, and government.[14]

Sarabhai and Tandon, the two top functionaries of IIMA and men with considerable clout, were both in favour of Chowdhry. Yet they could not prevail. That says something about the quality of the board of IIMA in those days. How many boards even today are capable of overruling the CEO and the chairman on any matter?

In late 1963, it appeared that IIMA had found somebody. This was J M Shrinagesh, an ICS officer, whose brother rose to become chief of staff of the Indian army. Shrinagesh was then managing director of Hindustan Steel , forerunner to today's Steel Authority of India Limited (SAIL). IIMA first approached him sometime in January 1963. After much correspondence and several meetings, it was decided to offer Shrinagesh the directorship.

It was proposed that Shrinagesh assume the directorship of IIMA after he retired from government in November 1963. Lalbhai was in favour of trying out Shrinagesh for one year. Since it was intended that Shrinagesh attend the AMP at Harvard for four months, it was decided to offer him a two-year contract.

Shrinagesh was to join in December 1963, on his return from a trip to the US. While in the US, it would be arranged for him to visit HBS. The salary offered to him was ₹2,500 plus ₹1,000 as personal allowance.

The appointment did not materialise. Shrinagesh declined the IIMA offer when he was offered the governorship of a state. Of this episode, Tandon writes acerbically:

> The challenge of an academic assignment that he (Shrinagesh) had talked about evaporated quickly. I was relieved, for if there could be a choice between a governorship and the chance of a lifetime of building a new institution of this kind, his rejection was the institute's gain.[13]

It was back to square one on the appointment of a full-time director. In March 1964, there was a board meeting which was attended by Dean Baker and Hansen. HBS made clear its keenness to have a full-time director without any further delay. A five-man committee of the board headed by Tandon was appointed and asked to recommend somebody in the next few months. Sarabhai was asked to continue as honorary director.

The board also felt that the time had come to define an appropriate organisational structure for IIMA. Sarabhai prepared one in consultation with Hansen. At the time, the Institute was run by three committees: the Faculty Council, which met every month or as required, the Special Programme Committee for executive programmes, and the MBA committee (later called PGP Committee) for the two-year programme.

For the executive functions, the director relied on two officers, the coordinator of programmes (Chowdhry) and the administrative officer. Since Sarabhai was only the honorary director, the coordinator of programmes assumed day-to-day responsibility for the Institute.

Sarabhai proposed that Chowdhry be re-designated as deputy director. In a note to the board, he said that it would become necessary to have three deputy directors, one each for the PGP, research and executive development programmes. This would be consistent with the two or three associate deans a typical American business school had under the dean (who is equivalent to the director at IIMA). Designating Chowdhry as deputy director, Sarabhai felt, would be a start.

The suggestion did not find favour with the Board; they seemed to think that the task of finding a full-time director might become complicated if somebody with the title of deputy director was already at the helm.

Sporadic attempts to find a director continued for another year. Many retired administrators and generals were interested but were not considered suitable. Tandon confesses that there was a general impression that he and Sarabhai were stone-walling for Chowdhry's sake. IIMA began to draw unfavourable comparisons with IIMC where a full-time director had been appointed two years earlier.

Tandon remarks that Sarabhai felt 'unwanted' by the board and he also thought he had let Chowdhry down by not resigning.[16] Chowdhry herself felt the same way about Sarabhai and Tandon. She thought they should have stood up for what they believed in. Both Sarabhai and Tandon began to find the search for a director somewhat unappealing.

Now we come to an unresolved mystery. From out of the blue, as it were, in 1965, Sarabhai and Tandon settled on who they wanted as director of IIMA. Their choice, a young man with no serious academic credentials to speak of, enthused the Board. It enthused the Ford Foundation and HBS as well.

Whoever came in contact with the young man was left in no doubt about his suitability for the job. Nobody has been able to tell me how exactly Sarabhai and Tandon hit upon this person and what gave them the confidence to press his case confidently after a two-year search that had almost reduced them to despair.

And yet, it turned out to be absolutely the right choice, a tribute to the judgement of the founders of IIMA. It can be said that the choice of Ravi Matthai was a game-changer, one that was to augur well not only for IIMA but also for management education in India.

We must turn now to the antecedents of this remarkable man.

3

The Master Builder Arrives

Ravi Matthai was born in Trivandrum (now Thiruvananthapuram) on August 6, 1927, the youngest of Dr John and Achamma Matthai's three children. He had a brother, Duleep, and a sister, Valsa.

Dr Matthai, best known as finance minister in Nehru's cabinet, came from a Syrian Catholic family. The family hailed from Kottayam and later adopted the faith of the Church of England represented by the Church Mission Society that began to work in Travancore–Cochin. (As mentioned earlier, I will refer to the father as Dr Matthai and Ravi Matthai simply as Matthai.)

Dr Matthai was born in Calicut (now Kozhikode), one of Thomas Matthai's many children. The family was distinguished for its contribution in the fields of education and public service. Dr Matthai's elder brother, Cherian Matthai, became director of Public Instruction in what was then the state of Cochin. The families had left Kottayam in the late 1870s.

Dr Matthai made a mark in the pre-Independence period itself. After completing his BA in Madras, he studied at the London School of Economics and at Balliol College, Oxford. He was professor of Economics at Presidency College, Madras and a member of the Madras Legislative Council.

Thereafter, Dr Matthai went on to hold several important posts: chairman of the Tariff Board, director-general of commercial intelligence and statistics, finance member of the Viceroy's Council, director with the House of Tata and Minister for Railways and Transport in the Interim Government. While with the Tatas, he was one of the authors of the Bombay Plan, the first attempt at drawing up a plan for the economic development of India consequent to its attaining independence.

In the post-Independence period, Dr Matthai distinguished himself in several roles. He was the second finance minister in Nehru's cabinet, succeeding Dr Shanmugham Chetty. He resigned from the cabinet following differences with Nehru over the role of the Planning Commission, an act typical of a man of his integrity, and returned to the House of Tata. However, this was talent that the government could not afford to ignore. Even while in the service of the Tatas, Dr Mathai was appointed chairman of the Taxation Enquiry Commission.

As a director with the Tatas, Dr Matthai was famous for his ability to take quick decisions. He would not keep a single file or letter unattended in his tray by evening and made it a point to leave office at 5:00 pm on the dot every evening. His integrity was legendary and he believed that integrity began with small matters. For instance, he would not use office stamps or stationery for personal matters. For this purpose, he had a monthly renewable account of ₹100 with his secretary.[1]

There is a terrific quote about Dr Matthai from Homi Mody, another Tata director: 'Even if Dr Matthai said "good morning" and nothing else, it sounded like a Papal benediction.'[2] This ability to impress with speech, and quickly, at that, seems to have been passed on to Matthai for I have heard similar things about the son.

While still with the Tatas, Dr Matthai became the first chairman of the State Bank of India. (It is unthinkable even in post-liberalisation

India for a director of a leading industrial house to be chairman of the premier public sector bank in the country.) Later, he became vice-chancellor of Bombay University.

He quit the post of vice-chancellor in protest against what he believed was interference in the autonomy of the university; one does not know how much this episode contributed to Ravi Matthai's fierce determination to guard the autonomy of IIMA many years later.

Dr Matthai had several other firsts to his credit – chairman of the National Council for Applied Economic Research, chairman of the Court of Governors of the Administrative Staff College of India, Hyderabad, chairman of the National Book Trust of India. The last important position he held was vice-chancellor of the University of Kerala. This was after he had decided to return to his home state towards the end of his life. It is hard to think of many people in independent India whose contribution has been as varied and as distinguished as Dr Matthai's.

Unlike many others in important positions, Dr Matthai did not believe in promoting the careers of his children. There is nothing to suggest that Matthai ever used his father's name or connections to further his career or that he even flaunted his family background. Matthai became director of IIMA in 1965; Dr Matthai had passed away in 1959.

Matthai's corporate life before he joined IIMA had little to do with his father's with the Tatas. It appears that father and son led their separate lives and what passed from one generation to another was a set of values, including fierce integrity.

It is also interesting that Matthai did not have much time to spare for his family after he became director of IIMA; he did nothing to promote his family in any way. His professional life and especially his life at IIMA was his alone and he seems to have hardly ever discussed his work with his family. I realised this when I came into contact with his wife, Syloo and his daughter, Radha.

To return to the story of Matthai's parents. His mother, Achamma John, like her husband John, was from an orthodox Syrian Catholic family. She was the daughter of Elanjikal John Jacob, an eminent lawyer in Trivandrum. All the members of her family were staunch supporters of the Jacobite church and intimately involved with its affairs. Achamma was educated in Trivandrum and later attended the St John's Diocesan College in Calcutta (now Kolkata); she was amongst the first women in Kerala to obtain a college degree and that too from another state.

Achamma was a dedicated social worker throughout her life. During the Partition riots in 1947, she worked indefatigably in refugee camps. Later, in Bombay, she worked with the Bharat Sevak Samaj and set up Anand Kendra, a home for the rehabilitation of street children. She was an active member of the YWCA and collected funds for a working women's hostel which came to be named after her, Achamma Bhavan. Achamma collected funds to rebuild a Syrian Christian church at Dadar. She also served as member of the Central Social Welfare Board and toured the country, extensively inspecting projects.

From his parents, Ravi Matthai seems to have inherited a commitment to values, a strong sense of social purpose and an abiding interest in education. He was not religious in the formal sense. However, the Bible was his constant companion and he was fond of quoting from it.

Soon after Matthai was born, the children were sent to England where they lived with an English family for three years. On their return to India, it was decided to send the children to Nazareth Convent, a boarding school in the hill station of Ooty in Tamil Nadu. Dr Matthai was chairman of the Tariff Board at the time and he and his wife had to travel extensively. Sending children to boarding schools at any age was then, as now, an elitist affair; sending children in their early years must have been pretty rare.

On a holiday in Ooty in 2009, I got a chance to visit Nazareth Convent. It is located on St Mary's Hill, overlooking the Ooty lake. The Convent was founded in 1875 by a French nun. The original building has not seen much change, although some additions have since taken place. As you drive in, there are the housing quarters of the sisters who take care of the school. The living quarters of the sisters connect to the school building through a narrow corridor.

The school building itself is unpretentious, with wooden floors that creak loudly, and semi-circular arches for windows. Past the main building is another complex with laboratories (for physics, chemistry and biology) and an indoor play area for children that is used when it rains. Further beyond is a playground and a stadium. The convent still has plenty of land at its disposal. Some of it, we were told, has suffered from encroachments.

Compared to the two better known boarding schools in Ooty, Lawrence School and Good Shepherd, Nazareth Convent seems pretty ordinary (Lawrence, for instance, stretches over 700 acres and houses some magnificent buildings). But, in its early years, the convent had the reputation of being quite exclusive, catering mostly to the children of maharajahs and the upper class.

After a stay of about three years, Duleep and Ravi were taken to Trichur where they spent a year studying at home with a tutor, the sort of thing one associates with Motilal and Jawaharlal Nehru. Clearly, the Matthai family had the means to indulge such preferences. Valsa continued at Nazareth Convent until her senior Cambridge.

The next move took Duleep and Ravi to the north; they were admitted to the newly-created Doon School in Dehradoon. The school was founded by S R Das, brother of the more famous freedom fighter and Congressman C R Das, and modelled on famous public schools of England such as Eton and Harrow. Its purpose was to educate the future leaders of India.

HBS is said to have a slogan that runs something like this: 'We don't create leaders; we pick leaders and then claim credit for their success.' Much the same could be said of Doon School. The first batch of boys was hand-picked by the Headmaster, who visited the families of prospective entrants and picked those who matched the selection criteria. There was no mistaking the elitist character of the school even then.

Doon School provided the broad-based education for which it has since become famous. It gave its students every opportunity to pursue whatever interests they had. A wide range of sports activities was available – cricket, tennis, football, swimming, hiking, fishing and mountaineering. In the arts, the school offered sculpture, painting, music, dramatics, elocution and debating. Even today, you can count on your fingertips, the number of schools in India that provide such a range of activities.

Matthai's interests were swimming, hiking and mountaineering, painting, sculpture, dramatics and music. He took part in several expeditions, including one to Badrinath. At Badrinath, he was keen to take a peek at the sanctum sanctorum; he managed the feat by telling the Namboodiri priest that he was of Namboodiri descent!

One small incident during Matthai's stay at Doon School gives us an indication of how his character was shaping. He was once wrongly accused of some violation of school discipline. By way of punishment, he was asked to run around the playground a couple of times. Matthai kept running and would not stop until the school authorities accepted that the punishment had been wrongly imposed.

Matthai was to have fond memories of his headmaster, John Martyn, who played a major role in the development of his talents. Doon School also left Matthai with an enduring love of classical music, Indian and Western, and the habit of frequenting concerts. Matthai played the flute and some years later, took tabla lessons in Calcutta.

Later still, he developed a taste for contemporary pop music. If there is a connection between how rounded one's education is in the early years and one's creative output, and one presumes this is what quality education is all about, it is to be seen clearly in Matthai's life.

Matthai certainly thought Doon School had done a great deal for him because he retained a strong attachment to his school. He served on the Board of Governors of the school for a couple of terms and helped draft a ten-year plan for the school.

Matthai left Doon School in 1944 to join Allahabad University, then regarded as one of the best institutes of higher education in the country. He stayed at the well-known Muir hostel. At the university, as at Doon School earlier, he made lifelong friends, many of them became well-known public figures. At Doon school: Lovraj Kumar (later to rise high in the echelons of the bureaucracy), Piloo Mody (a future pillar of the Swatantra Party), Gulab Ramchandani (who would go on to head the Blue Star group of companies). At Allahabad University: Garry Saxena (later to head RAW, the Indian agency for external intelligence), A N Kaul (who joined the IPS), Vijay Kachlu (who became a senior executive at ITC). Of these, Lovraj Kumar was also at Muir hostel and at Oxford with Matthai.

Matthai enrolled for an MA at Allahabad University but never got round to completing it. Thereby hangs an interesting tale.[3] Matthai attended a party one evening and was driving back quite drunk when he hit a pedestrian. The man died on the spot.

Matthai did not flee. He picked up the body, put it in his car and surrendered to the police. He then went to the house of the famous lawyer, Tej Bahadur Sapru, a friend of his father, and told him what had happened. Sapru is said to have asked, 'Why did you go to the police? You should have come here straight!'

A police case was registered. Dr Matthai is said to have consulted Nehru who told him bluntly that the law would take its course. Dr Matthai then went to Sardar Patel, the home minister, who suggested the boy be brought to Delhi and then packed off to a foreign destination. The father decided that Oxford would be that destination.

So it was that the next halt in Matthai's journey turned out to be Balliol College, Oxford. There he read politics, philosophy and economics. Why Oxford and why those courses? Matthai has answered the question himself with characteristic candour:

> I didn't (choose Oxford) actually, my father did. He had been from the same college and wanted me to go there. My old man was very keen that I should join Oxford. So, he got me in… I don't think he regarded me as particularly bright. So he chose the subjects which he thought a person of my somewhat limited capability would be able to cope with.[4]

Matthai loved Oxford and thought it was great fun. 'I was very reluctant to leave because I did not see working for a living as fun.' Matthai found, as thousands of undergraduates over the years have, that there was a great deal more to Oxford than academics:

> I regard the work aspect in a place like that of an importance of less than 50%. It's a great deal more to learn from the place than just the subject… Firstly, such a variety of students, such a variety of activities and such tremendous initiative. Students forming their

own discussion groups, quite apart from the fact that there are so many extremely interesting societies one could join and also considerable scope to take great deal of initiative in organising our own things. That was such a fantastic amount one can get by getting involved – from music to abstract logic.[5]

Matthai became president of the Oxford Majlis, the second oldest society at Oxford after the Oxford Union. 'Majlis', in ancient Persian, means assembly. Originally a South Asian society founded to campaign for Indian independence in the UK, it has since become apolitical and includes members from all parts of the world. Matthai doesn't seem to have taken the title or the role very seriously.

As he put it, 'That was the only responsibility that I took which I very conveniently asked somebody else to hold. So I asked someone to act as a secretary and in fact do all the work for me, and I had a good time.'

You can't say Matthai didn't have his priorities right as a young man in England.

Through the placement office at Oxford, Matthai applied to a managing agency house in India, Messrs McNeill and Barry, and was selected. Shortly after he was appointed, Matthai got an offer for a doctoral fellowship from the UN. He was in two minds. He went to the director of the firm and asked whether he could defer his appointment for two years, so that he could do his fellowship. He offered to take up research that would be of interest to the industries in the group.

The director put Matthai in his place. He made it clear to Matthai that, having just been appointed, he was far from indispensable. He should make his choice and stop wasting the company's time. Matthai chose to join the managing agency. The 'clincher', as Matthai put it, 'was an almost simultaneous suggestion from the family that it's time I started earning my living and stopped playing the fool.'[6] Matthai was to stay on with the managing agency for 11 years.

Many international companies had the practice of starting their new recruits on very dull jobs. (I remember a friend of mine from one of the IIMs landing a prize job with a foreign bank and looking after the telex department for the first couple of years.) Matthai's job was to place his initials on the backs of bills signed by six clerks. This he did very conscientiously, staying on at the office until 8:00 pm.

He deluded himself into thinking he was doing something wonderful. It was left to a head clerk to bring him down to earth one day. The clerk told him, 'You are wasting your time. You are a thoroughly unworthy son of a worthy father.'

After some time, the work began to get more interesting. Matthai was posted in the tea department and given charge of purchases. This gave him an opportunity to visit tea gardens, which, as he rightly said, are 'very beautiful places.' He had to learn from scratch about making purchases – of elephants, for instance, and shipping them across to England. Later, he moved to the coal department. After that, he was put in charge of a small company in the group, that happened to be competing with a company that was then well-known, Metal Box.

It appears Matthai wasn't doing anything exciting or significant. Perhaps. But he was learning to take initiative and he was also forever getting into new situations and learning to cope and build. At times, he flopped badly. He noticed that large purchases of coal were being made without any study of market trends. So he studied the market carefully and then placed an order – only to find prices dropping sharply thereafter.

On another occasion, he was asked to organise safety posters for his coal company. He decided to design them himself instead of giving the job to an ad agency. He forgot that the idea was to make workers safety conscious. He came up with posters that he thought were very clever; they turned out to be unintelligible, even to the managers. He ended up becoming rather unpopular.

Matthai was also rather quarrelsome at the workplace, often getting into rows with his superiors. On one occasion, he got into a shouting match with his boss. It is interesting that his company was extremely tolerant of his behaviour and his failures. They must have noticed his capacity for taking initiative and, perhaps, they also approved of his willingness to question and challenge authority. In any case, in putting up with and ultimately rewarding Matthai, the British firm showed itself more enlightened than most organisations even today.

After five years spent on three assignments, Matthai was granted nine months' leave (part of the famous expat packages), with fares paid to England and back as per company norms. This time, Matthai returned to England with wife and first child in tow.

He spent his time in art galleries, music shows, and generally admiring the architecture of different cities in England. When you think of Matthai's life upto this point, there is much to envy: the upper middle class background, elite schools, Oxford, a well-heeled executive at a British firm.

On his return from England, Matthai was given what was, perhaps, the most important assignment he had had thus far, one that may have contributed eventually to his becoming director of IIMA. He was made CEO of a company that the group had bought and asked to break down this company and build it again on the basis of indigenous production. It required Matthai to take plenty of initiative; perhaps, he was given the assignment precisely because he had shown initiative in his earlier assignments.

As CEO, Matthai had to think through and implement the project from start – what to produce, licenses, collaborations, setting up factories, marketing, the works. He also learnt something that was to prove useful later when he became director of IIMA: dealing with government and all the vexations that the process involved. It was a comprehensive experience and, from all accounts, a very productive time for Matthai.

Matthai had an endearingly self-deprecatory manner. Talking about his stint as CEO later, he professed to have had no particular credentials for the CEO's job, giving the impression that it was just one of those happy accidents of his life, never speaking of his accomplishments in the job.

However, at least one account has it that Matthai successfully turned around a loss-making operation. Certainly, the five years or so he spent as CEO earned him enough of a reputation to make the next big move of his life, into education and a professorship at IIM, Calcutta.

The offer to join IIM Calcutta, in 1963, came from K T Chandy, a former director of Hindustan Lever and the first director of IIM, Calcutta. We do not know what prompted the offer and we have to surmise, as I have indicated above, that Matthai had made a name for himself in the corporate world.

Matthai grabbed the offer with both hands. He said later that he had always been interested in education, partly because it ran in the family. Moreover, the IIMC offer attracted because he was clear in his mind that he did not want to get into the university system.

What he had seen of university products had left him unenthused:

> In the course of building up this company (of which he had been CEO), we had to interview thousands and thousands of graduates, which I used to do personally till late at night. It was absolutely depressing and about all the people we took on will have to literally unlearn a great deal both in the ways they have been taught and what they have been taught.[8]

The fact that IIMC was outside the university system and 'was at least intended to have the autonomy to do things' was a clear attraction. Here, for the first time, we see Matthai talking about autonomy, the possibilities it might hold for an educational institution and how the university system stifled those possibilities.

His friends thought him a 'bloody fool' to chuck up a lucrative corporate job in order to take up an academic career. So did his family. The course bristled with risks, he knew. He had never been in education, he didn't know what teaching meant, what research meant, what sort of salary he could expect, whether he could buy his wife's saris or send his children to a certain type of school. It was a leap into the unknown.

But, as people were to discover when he was director of IIMA, Matthai was a creature of instinct, a man who listened to his inner voice, a man who was not guided entirely by cold reasoning. To worry about risks was to take the path of safety and to miss out on what one wanted deeply. 'The result is that whenever I have made a major change in my life, I know why I want it but I do not think about it at all and therefore, I do not consider the consequences.'[9]

So, that was that. If joining academics meant walking away from security and comfort, so be it. Matthai's company told him he could keep the company house until he found an alternative accomodation. Matthai declined. He learned to ride buses. He found a one-room apartment, where 'you could just about put a *charpai* (cot)' and happily settled for it.

He did not care to find out what his salary would be, and was pleasantly surprised at what he got. This willingness to depart from the beaten track, and a spirit of derring-do were among the attributes that were to define Matthai later.

His initial experience at IIMC was unsettling. In industry, he was used to very correct and formal meetings. At IIMC, at the first faculty meeting he attended, Matthai found people abusing each other. He thought, 'Why can't these people grow up? They are behaving like a bunch of school kids.'[10] (I had the same feeling myself when I came to IIMA from the corporate world.)

But Matthai was quick to correct himself. 'I didn't realise at that stage, what an important process it was,' he was to say later. Of course! You don't expect academics to be prim and proper. You expect them to argue heatedly and you certainly expect them to express themselves freely – wasn't that an essential part of academic freedom?

He was with IIMC for six months in 1963 and for eight months in 1965. In between, he spent about a year at MIT under IIMC's collaboration with MIT. His time at one of the most famous institutions in the academic world, in all probability, strengthened his credentials and prepared him better for his biggest career move, the directorship of IIMA.

Box 3.1: A corporate executive turns academic

Matthai's transition from the formal world of a British managing agency to the maddeningly informal world of Indian academia appears to have been extraordinarily smooth. Barun De, a former faculty member of IIMC recalls:

Casually dressed, for part of the next year he used to park his car in my house, saunter up with me some distance to where the IIMC bus would pick us up for the long haul to the Baranagar campus and occasionally startle even me by inserting two fingers in his mouth to emit a loud whistle when he wished to attract the attention of whomever was driving past, whether Mr Sachin Chaudhuri, then not yet union finance minister or Ain-ul-Haq who is still the indomitable driver of the bus. He also maintained impeccable method as well as courtesy in his dealings with the young managers who were being trained in the junior executive development programme at Barrackpore in 1963 and 1964.[11]

Matthai quickly came to assume a leadership role in the fledgling institute. K T Chandy, then director of IIMC, writes:

He was easily accepted by the academicians on the faculty as a leader and he played a quiet but highly constructive role in building up the requisite fellowship within the faculty and in developing systematic interaction with the industrial world through consultancy, research and training programmes. His work easily marked him out as the best choice for starting the work of the sister institute in Ahmedabad and so he went there with the warm support of all of us who were then at the Calcutta Institute.[12]

As I have said in the previous chapter, we do not know what considerations prompted Sarabhai to select Matthai as the first full-time director of IIMA. Matthai had spent a little over an year at an academic institution and had done very little teaching or research when Sarabhai approached him. What had Sarabhai heard about Matthai? In what ways did Matthai impress him, in the limited encounters they had? Not even those who knew Matthai well at IIMA have been able to shed light on this matter.

We have Matthai's version of events, and, as always, it errs on the side of self-deprecation:

> Vikram Sarabhai was the honorary director and used to spend a few hours at the Institute and they had located a large number of people but of the persons they sounded out, some refused and the government did not agree to the salary some wanted. When they got to me, they had run out of all viable names.[13]

The idea that Sarabhai chose Matthai for the job because nobody else was available is laughable, especially when you consider what an apt choice it turned out to be. No, Sarabhai was far too clear-headed, too good a judge of men, too competent an institution-builder and far too committed to IIMA to have settled on Matthai simply out of desperation.

It appears that Sarabhai and Tandon heard about Matthai's work at IIMC and flew down to Srinagar to attend a management development programme that Matthai was conducting there. They were sufficiently impressed with him to make up their mind on the spot. A write-up on Matthai in a special edition of an in-house journal of IIMA brought out after his death, tells us what transpired:

> With his uncanny sense to judge the hidden value of people, Sarabhai was struck by the clarity of Ravi's thinking and articulation and also his ability to relate himself with colleagues and associates. Tandon shared Sarabhai's judgement about the young professor.[14]

The family background, the John Matthai connection and the aristocratic upbringing must have counted. So also did Matthai's record as CEO and his stint at MIT. Then, as Matthai himself admitted, he had become the public face of IIMC despite his relatively short association with it:

> The first director of IIM Calcutta was hardly ever in the institute. Very fine person, very intelligent with tremendous vision, but he

had other objectives beside the institute. He was hardly ever there. I was the one from industry at IIMC and therefore, I had contacts. Faculty members, when they wanted something to do with industry, they started coming to me. I think this somehow got to the Board here (at IIMA) who were looking for a director.[15]

It's fair to surmise that Matthai had carved enough of a reputation for himself to be wooed arduously by Sarabhai and the IIMA board. We have Prakash Tandon's impressions about the choice:

Ravi Matthai appeared over the horizon. He was young, only thirty-eight, had worked in industry, and under Chandy's influence, moved from industry to teaching at Calcutta. With a clear, thrustful mind, he made a good leader and his values assured me that there would be no compromises with the institute's growth. He took more than a year's persuasion, because his heart he said, was in teaching and research and not in administration; that was why he had left industry. While he had transparent integrity, I think he was mistaken about his desire for teaching and research, for when he was in a position to do both, he did neither. He was too restless and lacked the necessary perseverance for research at least. He was really an institution-builder, and that is where we were lucky.[16]

This is a remarkable passage and it bears careful reading. Note that three things about Matthai seem to have impressed Tandon even during the selection process: his clarity of mind, his values and his leadership skills. Almost everybody I have talked to about Matthai seems to have formed the same impression about him, and fairly quickly. It must have been, as Tandon says, transparent, something that immediately communicated itself to others.

The idea that Sarabhai and Tandon were taken with Matthai after their very first encounter with him appears thus entirely plausible.

For HBS too, which was consulted this time round, it was love at first sight. The school's coordinator in India, Harry Hansen, was to write later:

> As Harvard's representative in the establishment of the Ahmedabad Institute, I was vitally concerned with the choice of director. I first met Ravi in the lobby of the Clark-Shiraz Hotel in Agra in 1965. A search had been on for several months to find a successor for Vikram Sarabhai who had been serving as honorary director of the Institute since the beginning. Douglas Ensminger, then the Ford Foundation's representative in India, had told me of the virtues of Ravi, then a professor at the Calcutta Institute, and he seemed a first-rate candidate for the position.
>
> We met in front of the elevators. Someone, who today is nameless, introduced us. Ravi looked at me with the measured eyes of, 'Who is this person?' And I probably did the same, having been with the Institute since its birth in 1961, with Vikram Sarabhai, Kamla Chowdhry and Prakash Tandon.[17]

With the benefit of hindsight, it is possible to put forward an explanation as to why Matthai appealed to Sarabhai and Tandon. IIMA had already been in existence for some four years and what was being attempted was new in Indian education, new in content as well as form, a departure from the format of the Indian university with all its rigidities.

An academic from a top US school would have fitted well into this environment but would have been hard to find. An academic from an Indian university, however accomplished, would have found it hard to relate to the flexible and decentralised processes that Sarabhai was attempting to put in place.

If the director had been from Indian academia, he would have tried to impose his pre-conceived notions on the fledgling institution. Sarabhai must have judged that it was better to have somebody with the qualities of a good manager and a value system that fitted in with IIMA's own, than somebody with great credentials as an academic or researcher.

Sarabhai's decision to plump for Matthai received an unexpected thumbs-up from his wife, Mrinalini. Sarabhai had not known this but Mrinalini was well-acquainted with the Matthai family. Dr Matthai and his wife, Achamma, were good friends of Mrinalini's family and Mrinalini had grown up hero-worshipping Dr Matthai. '...I always thought that he personified everything one would like in a man...'[18]

When Mrinalini was studying at Shantiniketan, she always spent a night at the Matthais' house in Calcutta. She recalls how she got acquainted with Matthai:

> On one of my visits, a young boy came to me and said very seriously, 'Do you know something, Miss Swaminathan? I can sing the "Vande Mataram" by heart.' This was Ravi Matthai and his seriousness even then when he sang that song with so much patriotism, standing erect, was noticeable. I remember even today Ravi as the serious young man of those days.[19]

One day Sarabhai came back from Calcutta and announced, 'I have found someone in Calcutta called Ravi Matthai.' To which Mrinalini responded, 'Oh! Ravi Matthai. He would be just the right person to shoulder the task of building the IIM.' It is clear from the narration that Sarabhai was in no way aware of Mrinalini's association with the Matthais.

Perhaps uncharacteristically, Matthai took his time over this decision. Sarabhai met him first and made the offer. Matthai declined. When Matthai had moved from industry to academics, the change involved only himself; now he would have to take responsibility for a whole community.[20] Then Tandon was sent to persuade him. This time, Matthai asked to know a little more about IIMA. An old family friend who was on the IIMA board joined in the effort at persuasion. (By now, the IIMA board was going all-out to entice Matthai!).

Matthai went over to Bombay and had a meeting with more members of the IIMA board, and some people from Harvard, too. They discussed the Institute's policies. Matthai asked one of the board members whether any research was being done at IIMA; to which, the member replied, 'There is not and will not be any research done at the Institute for many years to come. Case material is the number one priority.'

This disclosure, Matthai was to say later, 'made me so angry that I said, the hell with it! I am going to join.'[21] We must be forever grateful to the anonymous board member who provided the provocation. That one remark of his seems to have conveyed to Matthai that there was a challenge waiting to be taken on, an institution waiting to be built and moulded, and on which he could bring to bear all that his life had trained and prepared him for.

Matthai, according to Tandon, laid down two conditions. One, he would not remain as director for more than five to seven years; and, two, that Tandon should stay on as chairman for another two years, at least till he had completed his five-year term.

As we shall see later, Matthai's decision to step down as director after seven years at the helm was one of his great decisions at IIMA, one that took the IIMA community and the world at large entirely by surprise. We have it on Tandon's authority that the decision was taken at the time of joining itself. It could be fairly said that it was a tenure born in greatness.

A member of the administrative staff at that time recalls Matthai's arrival at IIMA. The staff member was playing badminton with a colleague when a youngish man in a sweater walked into the court. 'Gentlemen, can I join?' the stranger asked, then played for a while and left. The next day, the staff member attended a meeting called by Sarabhai to introduce the new director. It turned out to be the stranger on the badminton court!

The initial faculty response ranged from wariness to hostility. H N Pathak, one of the early members of the faculty, writes:

> The first impression about Ravi, for several of us, was that he was very young. Some of us had come to know about his background and experience but the big question in our mind was: how will he shoulder the responsibility of developing this nascent experiment in innovative professional education in India?[22]

Others were not even willing to give the young director the benefit of doubt. Dwijendra Tripathi, the well-known business historian of IIMA, recalls the corridor joke in the early months of Matthai's directorship: what are his credentials apart from being John Matthai's son? (Tripathi is quick to add that only once during their entire association did Matthai mention his father, and that too, very tangentially.)

Tripathi remembers his first meeting with Matthai. He had just returned from Harvard and had accompanied a lady colleague to the faculty mess. Matthai happened to be present and the lady introduced Tripathi.

'Have you met this new faculty member? Dwijendra Tripathi.'

Tripathi looked at Matthai and asked politely, 'And you, Sir?'

Matthai: 'My name is Ravi Matthai.'

Tripathi: 'So you are our new director.'

Matthai: 'Yes, but I am also a faculty member.'

Tripathi (jocularly): 'True, but everybody here knows you are the boss.'

Matthai was short and did not impress you at first sight, says Tripathi. But when he spoke, he held your attention. He had a cultured, British accent (he spoke neither Hindi nor Malayalam) and the language was arresting. Matthai's writing, I would add, is not as impressive.

Michael Halse, an HBS faculty working on agriculture, mentions that a certain negative perception had preceded Matthai. Matthai was said to have turned around a company of which he had been given charge. The turnaround had meant sacking people at all levels, so the story went. Matthai's arrival at IIMA was billed as 'Enter Ravi, the butcher'.

At one of their early meetings, Halse made bold to remind Matthai of his managerial reputation. Matthai seemed not to comprehend. Halse explained hesitantly that in Matthai's last job, 'er-humph, people sacked wholesale, er-humph.' Matthai was hurt by the description. He exclaimed with a hurt expression on his face, 'My God, I am not a butcher.'[23]

As an outsider to the system and somebody who was not an academic by training, Matthai started off at IIMA with something of a handicap. It was also a disadvantage that he had not had much exposure to academic administration although he had been a successful manager in the corporate world. Add to these the perceptions about his record as a manager and his being basically his famous father's son, and you understand how heavily the odds were stacked against Matthai.

Moreover, in the initial years, IIMA suffered from comparison with IIMC in many ways. IIMC had had a permanent director from the word go whereas IIMA had carried on with a part-time director for nearly four years. IIMC had managed to attract several 'star' faculty members whereas IIMA had not. These were cited as important reasons for IIMC having forged ahead. The young director's performance would be closely watched in the initial months.

Soon Matthai would face baptism by fire. His lack of experience in academic administration would be shown up in a way that seemed to confirm the sceptics who were waiting to say, 'I told you so.'

4

Erecting the Edifice

We are assembled in a small room in Wing 11 on the second floor of the main building, seated in several rows of wooden chairs on two sides of an aisle. In front of us is a long, rectangular table. Behind the table are a chair and a blackboard. By the standards of conference rooms in the corporate world, the room would qualify as forbiddingly austere.

A colleague rests against the table, facing us. He does not occupy the chair. Anybody peering into the room might be forgiven for supposing that a class was in progress, and a somewhat unruly class at that.

This is a typical meeting of the Faculty Council of IIMA presided over by the director. This is where, in principle, all important decisions relating to the Institute are made, for IIMA prides itself on being a faculty-governed institute. These meetings can go on for hours. In the old days, the meeting would even be adjourned for the day and continue the next day or a few days later.

As the meeting winds down after, say, four hours, only a handful of stragglers may be left. Right at the end, a decision or outcome may be mentioned. Later, the minutes of the meeting will state that the 'consensus' had been in favour of the decision or outcome. You could call it 'management by attrition'.

Through the meeting, some faculty members will leave, others will enter. From time to time, faculty will head for a table at a corner containing tea, biscuit, samosa or, if they are lucky, fruit cake. The discussions, often noisy and tempestuous, are punctuated from time to time by the clatter of crockery.

Unless you are seated in the last row, you have to turn around and crane your neck when somebody is talking. Some of us joke that this is one occasion when colleagues can literally become a pain in the neck. A chair in the last row and right next to the door is greatly preferred; from there, you have a privileged view of the proceedings and can make a quick and unobtrusive exit.

Sarabhai started the practice of holding Faculty Council meetings where almost all issues, certainly all academic issues were thrashed out, which gave him a basis for taking decisions. In later years, some matters came to be discussed in smaller committees. The committees made recommendations which mostly came to the Faculty Council for deliberation or ratification.

The minutes of Faculty Council meetings held in the time of Sarabhai and Matthai are a revelation. They are detailed; at times, the level of detail is excruciating. They often run into more than ten pages. It is not just that points made by faculty are recorded; there is no coyness about naming faculty, either.

Through the minutes, we can glimpse the attitude of Sarabhai and Matthai towards faculty participation in decision-making. We see them listening patiently, allowing faculty the fullest freedom to express their views, intervening only occasionally to provide clarification, summing up the views on a particular item and then presenting the consensus. Virtually the entire gamut of issues related to the running of the Institute gets discussed.

Over years of association with various Boards of Directors, I have a developed a test for judging the quality of governance in an institution: look at the quality of the minutes. If they are detailed and if there is evidence of thorough discussion, there is a good chance the institution would have got its governance right. If the minutes are sketchy, if they merely record outcomes and not the deliberations that preceded these, one needs to worry.

IIMA in the days of Sarabhai and Matthai passes the test with flying colours.

Matthai presided over his first faculty meeting in October, 1965, just a month after he took over as director. He was new to the Institute. He was in the midst of people whose academic credentials were superior to his. He was junior to some in years. But he showed not the slightest sign of self-doubt or lack of confidence.

Matthai began by asking the areas (as the departments are characterised at IIMA) to review their performance in the PGP. (It was then called the MBA programme and continued to be called so for some years thereafter; in the interest of consistency with the present, I refer to it as PGP). By this, he said, he meant not just a review of course content but introspection in relation to a wide range of problems. He would arrange for a list of problems to be circulated.

On the ITP, he indicated that he was in favour of a course correction. Faculty development did not mean 'unvarying participation' of all faculty in a particular programme. Development plans should be tailored to individual needs. It all depended on the requirements of individual faculty, the resources of the Institute and the opportunities available.

The policy on faculty development would have to be a flexible one. There should be no presumption that every faculty member joining IIMA would go to HBS for training. He also wanted development of research staff to be brought under the purview of academic development as research staff formed an important component of academic life at IIMA.

Regarding executive programmes, Matthai noticed that IIMA offered mostly general management programmes. He said the Institute needed to offer specialised programmes in which industry would be interested and to increase its earnings by increasing its programmes, participants and fees.

In-company training programmes mean easy money for faculty as well as the Institute and one would expect faculty to be partial to these. At this very first meeting with faculty, Matthai made his views clear. He did not think these programmes contributed much towards the image-building of the Institute and hence rated them low priority.

Since the Indo-Pak conflict of 1965 was on, Matthai suggested that the government might be prepared to provide funding for research projects in areas such as food production, defence strategy, import substitution and export promotion. A faculty member asked how faculty could be expected to take up such projects when they had a heavy teaching load. Matthai replied somewhat tartly and uncharacteristically: by increasing the length of their working day.

Matthai's responses at his very first faculty meeting reveal a degree of self-assurance, a sure grasp of issues and boldness of thinking, qualities that were to mark his tenure as director. In just one month, he seems to have come to quick conclusions regarding important issues. He showed that he was willing to listen to suggestions but had a mind of his own.

Matthai was to remain steadfast on the views he expressed at the very first meeting he had with faculty. For instance, he actively encouraged research assistants to upgrade themselves and helped many pursue higher studies abroad. One of them, Jahar Saha, rose to become director of IIMA.

Again, Matthai would not approve in-company training programmes unless they translated into wider benefits. A faculty member once sent him a proposal for a training programme for a financial institution. Matthai wanted to know whether it would contribute towards the institution's improving its appraisal of projects. If it did not, it was not worth pursuing.

C K Prahalad, an unabashed admirer, told me that while Matthai was always warm, friendly and accessible, 'everybody knew who was boss.' That is just the impression Matthai conveyed at his very first formal meeting with the faculty.

Students at IIMA are a docile lot compared to the typical student body in a university. There has been no strike or organised protest for decades now. There are grievances and mutterings, typically about infrastructure, and these are handled through the mechanisms available, such as the warden, the PGP Committee, etc.

Unruly behaviour is virtually unknown both in and off the classroom. This stands to reason. People who get into IIMA are high achievers. Besides, the stakes at IIMA are high. To engage in bad behaviour is to face the risk of throwing away the opportunity of a lifetime. But it hasn't always been like that. When IIMA started off, the PGP was new to the country and job prospects uncertain. The case method was novel and it contributed to a certain sense of unease. Students were unsure whether they were learning anything at all.

After a lecture or series of lectures, you have a sense of having learned something substantial. You can list the concepts taught. But after a few case discussions, you might think you just heard a lot of talk in the class and the instructor did little more than jot down on the board, points made by different students. Students were not happy with some of the instructors. Many were new to management teaching and took time to settle. Students were not happy with the grading system followed by some instructors, either.

The rumblings reached a level where faculty began to say that 'saving the MBA programme' ought to be the priority for the new director. Matthai took it upon himself to spend time with students one-on-one. Every evening, he could be seen striding across the campus to meet the waiting students. He would sit in a chair with the students sitting around him in a horse-shoe formation and have long exchanges with them:

> He spoke gently, quietly, so quietly that, when I passed by, my own work for the day being finished, even though I passed quite close behind Ravi, I could not hear his words at all. No wonder the students sensed that he was speaking to them only: that achieving their trust and understanding was the only peak he aspired to scale.[1]

This went on for several days. What passed between Matthai and the students we shall, perhaps, never know. But the meetings seemed to work. Gradually, the student protests died down. These interactions between Matthai and the students did not go down well with the faculty. Since much of the student discontent was about teaching, faculty members felt that Matthai should have involved them in the discussions. Earlier, when Sarabhai had faced student unrest, he had done just that.

IIMA was conceived as a faculty-governed institute and, after Sarabhai, it was Matthai who gave substance to this idea by making it a point to involve faculty in important decisions. However, in this particular instance, as in some others, Matthai showed that he could be utterly non-doctrinaire in his approach.

Matthai attached the greatest importance to involving faculty in decision-making but if a certain situation required a departure from the norm, he did not hesitate to do differently. The idea of a faculty-governed institute did not imply calling a meeting of faculty for every problem under the sun. It was up to the director to handle a problem on his own if that promised to be more effective.

Matthai often referred to himself as a 'layman' in the field of management who operated on 'instinct'. By 'instinct', he did not mean an absence of thought or cogitation. Not at all; Matthai was nothing if not thoughtful. He meant that, unlike experts in management, he did not have ready frameworks to guide his actions. He had to think through the requirements of various situations. To Matthai, a faculty-governed institute did not mean the surrender of the director's discretion.

IIMA prides itself on its stringent performance requirements for students. Performance is closely monitored and students who do not measure up are asked to withdraw, repeat a year or repeat courses. Faculty can be quite fanatical in applying rules. There are times when I have myself thought them heartless in asking students to leave because they did not measure up to the Institute's exacting standard. However, colleagues will solemnly aver that it is this exacting standard that makes IIMA stand out among the higher education institutions in India, and accounts for the premium its students command.

In February 1966, some six months after Matthai assumed office, the PGP committee had reviewed the academic performance of students and wanted four first-year students to withdraw from the programme, on the ground that their performance was unsatisfactory. They had been told earlier that their performance must improve. It had not, so they could not continue.

The PGP chairman, V L Mote, went to Matthai and asked that the concerned students be expelled. Matthai immediately signed the necessary expulsion letters. The concerned students were asked to vacate their hostels in 24 hours. This was a mistake. Matthai should have asked Mote to sign the expulsion letters as that would have left open the possibility of an appeal to the director. (After this episode, expulsion letters came to be signed by the PGP chairman).

The students immediately decided to go on strike. They insisted that the four cases be reviewed and stayed away from classes for two consecutive days. A meeting of the PGP committee was called to take stock of the situation. Matthai came to the meeting and quickly excused himself saying, 'I do not want my position as director to be compromised by my being present. So I will leave.'

This bit of drama was meant to assert a principle, namely, that the director stands above some operating decisions. Matthai's assertion of this principle was however somewhat belated. He should have taken this position when Mote had asked him to sign the expulsion letters in the first place.

The faculty was for standing firm on the issue and it affirmed its solidarity with Matthai. Matthai conveyed to students through a team of three faculty members that he would not meet them until the demonstrations stopped. This did not work, so he decided to address the students. He told them that this was not an industrial dispute and that the relationship of teacher to student was more of a parental kind. Students could list their demands and take a constructive approach.

In a bid to break the impasse, Chowdhry arranged for Tandon, then chairman of the board, to visit IIMA. She and Matthai had been rather distant until then but this situation brought them together. The three met at Chowdhry's house. It was decided that the expulsion letters be withdrawn. It is fair to surmise that the suggestion was made to Matthai and he went along. The students then called off their strike.

Matthai called a meeting of the faculty the next day. He entered the room with his head drooping, his body language could not have been more defeatist. He muttered, 'I don't know what I have done ... but I have withdrawn the expulsion letters ... everybody deserves a second chance.'

The faculty was agitated. It thought Matthai had caved in lamely. How could he have taken such a decision without taking it into confidence? The episode, so early in Matthai's tenure, was a huge setback. It seemed to confirm the faculty's assessment that a somewhat callow individual had been thrust into the director's seat.

And yet this was to be a defining moment in many ways, an experience from which Matthai learnt and adapted. Thereafter, every action of Matthai's was carefully thought through, he acted with the utmost caution. He unfailingly consulted the faculty but never failed to convey, where required, that there was such a thing as the director's discretion. He achieved that fine balance between faculty sentiment and directorial prerogative that was to give IIMA its unique character and underpin much of its early dynamism and success.

In the process, Matthai not only recovered from the initial setback but rose higher in the esteem of his colleagues, eventually reaching a position of unassailable authority. His stature in the Institute was to remain undiminished even after he stepped down as director.

While he went on the defensive for appeasing the student community, Matthai was quick to make the point to faculty members that there were several lessons to be learnt from the student flare-up. The relationship between faculty and students was not healthy. Communication between the two sides was poor. The grading methodology had not been properly explained to students.

Students should have been told that if they were disqualified, they had a right to appeal first to PGP committee and then to the director. Matthai told the faculty that he had informed the students that a sub-committee of the PGP committee would look into the four cases and its decision would be final. He said he was preparing a note on the episode and it would be a good case study.

The episode brought about several positive changes. In July 1966, the faculty approved a grading system and criteria for promotion from the first to the second year, which has remained largely intact ever since. The points corresponding to each grade and sub-grade were defined and this served as the basis for computing the cumulative grade point score.

The grade point required for promotion was specified. A system of continuous review and communication of performance was introduced. Faculty were told to clearly specify the grading system for a given course, the weights that would apply to quizzes, tests, mid-term examination, end-term examination, class participation, etc.

However, this did not put an end to the students' grievances. In 1967, Matthai's second year as director, a fresh set of complaints cropped up. These related mostly to the implementation of the evaluation and grading system. Matthai had two meetings with the students. Unlike during the 1966 crisis, the PGP chairman was present at these meetings between students and the director.

Students alleged that the grading system was flawed in many ways. Favouritism was being shown to some students, copying was ignored, different faculty members had different weights for class participation and other components, and so on. They said it was not correct to ask students to leave on the basis of their grades when the grading system itself was suspect.

The matter was discussed at a faculty meeting. Faculty proposed measures that were to stand the Institute in good stead in the years to come: more interactions between faculty and students; meetings of students with the PGP chairman and the director; strengthening of the Student Affairs Committee; and taking the inputs of heads of administrative activities into account in evaluating faculty performance.

Matthai also constituted a committee presided over by himself to look into the students' suggestions.

Eventually, in 1969, a PGP policy manual came to be prepared. It defines the entire set of requirements and processes related to the PGP which has been and is the reference document for students and faculty alike. In relation to the PGP, it has the status of a written constitution.

'Violation of the manual' is one of the harshest criticisms that an IIMA faculty member can face even today. Major modifications are not easily effected and can be subject to deliberations almost as involved as those that accompany amendments to the Indian Constitution. The codification of the PGP processes, transparency in grading and the policy of continuous engagement with students had the desired effect. The student disturbances died down for good, to a point where they are unknown in the Institute today.

One reason why student restiveness was quickly contained could have been the success that IIMA had with placements right from the very first batch. For B-school students, placement is everything. The average, median and highest salaries define the ranking of a business school.

Many things go into success at placement: the quality of faculty, course content, infrastructure, the location of the school, etc., but placement is the bottom line on which B-schools are judged. Every year, magazines carry cover stories on the ranking of B-schools in India. The stories carry tables that compare B-schools on various dimensions but it is only the first table that matters to students, the one that compares salaries.

Box 4.1: An emphasis on excellence in teaching

One of the hallmarks of IIMA is the emphasis on excellence in teaching. Matthai did not hesitate to show the door to those who failed to measure up. The Institute has, by and large, maintained its standards of teaching over the past five decades. While IIMA cannot match the research record of top schools elsewhere, teaching is one dimension where it can claim to be close to international standards.

In all programmes, the faculty is rated by students. The ratings are displayed on the faculty notice board at the end of each semester. This contributes to peer pressure to perform well, although such pressure is never overt. Poor student ratings can come in the way of confirmation and promotion. New faculty members are encouraged to attend courses taught by their colleagues. In some cases, faculty members who have difficulty in the classroom are mentored by senior colleagues, although this practice is far less prevalent today than it was in the initial years.

There is also a process of monitoring of courses in a given semester, especially courses offered by new faculty. Student grumblings are picked up by the PGP office and relayed through the PGP chairman to the concerned faculty and sometimes to the director.

Even for senior faculty, there are incentives to do well in class. Faculty members who establish themselves as good teachers are greatly in demand for well-paid executive programmes. Indifferent performers in the class will lose out on these opportunities. The PGP and other long-duration programmes offer an opportunity to test out and refine cases which can then be offered in executive programmes.

Some of the faculty in the initial decades became renowned for their teaching styles and went on to become legends. Perhaps the best known was K Balakrishnan, professor of finance and business policy, who brought unusual intensity and drama into the classroom. Balakrishnan would race from the floor to the top of the gallery, then from one end to the other and come rocketing down to the blackboard. He would hector, mock and, on occasion, even burst into tears. There was never a dull moment. V L Mote and Sampath Singh were other faculty members whose theatrics lent an edge to their gifts of exposition.

B-schools like to declare that they are not placement agencies, they are in the business of providing quality education. The reality is that the quality of placement has become a measure of the quality of education. So much so, B-schools are wary about raising their intake of students drastically for fear that average placement salary would take a beating. It is almost as if, in determining their intake, they work backwards from an average placement salary they have in mind.

Everybody at IIMA understood that the future of the PGP hinged on whether the graduates of the first batch could get good jobs. If the Institute's products did not find suitable employment, the Institute would not be able to attract good quality applicants to the PGP. Also, if placement of the first batch did not go off well, it would be difficult to interest companies in the Institute thereafter.

Although the first batch would be in the job market in April, planning for placement did not commence until January that year. One faculty member proposed at a meeting that the responsibility for organising placement be given to S K Bhattacharyya. This was not an honour that Bhattacharyya coveted at all and he protested that at no point had it been indicated to him that his job involved such administrative responsibilities.[2]

All to no avail. Faculty members were unanimous in wanting Bhattacharyya to take up the assignment. They thought that since he had spent time with the business world and also with the Department of Company Affairs, he would have the necessary contacts and sufficient clout with companies to be able to make a success of the assignment.

Bhattacharyya set about his task in right earnest. He listed the immediate tasks. IIMA should send a brief bio-data of the graduating batch to select companies that were seen as potential employers. The Institute should also write personal letters to CEOs of large companies, inviting them to visit the campus for recruitment. Seniors members of the faculty and board members must approach their contacts in industry and government seeking support for placement. Based on a scrutiny of the complete background of graduating students (including education and experience prior to IIMA), select CVs must be sent out to companies with whom the students had a potential fit.

Letters bearing the signature of the director were sent out to 150 companies. The letters elicited tentative responses. The companies said they were interested in hiring the Institute's students as management trainees but they were not sure in which area the students could best contribute.

This must have seemed a little odd considering that leading companies, including MNCs, had routinely hired trainees from reputed institutions such as Oxford and Cambridge without much thought as to the students' field of specialisation and how it related to marketing or finance or any corporate function.

History, economics, even philosophy graduates had long been welcome, and continue to be welcome, not just at industrial firms but also at banks and investment banks. All that matters is the pedigree of the college. With IIMA's first batch, it may well be that companies were tentative in their responses because they had no means of knowing how good IIMA's programme was.

Bhattacharyya then set out on an eight-week tour of industrial cities, carrying with him profiles of the graduating students. He was promptly dubbed the 'travelling salesman of the Institute's products.' He was assigned a secretary specifically for placement purposes; the secretary was not only 'singularly innocent of all knowledge regarding filing, drafting or taking any action on his own'[3] but apparently also had the habit of disappearing when the workload increased. Bhattacharyya returned from his tour to find piles of correspondence that had gone unanswered.

The placement office has come a long way since. Today, there is a full-fledged placement committee headed by a faculty member and a permanent secretariat that is well-staffed and works like a well-oiled machine. Placement efforts are supported by a substantial budget, students mostly manage the show, and IIMA has long been in a sellers' market.

For all the limitations with which placement activity started, the first programme was a success. Top companies, both Indian and foreign, participated. They could easily make out that they were dealing with students of high quality, students who had made it through a stiff admission process and then gone through a rigorous programme.

Thanks to their training in the case method, the students showed their calibre when it came to fielding questions during interviews, often revealing an insight into business that surprised employers. The offers made were attractive even when compared to those made to IIT graduates and, more importantly, they were for positions that were managerial rather than functional in content.

In the first batch, there were 42 job offers. The average salary offered was ₹372, the salary range, ₹150-650. Just to put these numbers in perspective, the average salary was one-fifth the salary of a full professor and the highest salary, about half. Today, the average salary is equal to that of a full professor and the highest salary, a significant multiple.

Most students ended up with at least two offers. Everybody at IIMA understood that the Institute had, as Bhattacharyya puts it, 'arrived on the professional education scene.' This was reflected in the quality of students the Institute was able to attract in the batches that followed.

Students understood that it was difficult to get into IIMA and just as difficult to survive the programme; but if you got in and survived, there was something to look forward to. That, most people would agree, remains the position in IIMA's golden jubilee year.

Matthai had to quickly come to grips with two related issues: the Institute's finances and the creation of a proper campus. Faculty and students had operated out of temporary premises in the first two years. The first dorms at the Vastrapur campus were ready by September 1965 when Matthai took over as director.

Thirty faculty houses were to be completed by December 1965, but Matthai decided these would be initially used by students since they would soon have to vacate their Gujarat Housing Board flats. More dorms to accommodate 150 students were planned for June 1966.

Faculty members would start moving into the campus by April 1966. A temporary kitchen and dining room were planned at the campus. Later, servants' quarters, library, administration and faculty offices, a proper kitchen and dining hall and a water reservoir would follow.

Many of these plans were strictly on paper. There was a question mark over whether the construction of buildings could proceed at all. Projections made by the accounts department showed that, by the end of financial year 1965-66, the Institute would not have any funds left to make payments for construction.

As one officer puts it, IIMA faced a Catch-22 situation.[4] Government and other agencies that were approached for funds wanted to know about IIMA's performance. Without proper buildings, however, it was difficult for IIMA to perform.

Matthai made the all-important decision: 'Let us go ahead, let us build.' This required confidence on his part to be able to raise the necessary funds. The building costs had originally been estimated at ₹3 million and industry was expected to cover this amount. However, the cost soon escalated beyond ₹10 million and IIMA required assistance from the government.

This was a problem as the government had not offered any grant towards building; it had only committed ₹1.4 million annually towards recurring costs. In 1965, it was clear that this could not cover the staff salaries. It was also apparent that the sum of ₹1.1million the government had committed towards equipment and non-recurrent facilities including the library, would not meet the infrastructure requirements of the Institute. To top it all, the government was insisting on a complete government audit of accounts.

Matthai used his persuasive powers to entirely change the financial profile of the Institute:[5]

▶ The government accepted that the annual ceiling of ₹1.4 million for recurring expenses was unrealistic and agreed to meet the actual expenses without any upper limit. In the initial years from 1966-67 onwards, the contribution from government was around ₹3 million.

▶ The ceiling of ₹1.1 million towards non-recurring expenses was also removed.

▶ The Institute sought and was given two grants towards building, one for ₹1.6 million and another for ₹8 million. Building grants continued for several years thereafter.

- ▶ The Ministry of Agriculture agreed to give a grant for the Centre for Management of Agriculture (on which, more later). These grants continue to this day.
- ▶ The Ford Foundation sanctioned grants towards research and infrastructure.
- ▶ USAID gave funds for the construction of some dormitories.

Note that the contribution of the government completely dwarfed that of industry in the initial years itself, not to speak of the substantial contributions from government in subsequent years. The government has also contributed by awarding consulting assignments to IIMA.

These facts have been lost sight of, in the attempt in recent years to portray IIMA as a public-private partnership and, more fancifully, as a private institution. True, the Central Government was not the sole promoter of IIMA. However, where others faded away after initial contributions, the Central Government remained a contributor until the early noughties.

Matthai quickly disposed of the matter regarding the Central Government auditing IIMA's accounts by convincing the government that commercial audit would suffice. IIMA had created a favourable impression in government with its early performance and Matthai's persuasive powers were not inconsiderable.

It is ironical, and also a measure of Matthai's achievement, that IIMA came to be subjected to audit by the Comptroller and Auditor General (CAG) of India again in 2003-04 after it had ceased to be dependent on government funds. In the relationship with government, trust and confidence are everything. It was there in the time of Sarabhai and Matthai, and it continued thereafter. For a variety of reasons, that trust and confidence has eroded in recent years. We explore this theme further in Chapter 7.

I have mentioned earlier that fund-raising is one of the key tasks for any head of an academic institution in the US. Matthai, as we have seen, did a good job of raising funds from the government. There are some who believe that, with his extensive contacts in industry, Matthai might have raised resources from the private sector as well and helped create a substantial corpus.

Matthai did make attempts to raise funds abroad; on this, more later. As for raising money from the Indian private sector, we do not know whether Matthai gave thought to this matter. What we can say with a measure of assurance is that funding ceased to be a constraint for IIMA soon after Matthai took over and it has not been a constraint to the Institute's growth at any point since.

Recruitment and development of faculty were priorites for Matthai after he assumed office, as it should be with the head of any educational institution. Faculty recruitment was something on which Matthai expended incredible energy. In May 1967, Matthai visited the USA, the first of his many visits as director. One of the main purposes was to recruit faculty from abroad. He made it a point to inform the faculty in advance about his foreign trips, outline the objectives and provide a detailed briefing on his return.

Matthai's decision to recruit faculty from abroad was a bold one. He was averse to recruiting from within India, and not just because it was difficult to get quality faculty. He felt that recruiting from within the country did little to enlarge the faculty pool. It would only redistribute faculty from one institution to another. Recruiting from abroad was necessary in order to augment the pool of faculty.

Faculty or doctoral candidates in the US were hesitant to return to India; understandably, given the superior opportunities in the US and the fact that IIMA was still a new institution. And yet,

Matthai was able to motivate many to take the plunge. He also had an uncanny knack for judging who would be right for IIMA. Very often, he made open-ended offers to people, leaving it to them to decide when they wanted to join. He was careful to recruit only from reputed institutions. The many recruits from abroad that Matthai garnered must rank among his great contributions to IIMA.

Matthai made job offers entirely on his own and without any reference to the faculty at IIMA. This was a complete departure from the standard practice in most schools in India and abroad, which was to invite applicants for a seminar and interviews with faculty members in the particular field to which the applicants had applied. IIMA, too, fell in line with this practice some years later but in Matthai's time, recruitment vested largely in the office of the director.

On his first trip, Matthai interviewed some 65 candidates all by himself and made 18 offers. I doubt that a comparable recruitment effort has happened any time since. Indeed, it would be worth investigating how many areas have interviewed 65 candidates in the entire post-Matthai period!

Matthai reported to faculty that he expected 15 to join, some in 1967 itself and others a year or two down the road. Matthai visited the US again in October 1967. He interviewed a number of candidates and made five tentative offers for faculty positions.

In 1968, after another trip to the US, he reported that he had drawn a blank as the majority of applicants were not of good quality. In May-June 1969, he interviewed 60 candidates in the US, made 15 offers and expected about five or six to join by 1970. The increase in faculty strength during his tenure, with a large component of faculty trained in the US, was almost entirely Matthai's accomplishment.

G S Gupta, a retired faculty member of IIMA, narrated to me his experience of being interviewed for a faculty position at IIMA. He was doing his doctorate at Johns Hopkins in Baltimore and had to travel to New York to meet Matthai. Matthai said he would cover Gupta's travel expenses.

'When I met him, I was surprised at how simple he looked. It was summer and he was sporting a bush shirt,' Gupta recalled. 'He grilled me for half an hour.'

I asked, 'He grilled you on economics? But he was only a BA from Oxford.'

Gupta replied, 'He knew enough economics to grill me for half an hour.'

Matthai offered Gupta a position, agreed to cover his travel expenses to India, and also offered to pay baggage allowance. Gupta was to stay on at IIMA until retirement.

Today, recruitment to IIMs from abroad is down to a trickle. Many in the IIM system will say that there is little they can do about this. The rationale is, a faculty position in a US business school is more attractive in every way and it is hard to entice faculty in management abroad to move to India. Very true but not entirely true. There is always a small number willing to relocate to India especially since economic prospects in India have started brightening in recent years.

The challenge is to interest this small number. How open an institution is to those from abroad; how far it is willing to go to make things attractive for those wanting to return to India; and what sort of ambience and facilities it is willing to create for research – these are important factors. It is all a matter of whether leadership in India's elite institutions is up to the challenge.

Matthai was successful because he scored on these counts. He was clear in his mind that IIMA would seek out talent from abroad, he welcomed those interested with open arms, he was able to persuade people that IIMA was an attractive destination and he was able to create an exciting environment for those who made the move.

In taking upon himself the responsibility for recruitment, Matthai disregarded the hallowed practice in academia of leaving it to the concerned areas to recruit faculty. This is yet another example of Matthai's being guided by his 'instinct'. Perhaps that is precisely why the Institute had more success with overseas recruitment than at any time since. Matthai brought more foreign-qualified academics into IIMA than any other director has since done.

In theory, recruitment by the area is desirable as it subjects a candidate to a wider judgement and helps insulate recruitment from pressures that heads of institutions are exposed to. However, elite institutions in our system are subjected to very little market discipline. There are no incentives for those within to recruit faculty of high quality – indeed, they may stand to gain by not doing so. As a result, leaving recruitment to areas can easily result in faculty keeping out talent because they find it threatening.

A director, committed to raising standards and with the gift of judging talent, can make an enormous difference by overriding vested interests. The downside, of course, is that concentrating such powers in a director can spell disaster if the person concerned is lacking in integrity or competence. Recruitment of faculty by the director worked in Matthai's time because the director happened to be Matthai.

Matthai also had to take decisions on faculty development early on in his tenure. The ITP, which had been the principal mechanism for development of faculty, was reviewed at a faculty meeting in August 1965 just before Matthai assumed office. In the initial years, the ITP commended itself as a mechanism for creating a nucleus of faculty trained in the pedagogy and course work of a top B-school in time for launch of the PGP.

That purpose had since been met. IIMA faculty members were now available for providing training in curriculum building, case writing, teaching, etc. So there was a sense that the Institute needed to rethink its training needs. Future training should be tailored to the background and needs of individual faculty.

Secondly, there was some unease over the way the ITP was organised and the way participants were regarded as 'poor second cousins from the developing countries'. Participants in ITP 'neither had the status of learners in the MBA or executive development programmes ... nor were they accorded the recognition as scholars which accrue to those who are attached to the doctoral programme.'[6]

Box 4.2: Spotting talent: C K Prahalad

I had the opportunity to meet C K Prahalad, the well-known management guru, in Ahmedabad in January 2010, just three months before his unexpected demise. Prahalad told me that Matthai was instrumental in his moving into academia. Matthai assumed the directorship of IIMA in August, 1965. Prahalad graduated from IIMA's first batch in 1966. He was a gold medallist.

Matthai could have known Prahalad as a student only for a few months. Yet the Director chose to keep in touch with the newly-minted graduate. Matthai made it a point to give Prahalad a call whenever he was in Madras (now Chennai) where Prahalad had taken up a job with a manufacturing firm. Sometimes, they met for lunch.

At one such meeting, Matthai told Prahalad he should consider a career in academics. 'You are wasting your time here.' Matthai offered Prahalad a faculty position at IIMA. Prahalad accepted and joined IIMA as a faculty member in 1971.

A few months after Prahalad joined IIMA, Matthai announced his (now famous) decision to step down as director. Prahalad was distraught. He went to Matthai's office and protested, 'You get me to join this place and then you step down as director?'

'What does your entering academics have to do with my being director?' Matthai said calmly. 'I could have been knocked down by a truck. You are in academics because that is right for you.' From IIMA, Prahalad went on to do his DBA at HBS. The rest, as they say, is history.

Prahalad was gracious enough to acknowledge that the inspiration for his bottom-of-the-pyramid paradigm, for which he became famous in his last years, had come from Matthai's Jawaja project (Chapter 8). Said Prahalad, 'Matthai attacked the problem piecemeal; I am trying to see whether we can scale up using technology.'

The faculty was of the view that there was need for greater depth in the ITP and better ownership by HBS faculty. Participation of the faculty in doctoral seminars was mooted. Sarabhai himself favoured continuing with the ITP and suggested that HBS and IIMA work together to address deficiencies noticed thus far. He mentioned that HBS was undertaking such an exercise on its own.

Matthai came to some quick decisions soon after he joined. He decided that HBS would not be the only place faculty members would go to, there could be other quality institutions with which IIMA could work out arrangements. Equally important, all faculty need not go to HBS only for the ITP, they could opt for the MBA or DBA programmes as well.

Suresh Seshan, Keshav Prasad and K Balakrishnan were among those who completed their MBA at HBS and returned to IIMA. One IIMA faculty member who was sponsored for the DBA and made it big was C K Prahalad.

Matthai also decided to create fellowships for faculty members who wanted to go abroad for doctoral work and to scout for fellowships for graduate students from IIMA who wished to do the same. Faculty members continued to go to ITP until 1967 but the numbers came down over time.

Then, there was the larger issue of collaboration with HBS itself. The collaboration had been planned for five years, which meant it would expire some time in 1967. There were two issues that Matthai had to wrestle with. Should the collaboration continue? And should IIMA be tied exclusively to HBS?

Matthai was clear in his mind about the answer to the second question. IIMA would be open to faculty from other foreign institutions as it could not be assumed that HBS would be able to spare sufficient faculty for long. As with development of IIMA faculty, so also with sourcing of foreign faculty, Matthai favoured diversifiying IIMA's options.

This did not sit well with some of the IIMA faculty. They felt that if faculty members were brought in from institutions other than HBS, it would imply dilution of the case method which IIMA had borrowed from HBS. And the case method had been one of the unique selling points of IIMA. Matthai demurred. He felt that IIMA should encourage diverse pedagogical approaches. As he put it, he did not want to make IIMA 'a Roman Catholic Church of the case method.'

Matthai pursued his idea of opening up IIMA to faculty other than those from HBS, with vigour. On one of his visits to the US, Matthai addressed faculty at several universities to try and interest them in spending a year or more at IIMA. He interviewed 40 American faculty members and shortlisted seven. In this, he did have some success. In 1968, of the five foreign faculty at IIMA, two were from Harvard, one from Columbia, one from Michigan State and one from London.

Matthai also tried to work out exchange programmes with B-schools other than HBS. The intention was that IIMA faculty upgrade and refresh themselves through visits to leading US schools. Matthai also informed faculty that he was exploring possibilities for collaboration in research between IIMA and US universities.

None of these initiatives fructified. It's not hard to fathom why. The leading US schools could not have seen any advantage in letting IIMA faculty come in and teach or do research unless the concerned faculty measured up to international standards. This would also explain why IIMA has not had such exchange programmes even in recent years, except with some of the lesser schools in Europe.

The collaboration with HBS was a more serious matter. The benefits to the Institute were obvious: training of IIMA faculty via the ITP; participation of HBS faculty in the executive programmes (though not in the MBA programme); access to HBS cases. However, the relationship had not been smooth sailing. Several irritants had cropped up.[7] Both parties had their complaints.

HBS felt its advice was sought only on the academic side, namely, the planning and staffing of academic programmes, course content, etc. Matters such as the leadership style and faculty evaluation were regarded as 'administrative' and on these, HBS inputs were not sought. We should not be surprised that HBS felt a little slighted. As the leading B-school in the world at the time, HBS was clearly the superior partner in the relationship and it would have been natural for them to want to call the shots on all matters.

IIMA, for its part, did not relish the stipulation that HBS faculty would teach in executive programmes and not in the MBA programme. It also did not like HBS faculty sent to IIMA being designated as 'consultants'. Both these gave rise to the perception that the visitors were in a special category and it created a certain amount of resentment amongst IIMA faculty.

Besides, HBS did not spare many senior faculty members for IIMA. The first three individuals who came from HBS were doctoral candidates. Some of the senior faculty members sent out by HBS were products of the school but not HBS faculty. Warren Haynes, who stayed for two years and was the first MBA chairman, was from the University of Southern California. Thereafter, one emeritus professor visited IIMA for a year and, later, one junior professor for a longer period.

A third and, perhaps, more serious problem was HBS' insistence on being involved in the selection of a director to succeed Sarabhai. As we saw in Chapter 2, in 1962, when this request was first communicated, Sarabhai had side-stepped it saying that the search for a director had already commenced, so it would not be possible to involve HBS. In 1963, when the offer of directorship was made to Srinagesh, HBS was unhappy at not having been taken into confidence. HBS' opposition to Sarabhai's attempts to install Chowdhry as his successor added to the strains in the relationship.

This entire background may have weighed on Matthai when he took over. In the initial months, he showed a disinclination to keep in touch with HBS either by correspondence or through visitors.

The signals he sent out were not promising. The decision to recruit Indian faculty from abroad; the move away from the ITP as the sole mechanism of faculty development; the reduced emphasis on the case method; and the plans to source foreign faculty from institutions other than HBS all indicated to the latter that the collaboration no longer carried the same importance as before.

Once he had settled down, Matthai indicated that he had an open mind on the question. He told faculty that some changes were required in the collaboration. He agreed with the general perception that having HBS faculty as consultants was not helpful. HBS faculty should be normal faculty members of the Institute and they should be assigned a major objective which would be determined by the needs of the Institute.

He had initial discussions on the collaboration with Hansen of HBS and then pursued matters with Dean Baker while on a visit to the US in October 1967. During this visit, Matthai addressed HBS faculty. He presented Dean Baker with a copy of the first book to come out of IIMA, 'Studies in Block Development and Cooperative Organisations'. He also presented HBS faculty with a large silver and rosewood replica of the IIMA emblem, on behalf of IIMA faculty.

Matthai seems to have sounded out HBS on the possibility of a higher level of collaboration. He broached the subject of IIMA faculty spending time at HBS to teach and carry out research. It appears that HBS was willing to make a start with Chowdhry whom they knew well and respected.[8]

The atmospherics were just right for an upgraded relationship, because one source of friction in the relationship had just been removed. This was the stipulation that expenditures made by IIMA (and IIMC) under Ford Foundation grants required the concurrence of their respective partners, HBS and Sloan School. The stipulation had created a sense in the two IIMs that they were in a subordinate relationship.

The clause was revised in 1967 to allow each of the two IIMs to make their own technical assistance arrangements. IIMA promptly renewed its contractual arrangement with HBS and IIMC with Sloan. Now at last, the IIMs had a sense of being equal partners.

This change should have resulted in a more mature and tension-free relationship between the two IIMs and their collaborators. However, this was not to be. For reasons that are not clear, it marked a period of withdrawal and severance on the part of HBS and Sloan. Sometime in 1967, the collaboration came to an end.

While ending the formal collaboration, Matthai was able to persuade HBS to continue the relationship in informal ways. Faculty continued to go to HBS for advanced studies. HBS faculty would help out with preliminary interviews of US-based applicants for faculty positions at IIMA. Matthai's tour programme during his visits to the US continued to be planned by HBS.

We can only speculate on what brought the collaboration to an end. It could well be that HBS did not see any significant value to itself from continuing the association on the upgraded basis that Matthai had in mind. A top US school would not mind sparing doctoral candidates and junior faculty, as HBS did with IIMA in the initial years. But it would think very hard about committing senior faculty in large members to any overseas venture. The costs to the institution as well as to faculty are high.

Even today, with talk of higher education being opened to foreign universities, it is a moot question how many quality institutions will enter the country. People rightly ask: what is in it for them? Similarly, there is hardly any benefit to a top US B-school in allowing faculty from a lesser institution to come in and teach or do research.

Some former faculty members at IIMA have a different view. V L Mote, who was among the earliest recruits to IIMA, recalls Tandon telling him that the collaboration with HBS ended 'because of Ravi's ego.' Another IIMA veteran, D Tripathi, says that Matthai had once mentioned to him that HBS was keen to continue the collaboration and he had chosen to end it because 'you can't build an institution on the coat-tails of another institution.' Both believe that the decision to end the collaboration with HBS was Matthai's.

There is nothing in the official records to substantiate these views. It is fair to surmise that both Matthai and HBS had concluded that the collaboration with HBS had served the purpose of hand-holding during the initial period. It was now time to move on.

The record of HBS' collaboration elsewhere in Asia (with the Asian Institute of Management, Manila) and in central America, suggests that HBS did not generally view an extended relationship with favour. It was happy to open up its ITP and doctoral programmes to faculty from institutions with which it collaborated because this did not impose any costs on them, indeed it enhanced HBS revenues. But, anything else, and especially faculty exchanges, was not seen as worthwhile.

For those who believe that IIMA missed a great opportunity to become world-class by staying with HBS, there is an obvious lesson here. There are no short-cuts to becoming a world-class educational institution.

By 1966, the 3-TP, which had given the Institute a flying start, had stabilised. The number of participants rose from around 40 in the first batch in 1964 to 60. Door-to-door selling was no longer required. But the Institute kept fine-tuning the programme to better align it with the requirements of the market.

The issue of Indianisation of faculty in the 3-TP had been raised from time to time. Sarabhai had not been in favour of reducing the presence of HBS faculty. He took the position that it was the presence of the international faculty team that had given the executive programmes their special flavour and had contributed to their early success.

Matthai felt differently. In 1966, he decided that HBS faculty would not participate in the 3-TP after 1967. He did not favour the short visits that HBS faculty made for participation in 3-TP. He felt that HBS faculty should be invited to IIMA for short visits only for projects that were of interest to both HBS faculty and IIMA.

Meanwhile, the Institute had also launched the Programme for Young Executives (PYE), which was targeted at senior executives in family-managed businesses. These businesses, it was felt, would not be able to participate in 3-TP as they might not be able to send participants at all three levels. However, they would have training requirements at the senior level. The Institute had judged correctly. The PYE's first batch in 1967 drew 41 participants.

The 3-TP was reviewed in September 1968. By then, five rounds had been done. The programme had been intended to bring about change in an organisation at all levels, hence companies were required to send participants at all levels, at least when they were participating for the first time.

An analysis of five years of data showed that many companies were not meeting this requirement. Management development had become more common than when 3-TP had been launched, so many firms did not think it necessary to participate at all levels. IIMA decided not to insist on participation at all levels.

This practice of tweaking programmes, whether executive programmes or the flagship PGP or the newly launched PGP-X (for people with work experience), and effecting modifications to respond to changes in the market, has since become part of IIMA's culture.

The 3-TP was held in Agra and the PYE in Mussorie. The logistics could be quite daunting. Not just faculty but staff had to travel all the way and, in the case of the 3-TP, spend several weeks away from home. Transporting teaching materials was not easy. In those days, copying machines had not come into vogue and cyclostyling machines were required.

A secretary, who helped out with 3-TP, told me that 16 trunks, containing materials and cyclostyling machines, had to be transported by train to Agra. Taxis were not available at the railway station and the trunks had to be transported in 16 cycle-rickshaws!

The organisation for management programmes came to be strengthened. An external programmes committee of three persons was created to assist the external programmes director in management education programmes. This was the forerunner of today's Management Development Programmes committee.

Matthai had been insistent that the Institute should not confine itself to general management programmes. It should launch sectoral programmes as well. Accordingly, a 2-tier banking programme was launched in Agra in late 1970. It was a success. All nationalised banks and the RBI participated. There were 38 participants in the first tier and 25 in the second tier.

In December 1967, a USAID survey team rated IIMA the best management institution in India. It also found that industry in India felt the same way. This was in the days before the magazines had started ranking B-schools in India and it was as good an endorsement as any, of the impact IIMA had made on the management scene.

Faculty could see for themselves the change that Matthai had wrought in the Institute in a very short period of time. With his unassuming ways, friendly manner and transparent sincerity, Matthai had won the confidence of the community, indeed, he had come to be admired.

As Bhattacharyya wrote later:

The result of all this (Matthai's initiatives) was dramatic and within a couple of years of Ravi's arrival, we had evidently done something which was discernible as excellent achievement not only in India but in the academic and business world elsewhere... The original hostility to Matthai had somehow transformed itself into pride at being led by such a man.[9]

Matthai himself was not entirely elated. At a meeting with faculty, he observed ruefully that while the Institute had quickly made a name for itself outside, 'we are not so happily off inside.' The deteriorating atmosphere inside the Institute, he said, was cause for concern. Many problems that had surfaced in the recent past had an unhealthy personal element to them.

Faculty had begun to avoid committee meetings because they found them painful. There had been 'unconstructive activities', and attempts to pull people down rather than build an institution. He wanted to bring it all out into the open and encourage free discussion so that the situation could be improved. Faculty needed to evolve norms for behaviour and for solving problems. While the high opinion of the outside world might boost the morale of faculty, it was imperative for the latter to set its house in order.

There were other challenges. The Institute needed to augment the scope of its activities. A doctoral programme, for instance, was sorely needed. The administrative structure of the Institute itself required examination. Discontent over faculty evaluation was rife. Matthai had established himself in command but there was still much to be done.

5

Towering Over the Rest

In February, 1966, around the time the first batch of PGP students was due to graduate, Matthai began to think of launching a doctoral programme. The idea faced resistance from the faculty. Some members felt that, given the shortage of faculty resources, a doctoral programme would undermine the efforts going into the fledgling PGP. They felt that the Institute should remain focused on PGP for a while.

Matthai was not persuaded. He knew very well that no academic institution can achieve excellence only by producing graduates or under-graduates, and providing training for corporate executives. Quality institutions include in their remit, the generation of research and teachers.

It is only by adding to the body of knowledge through research that an academic institution can make a significant impact on the world at large. Besides, research feeds into and enriches teaching. Academic institutions also need to produce teachers and future researchers through a doctoral programme as otherwise the education sector cannot be sustained.

The MBA programme in a B-school makes news. The world tends to judge B-schools by placement salaries for MBAs but that is not how B-schools judge each other, at least not in the US, the Mecca of higher education. In the US, academics judge a school's greatness by two criteria. First, how many publications in top journals do the faculty manage in a year? Secondly, where can the B-school place its doctoral candidates? Can it place them in the top 10-15 schools? Can it place them at schools whose ranking is higher than its own?

For all the frenzy in the media over the ranking of MBA programmes, getting a high rank in this category is not in itself the primary objective of a B-school in the American academic world. The rank is seen as a by-product of the quality of faculty and research.

Faculty's ability to do research is, to some extent, related to the doctoral programme. For two reasons. First, running a doctoral programme requires faculty to be acquainted with the latest research. Secondly, faculty often works closely with doctoral students in producing research and co-authoring papers.

Matthai argued that the right question was not whether to offer a doctoral programme. A doctoral programme was imperative. The question was how fast IIMA could proceed with such a programme, and this was clearly contingent on resources available.

A committee was constituted to examine how IIMA should go about launching a doctoral programme. It was headed by B G Shah, a finance professor and former dean of M S University, Baroda. As IIMA did not have degree granting status, it was decided to proceed in two phases.

In the first phase, IIMA would collaborate with universities. IIMA faculty would be empanelled with select universities, as guides for doctoral students. The universities would be chosen based on criteria such as the availability of strong social sciences, commerce and management programmes, good library facilities, existence of research activity, etc. In the second phase, IIMA would launch its own doctoral programme.

This plan did not work out. B G Shah reported back to the Faculty Council saying that the discipline of management was not well developed in universities, so getting into collaborative arrangements with them did not make sense. It would be better for IIMA to start it own doctoral programme and focus on getting degree-granting status instead.

Matthai wanted the doctoral programme to commence as early as in 1967 as he expected the Institute to acquire degree-granting status by then. This estimate was to prove hopelessly unrealistic. The process of seeking a degree-granting status stretched on well past 1971.

Matthai also announced a scheme to sponsor IIMA graduates for doctoral fellowships abroad. He argued that this had the potential to enhance the pool of teachers that management institutions in India could tap. IIMA graduates sponsored for doctoral fellowships abroad would have to sign a bond requiring them to serve IIMA for a stipulated period once they had completed their doctorates.

The faculty had reservations about this initiative as well. They feared it would undermine IIMA's own doctoral programme. Matthai allayed these fears. The IIMA programme would take some time to commence and, in the meantime, a set of Indian management faculty needed to be created.

In November 1969, the doctoral programme was entrusted to C Rangarajan, later to make a name for himself in the highest echelons of economic policy-making in the country. It was launched under his stewardship in 1971 and christened the 'Fellowship Programme in Management' (FPM) since IIMA still did not have degree-granting status. (The idea of creating 'Fellows' was Rangarajan's.)

The first batch comprised just four students. The number jumped to 13 in the second batch. The programme involved two years of course work, the first in common with PGP, followed by a dissertation.

Matthai's vision of IIMA's role in the education sector extended beyond the PGP and the doctoral programme. He wanted IIMA to help establish viable schools of management. In this, he anticipated the mentoring of new IIMs by the older IIMs, a recent initiative driven by the ministry of human resources development. He was keen to promote faculty development in universities through faculty exchanges with them. He wanted to use the universities to disseminate IIMA's efforts in the field of management education.

IIMA's initiative towards faculty development at the universities was the University Teachers Programme (UTP). The first UTP, organised during 1965-66, was confined to managerial economics. Later, the scope of the programme was expanded to include finance and accounting, personnel and organisational behaviour, operations research and general management. In the first ten years, 1962-72, four such programmes were organised and they involved 110 teachers in 102 institutions of higher learning.

The UTP focused on individual teachers. A more ambitious initiative involved collaborations with universities for building departments of management. One such collaboration was with Punjab University in Chandigarh in 1968 when the university decided to expand its department of commerce into a department of management.

IIMA faculty went over to Chandigarh to assist in the setting up of the department. Faculty from the university spent time at IIMA to work on course design and development of materials. In 1969, one faculty member from the university even attended PGP classes. IIMA thus, played a pioneering role in the creation of management education in the north-western region of the country.

IIMA also helped Kerala University to set up its School of Management Studies in 1968. Here, the assistance was related to curriculum design for the Master's programme as also for regional executive development programmes. IIMA also collaborated in varying degrees with the universities of Gujarat and Poona and with the National Institute of Bank Management in their initial stages of planning. As an Institute publication released on the occasion of the tenth anniversary put it, 'It (IIMA) views new institutions as partners rather than competitors in achieving an important social and academic purpose'.[2]

IIMA had benefited from the institution-building efforts of a foreign institution, HBS. It was fitting that IIMA should have assumed this role for itself so quickly in relation to lesser institutions in India. It is also interesting that, in later years, as the Institute grew and expanded, it became more inward-looking and its interest in collaborative ventures of this kind faded away. IIMA contributed more towards building institutions in its first decade than in the subsequent decades.

The IITs and the IIMs do a great job of teaching. They also have the advantage of getting students of very high quality. So the engineering or management product of these institutions is highly valued. If the IITs and IIMs do not make it in the global rankings, it is because they lag behind in research output.

In the initial years, 1962-65, as IIMA struggled to cobble together a team to launch the PGP, the priority was generating Indian cases. Sarabhai attached great importance to the writing of cases. He called it the 'bread and butter' of the Institute's training programmes and the 'foundation' of the Institute.

After Matthai took over and consequent to the signals he gave about cases being just one component of pedagogy, complaints began to be heard about the de-emphasis of the case method. In September 1966, Matthai thought it necessary to reaffirm the importance of the case method. Two visiting faculty from HBS, Denis Thomas and Philip Borden, were asked to prepare a note on the subject. It was suggested that 50% of all cases should be indigenous and every faculty member should write at least three cases every year.

The thrust on cases paid off. By late 1969, IIMA had written enough cases to be able to produce case books prepared in four areas: managerial economics; production management; organisational behaviour, and financial management. The objective of indigenisation of teaching materials was also substantially met by the end of the first decade. By 1972, around 60% of all teaching materials were of Indian origin and IIMA had accumulated a collection of 900 cases and technical notes.

Cases do require collection and analysis of data. However, they are teaching materials and would not qualify as acceptable output towards confirmation and promotion in leading B-schools (with the possible exception of HBS). At IIMA too, once the PGP had stabilised, questions began to be asked. Are we doing enough research? What qualifies as research? How do we measure the impact of research? How do we become thought leaders in management?

IIMA's response, sometime during 1967, was to emphasise project research to a greater extent than before. This is not quite how research is understood at leading B-schools. Research at leading schools is seen as that which extends the frontiers of knowledge. Acceptable research is strictly publications in a defined set of peer-reviewed journals.

At IIMA, the focus was on 'relevance' of research, meaning knowledge produced must be applicable. Project research met this definition. This approach was, perhaps, a compromise between doing no research at all and producing only publishable research.

Once again, the institutional focus on a particular objective produced results. By 1971-72, IIMA had completed 71 research projects. The larger research projects were mostly supported by outside sponsors or funding agencies such as the World Bank, Indian Council of Social Science Research and industry associations. In several cases, the Institute first identified problem areas, provided seed money for developing research proposals and then located outside agencies to support the proposed projects.

The projects covered a wide range of issues: demand projections for various products; industrial conflict and trade union systems; scheduling and inventory problems; competitiveness of exports; entrepreneurship and the growth of enterprises, etc. Project research continues to be an area of strength at IIMA today.

Closely allied to project research in some ways was the consulting activity of the Institute. Consulting brings B-school faculty closer to real-world problems and gives the faculty an opportunity to test out ideas. At times, it helps in the generation of case studies. Not least, it adds to the income of the Institute as well as the faculty.

The Institute was careful to discourage repetitive types of consulting work in the early years. It was clear that consulting should not be entirely mercenary in character, it should contribute to the professional development of faculty. As mentioned earlier, Matthai was averse to the faculty taking up in-company training programmes.

In the early noughties, there was a significant departure as enormous training opportunities opened up, consequent to the economic boom. In-company training programmes became a significant generator of revenues for the Institute and the primary source of consulting income for faculty.

At a daily rate of a minimum of ₹100,000, such programmes are enormously lucrative for the faculty and the Institute alike. They are easy money for faculty because they involve repetitive teaching of the same topics that faculty offer in the Institute's PGP and other programmes. They require virtually no investment on the part of faculty members and contribute little by way of professional development. Directors themselves have been heavily involved in in-company training programmes. This is one area in which the Matthai legacy has not survived.

To go back to the Matthai era, the Institute began to think of appropriate structures and systems to support research once it was identified as an area requiring greater importance. The post of research director was created in 1968. It was decided to bring out a document listing research publications of the Institute. A document detailing policy regarding publication of research papers and monographs was also prepared. Seed money for preparing research proposals had thus far been provided by the Ford Foundation. It was decided to use the Institute's own funds for the purpose.

But unease over the Institute's lack of research output persisted. Many in faculty felt that project research was not good enough and were keen on more published research. Faculty members wanted to know what IIMA had to say about management problems whether in the public or private sector. Was research being adequately incentivised by being factored into evaluation?

Matthai was only too well aware that research was one area in which the Institute lagged behind. He shared his concern internally but was too shrewd a leader to let outsiders on to it. Somebody once challenged him: 'What are you – an academic institution or a training institution?'

Matthai had the happy gift of juggling with words. He replied, 'We are an educational institution.' How much of it was academics and how much training was for others to figure out.

There are some who contend that, not being an academic himself, Matthai did not have it in him to pay enough attention to research. Perhaps the best answer to this criticism is that dissatisfaction with the Institute's research output persists to this day. If Matthai did not address this issue adequately, nor did his successors who were supposedly better placed to do so.

In Matthai's time, an adequate complement of faculty to cope with teaching requirements had been barely created. The early years had been consumed by the urgency to produce cases. Matthai's successors had greater financial resources at their disposal and a larger complement of faculty and yet did not fare any better. One could say the same of the other IIMs and IITs as well.

The elevation of IITs and IIMs from teaching institutions to centres of high quality research and thought leadership is part of the unfinished agenda in higher education in India. It requires a mix of leadership, recruitment, incentives and competition in higher education of a different order from what we have seen so far.

The evaluation of faculty at IIMA poses its own problems. In the leading institutions of higher learning, faculty is evaluated overwhelmingly on the basis of research. Teaching is a secondary matter and in some places, carries little weight in the evaluation. The best ratings on teaching will be of little avail if faculty does not produce high quality research.

The definition of research itself is straightforward: publications in 'A' grade journals. The brand equity of a natural sciences or economics department rests overwhelmingly on research, so defined. At B-schools, it may not be appropriate to adopt this approach. Two questions arise. First, what constitutes meaningful research? Secondly, can research be given the same weight as in other disciplines?

Box 5.1: Can management be taught?

Can management be taught? Do we need B-schools? These questions have been asked for decades now and continue to be asked. The point is made that management is something you pick up by doing, through experience; it is not a set of theories you acquire in the classroom.

Matthai addressed this issue squarely on more than one occasion. 'There is not an institution concerned with applied knowledge that imparts professional skills where I have not heard the unending and age-long argument about 'theory' and 'practice'. Perhaps it started when the first systems of formal education came into contact with the guild and the apprenticeship systems. It will probably continue until doomsday'.[4]

Matthai made two points about this debate. One, it was important that the argument take place. 'If the institution legitimises the fact that the argument should take place, then implicitly it has accepted as part of its educational philosophy that its educational programme must be constantly reviewed and changed as circumstances warrant such change ... by discussing it ... you will implicitly accept change as part of your educational philosophy.'

Two, 'education' and 'experience' (or 'theory' and 'practice') were not substitutable, they complemented each other. 'I thank god that I do not have to discover the laws of demand and supply all over again. ... I am sure we are all thankful that we don't have to wait apprehensively under every crow on a mango tree, waiting for Newton's gravitational inspiration to strike us ... however much or however little each one of us might assimilate from the vast accumulation of human knowledge, to that extent we lay a base for ourselves from which we enhance the value of experience ... Thus, education enhances the value of experience. If you look at a part of your working life as a series of such experiences, then from each experience, you gain that much as a result of your education. You are then accelerating your process of learning, and this is what education is about.'

This is as sensible a defence of management education as anybody can make. The whole point about an MBA programme is that it sensitises participants to various aspects of business and abbreviates the period of learning in the workplace itself.

To address the first question, many wonder whether it suffices for B-schools to produce theoretical knowledge as other disciplines do. They would like B-schools to produce research that influences practice. That is certainly a declared objective at IIMA. Of what use is management research if it cannot improve management practice?

Alas, the connection between published research and practice is pretty tenuous in the case of management. Medical journals are said to contribute substantially to improved medical practice. Law journals are greatly valued by lawyers. In management, however, publications in leading research journals are hardly read by practitioners. Many of the papers published in journals would not even be comprehensible to managers. *Harvard Business Review* is one management journal that managers like to read. But there cannot be many schools in the US where faculty members can make tenure on the strength of articles published in *HBR*.

A much cited article in *HBR* a few years ago lamented the fact that B-schools had succumbed to 'physics envy' in their research objectives, meaning that they tended to pursue abstract research without in any way bothering to relate it to practice.[5] The schools professed to be interested in practitioner-oriented research but only rewarded research 'designed to please academics'.

The authors added caustically, 'Today, it is possible to find tenured professors of management who have never set foot inside a real business unit, except as customers.' Management education was in 'crisis' because B-schools had adopted a 'self-defeating model of academic excellence.'

Defining research is not the only problem for B-schools. How much weight to give to research relative to other activities, is also a contentious issue. If influencing practice is an important objective, then writing cases assumes importance. Teaching becomes far more important than in other disciplines, as producing high-quality managers is an important objective.

Great teachers can help build the brand equity of a B-school as much as researchers do. Publications in the popular press, memberships of policy-making committees and boards also contribute to influencing practice and building brand equity. At IIMA, key administrative activities such as admissions and placement, are looked after by faculty. Faculty would have little incentive to undertake these tasks if they did not count in evaluation.

Matthai addressed the problem of faculty evaluation in his inimitable way. At one Faculty Council meeting, he made clear that any director would need to evaluate faculty. However, he had no preconceptions as to how evaluation might be done and he was entirely open to suggestion.

Many views were expressed on who should carry out the evaluation. Some said the evaluation should be done by the director, as had been the practice until then; others suggested a review by peers in the Institute; yet others wanted outside faculty to be involved. Matthai insisted that he did not want the Institute to be a 'one-man show'. He would constitute a core committee of faculty, presided over by the director, for the purpose of evaluation. The faculty went along with the proposal.

The committee, Matthai said, could involve outsiders as required. Having a core committee would help achieve a degree of consistency in the application of criteria for evaluation. The system continues to this day. Evaluation of faculty is done by a Faculty Development and Evaluation Committee (FDEC) chaired by the director. Outsiders are not co-opted but inputs from outside experts are sought.

In 1971, in an attempt to make the process of evaluation transparent, Matthai prepared a detailed note on faculty evaluation based on the extensive discussions he had had with the faculty. The note defines the work load for faculty and also the norms for evaluating each component of the work load – teaching, research, consulting, administration, publication – and also touches upon requirements of team work expected of faculty at the Institute.

The note is the closest the Institute has ever got to spelling out work load and evaluation norms. However, complaints about lack of clarity or consistency in evaluation have not ceased to this day. When an attempt to define the work load was made recently, Matthai's four decade-old note was pulled out and dusted up. Not only do the same questions about evaluation persist but the answers, it would seem, are not too different from what Matthai had proposed.

One of the unique features of IIMA is the attempt to apply management principles to important sectors of the economy other than business. Sarabhai and others believed that management principles were applicable not just to business or industry but to a wide variety of under-managed sectors. One sector that was identified early on for special attention was agriculture. As we shall see in Chapter 6, Matthai identified six other sectors that IIMA would focus on and articulated the philosophy underlying the sectoral approach in some detail.

The focus on various sectors, including agriculture, has served IIMA well for a quite different reason. The government has spent enormous sums on the IIMA as it has on other IIMs. The IIMs have sprawling campuses with good quality accommodation and other infrastructure. For the IIMs to merely produce 200-300 graduates to cater to the Indian corporate sector and to MNCs, as they did until recently, exposes them to the criticism of squandering public money for private benefit.

Around a quarter of the IIMA batch these days gets placed overseas. The high salaries they command may make front-page news in the pink papers but this is resented in the government and elsewhere. The question gets asked: what does the Institute contribute to Indian society at large and, particularly, to the under-managed sectors of the economy? Having a centre dedicated to agriculture, and other areas, such as healthcare and infrastructure, has helped the Institute address some of the criticism.

Sarabhai consulted a professor of agribusiness at HBS, Henry Arthur, on starting an agriculture group at IIMA. In response, Arthur sent a DBA student, Michael Halse, to help the Institute in 1963.[5] Arthur wanted to start an agribusiness section at IIMA as part of the marketing area, as was the case at HBS. Halse, however, favoured Sarabhai's approach of dealing with the agricultural sector as a whole instead of just agribusiness, and started working on agricultural cooperatives.

With Halse's help, another faculty member, D K Desai, came to be appointed. Sarabhai then sought financial support from C Subramaniam, then Minister for Agriculture in the Government of India. Subramaniam sanctioned a two-year grant for the study of community development. Later, the Ford Foundation provided a grant which helped create the infrastructure for the group and also served to meet travel expenses.

The grant enabled the Institute to set up a team of five faculty and five research associates to study the problems of community development. This was the genesis of the Agriculture and Cooperative

Group (AGCO). This group was unique in that it was separately funded and was not dependent on the resources provided to IIMA by the Ministry of Education. Over time, many of the other centres at IIMA have also gone down this route. Some are supported by the sectors on which they focus.

The head of the AGCO group carried the designation of 'leader' and he was given responsibility as well as authority for determining the allocation of resources within the group, and the output of the group. Halse was designated leader, to start with. In this respect, AGCO differed from the different functional areas at IIMA where the Area chairman had responsibility but no authority.

There was a rationale for the separate treatment given to the AGCO group. Unlike the areas, it had an outside provider for funds to whom it had to fulfill certain commitments, rather like the shareholder to whom the CEO is accountable. Sarabhai reckoned that this warranted a special dispensation. The leader should have adequate authority for the group as a whole to deliver. Later, Matthai went along with this arrangement but was keen that an Indian should be leader so that the group would not have to depend on foreign faculty for its development. Desai replaced Halse as leader.

In an educational institution, it is difficult to justify centres or individuals doing only research. There is a presumption that if people are working in a particular area at a centre, they must offer courses or programmes related to it. Otherwise, the centre begins to attract unwelcome attention. People are apt to ask: why should we be teaching day-in and day-out when we can migrate to a centre and focus only on research or on projects?

The AGCO group gradually began to make forays into teaching. The group initially offered an elective course on agriculture management in the second year of the PGP but this was not well received. It had better luck with training programmes. With the cooperation of the well-known Gujarat-based co-operative, Amul, the group developed a number of case studies.

This provided the basis for the launch in November 1966, of a multi-level Dairy Management programme. The programme was patterned on the 3-TP, with the difference that the Dairy programme covered the sector as a whole at the top, plant and village levels, instead of covering the three levels of a company.

The first grant from the ministry ran out in 1965, and there was some resistance in the ministry to continuing the grant as it did not see much value in the case studies that the group had produced until then. The ministry was, however, open to providing funds for project research.

The AGCO group then offered to study the planning and implementation of the High-Yielding Varieties (HYV) programme, which was a priority for the ministry then. This was approved and financial support from the ministry continued. The reports on the HYV programme went down well with the ministry, and, thereafter, they were happy to leave it to the group to propose projects of its own choosing.

In 1969, Matthai mooted the idea of launching a one-year Programme of Management in Agriculture (PMA). The intention was to have for agriculture a programme equivalent to the PGP, which was oriented towards industry.

Matthai felt that PMA students would have a market in various fields: government agricultural development activities, particularly at the district level; the banking sector with emphasis on agricultural finance; industries supplying agricultural inputs; and industries dealing with purchase and distribution of agricultural products.

The matter was discussed at a Faculty Council meeting. Faculty outside the group was almost unanimous in opposing the idea. They had many concerns. The programme would cause diversion of scarce faculty resources and result in the dilution of the PGP. What would be the impact on PGP if other sectoral programmes were started?

Some felt that combining the PGP and agricultural programme students for particular courses might not be desirable as the mix was not right. It would be difficult to place agriculture management graduates. Others pointed out that IIMC had started a similar programme and given it up, and suggested it might be better to run an 11-month external programme similar to that at HBS.

Matthai argued that there was a strong demand for management-oriented agricultural graduates. Agricultural universities were not responding to this need, so there was an opportunity for IIMA. While summing up the discussion, he announced the decision to launch the programme and made a fervent plea for faculty support.

It was one of those situations where Matthai did not hesitate to exercise the director's prerogative to override faculty sentiment. Matthai was to later say that he had been patient with faculty when it came to launching the fellowship programme. Twice, they had said they were not ready and he had dropped the idea. It was only in 1971 that faculty said they were ready and he could go ahead. However, when it came to the agriculture programme, he said he adopted a very different approach:

> 'I was thoroughly dictatorial. I threatened to sack the whole CMA (Centre for Management of Agriculture) faculty lot. I refused to give them the same degree of choices.'[6]

The initial plan was to have 40 students and 16 faculty members. Additional funds for a hostel and an office would be required. Matthai himself made a presentation of the programme to USAID.

A substantial grant followed. It included a non-recurring grant for construction of two dormitories for PMA students and a recurring grant for several faculty members, for a period of five years.

The programme was launched in July 1970. In the same year, the name of the group was changed to the Centre for Management in Agriculture and the designation of leader was changed to chairman, bringing the administrative structure of the centre in line with that of the rest of the Institute. Over the years, the Institute has successfully replicated this approach – of creating a centre, then floating courses in that area and creating administrative structures appropriate to those activities.

The PMA itself went through several mutations. It became a two-year programme with the first year in common with PGP, then a separate two-year programme, then a two-year programme with the first year in common with PGP. Today, it is called the Post Graduate Programme in Agricultural Business Management (PGP–ABM).

Many of the original objections to the programme persist and it has never quite got over the reputation of being something of a poor country cousin of the PGP. Students tend to compare placement salaries of the agriculture stream with those of the PGP; the fact that agriculture and industry are two very different sectors is easily overlooked.

Faculty members ask whether the same efforts cannot be used to simply scale up the PGP. The FPM and other programmes launched since then by IIMA also suffer in comparison with the PGP. How to bring the various programmes it offers to the standard of the PGP, remains a challenge for the Institute.

When IIMA was founded, it was presumed that the Institute would be given degree-granting status fairly quickly, say, in three to four years' time. In the initial years, the diploma given out to graduating students even had a slip attached to it saying that it would soon be converted into an MBA. The degree-granting status, however, turned out to be elusive and the quest for it long and arduous.

The two IIMs, IIMA and IIMC, could acquire degree-granting status only through an Act passed by Parliament declaring them institutions of national importance. Such an Act had been passed earlier for the IITs. The IITs have three bodies overseeing them, namely a Council (which is intended to coordinate the activities of all IITs), a Board of Governors and a Senate (which comprises members of the faculty of the IIT as well as some from other educational institutions).

A similar structure was proposed for the IIMs. This would have meant that the society created for IIMA would be abolished and its powers transferred to the board. The directors of the two IIMs were to draft a Bill that would be placed before Parliament after being vetted by the University Grants Commission and the AICTE.

Matthai informed the Faculty Council in late 1966 that he had suggested fundamental changes in the draft bill relative to the IIT Act, in order to give more autonomy to the IIMs. These suggestions seemed to have met with some resistance within the government. In an update that he provided in December 1967, Matthai expressed the apprehension that the draft bill might see some changes as it passed through various ministries, and consequently the Institute's autonomy might be whittled down.

In January 1968, the draft bill was discussed in a Faculty Council meeting. Faculty suggested that the size of the board be reduced from 25 to 18 to 10 or 12. They also wanted criteria for co-option of members of the board to be laid down and sought representation of the faculty so that the board had a feeling of the 'pulse of the faculty.' The latter suggestion came to be accepted in due course and two faculty members joined the board. The practice continues to this day.

However, it is an open question as to whether the faculty members on the board can be said to represent faculty. This is because the two faculty members are not actually voted in by the faculty. They are essentially nominees of the director (they are called 'chairman's nominees') although the director does go through the motions of seeking nominations from the faculty.

Moreover, no mechanism has been evolved for faculty members on the board to articulate concerns of the faculty or to communicate to faculty outcomes or decisions relevant to them. It is not uncommon for faculty members who sit on the board not to respond to requests for information on board decisions from their colleagues. A colleague who sat on the board told me quite bluntly, 'I am not a faculty *representative* on the board. I am a faculty member who sits on the board.' The objective of enabling the board to feel the 'pulse of the faculty' has not quite been met.

The size of the board itself has been the subject of debate over the years. The intention in having 25 members was to provide representation to diverse interests, including business, academia, the social sector, alumni, etc.

But there has been a sense over the years that the board is too large and unwieldy in relation to the size of the Institute. Half the board members or sometimes more fail to show up for meetings. In 2008, the IIM Review Committee headed by R C Bhargava made strong observations about the functioning of the IIM boards. One of the recommendations it made for rendering the boards more effective was that the size of the board be pruned to 11 members.

Matthai himself was in favour of a much smaller board. He thought nine or ten members would suffice. He also argued that the criterion should be outstanding contribution in the field of management education, not representation of particular interests. As he put it, 'The principle should be commitment and contribution and not representation.' For reasons I have been unable to fathom, these and other weighty arguments for a smaller board have not found favour with the IIMA community. As recently as in April 2010, the Institute's Committee on Future Directions (CFD) proposed a 25-member board.

In February 1971, Matthai reported that degree-granting status may be further delayed. So the doctoral programme would be launched as a fellowship programme in Management as was done at the Indian Institute of Science before it received degree-granting status. That was the last that was heard of the proposed bill on degree-granting status.

Sometime in 1971, Matthai, Sarabhai and Lalbhai seem to have decided amongst themselves that not much was to be gained from pursuing the degree-granting status and that indeed, this might involve some loss of autonomy. Lalbhai is said to have asked, 'Why can't the Institute have enough confidence in its educational system that the products would be known for their quality rather than the degrees after their name?'[7] This argument won the day and it turned out to be one of the pivotal decisions in the Institute's history.

IIMA has lived with its diploma and fellowship ever since. The decision not to bring IIMA under the purview of Parliament has always been hailed as an act of statesmanship on the part of Matthai and others at the helm of affairs at IIMA as it served to give the Institute, and the IIMs that came up later, a greater measure of autonomy than is available to even the IITs.

Matthai travelled abroad quite often. He visited the US almost every year to recruit faculty. He used the visits for other purposes as well, such as raising doctoral fellowships from a number of US universities for IIMA graduates. On one visit to New York, he sought funding for doctoral fellowships from industrial firms.

On a trip in 1968, he mooted the creation of a dollar fund in the US which would initially be available for faculty development, research, books and equipment at IIMA and, later, to all institutions involved in management development in India and Southeast Asia. The dollar fund would be administered by an autonomous, non-profit organisation in New York. The organisation would apply for Federal Tax exemption in the US and tax deductible status for donations to it.

The main source of funds would be international businesses with investment in Southeast Asia. Six people would serve as incorporators and subsequently on the Board of the Trust to be created: two US academics including Dean Baker of HBS, Matthai himself, and three leaders of industry in New York. In mooting this idea, Matthai anticipated similar initiatives that came from the IITs much later. It is not true to say, as some have suggested, that Matthai did not pay adequate attention to fund-raising. It is a different matter that his initiatives did not fructify.

Matthai visited other parts of the world as well. In October–November 1966, he went on a tour of Southeast Asia at the invitation of the Asian Productivity Organisation. The APO wanted IIMA to act as a centre for management studies for member countries of the APO. Matthai visited Bangkok, Manila and Hong Kong on his way to Tokyo. Matthai made the pleasant discovery that the IIMs were unique in South and Southeast Asia and more advanced than others in the region. Even Japan lagged behind in management education – and, perhaps, still does.

In Tokyo, the APO asked that IIMA open its doors to Asian participants. It was interested in both short-term and long-term programmes run by IIMA. Matthai told the APO that these special programmes could be arranged only if there was a five-year commitment and necessary finance for getting additional faculty would have to be provided.

IIMA would design the programme which would involve the study of conditions in Southeast Asia and the collection of data. It was agreed to approach the UN for financing if the APO Governing Council was agreeable in principle. The Japanese chairman of the APO even visited IIMA to pursue matters. The idea, however, turned out to be still-born.

Another important overseas trip that Matthai made was for a period of six weeks beginning September, 1970. He travelled to three East African countries and from there, went on to the US and Europe. His visit to East Africa was at the behest of the Ministry of External Affairs and it was intended to establish contact with educational institutions there. His objectives in visiting Europe were to look for faculty and for doctoral fellowships.

Matthai's visit to East Africa resulted in IIMA assisting in the development of faculty at the Institute for Management Development in Tanzania. Three faculty members from Tanzania joined the PGP as full-time students, after which they were to return to their Institute to teach and develop academic programmes. It is a measure of the early success IIMA achieved that it received requests for collaboration from several institutions in Asia and Africa.

Matthai's extensive travels made him something of a brand ambassador for IIMA. His eloquence, the social skills he had developed from his elitist upbringing, his self-confidence and capacity for negotiation, all contributed to the benefits that flowed from these travels.

There were tangible benefits, of course, such as recruitment of faculty, provision of doctoral fellowships for IIMA students, visiting faculty from reputed foreign institutions, funding support from overseas sources, etc. But the visits also helped project IIMA onto the international stage and they enabled the Institute to remain tuned in to developments in management education elsewhere.

We have said little so far about the administrative structure or the processes at IIMA. For most of Sarabhai's tenure, when there were only around 15 faculty or so members, the Institute remained a loose collection of faculty, each one drawing up his or her plans in consultation with the director.

In March 1965, just a few months before Matthai arrived on the scene, areas were formed. These were Finance and Accounting, Managerial Economics, Policy and Business Environment, Organisational Behaviour, Labour and Personnel relations, Production and Marketing.

The entire planning for the PGP moved thereafter to the areas. This system continues and it applies to all long-duration programmes offered at IIMA. The courses to be offered, their syllabi and evaluation, assignment of faculty to various courses, all these are decided in the areas. Individual faculty members decide the courses and their content, the area approves and, at the Institute level, a Courses Committee gives formal approval.

The broader policy decisions are taken at the Faculty Council. There is nothing in the Institute rules or framework that formally cedes decision-making powers to faculty. All power vests with the director and the board. The role of faculty in decision-making is entirely a matter of culture and precedent and is something that both Sarabhai and Matthai did much to foster. I address this aspect of the Institute at greater length in Chapter 6.

It is interesting that in the other major activity of the Institute, executive training programmes, the director remained in charge for long, and made way for a Faculty Committee only much later. It was almost as if faculty governance was first tested in the running of PGP and, once faculty had earned their spurs, they were allowed to run executive programmes as well. Evaluation of the faculty, as we have seen, was done by a Committee of Faculty headed by the director.

These rather loose administrative structures seemed to serve the Institute well enough in the formative years. As the Institute evolved, though, there was a growing sense that the Institute was, as Matthai put it, 'under-organised.' The first review of the organisational structure was done in 1969 by a British academic, A K Rice, who was invited to spend three months at the Institute. Rice made certain recommendations to a group of four faculty members, including the director but these were not implemented. Matthai thought that the scheme Rice had proposed was excellent but 'might be too authoritarian and forced for the attitudes which were, by then, evolving.'

In December 1971, even as the Bangladesh war was raging, Matthai introduced the subject of re-organisation and planning for the future, and raised a number of issues:

- ► Decision-making was highly centralised although he had emphasised individual freedom as part of the Institute's culture.
- ► Institutional tasks had to be performed and it was not enough for the Institute to be an agglomeration of individuals. Could the existing situation, where not enough concern was shown for larger institutional tasks, be remedied when those with administrative responsibility had no authority?

- ▸ The Institute had taken a sectoral approach and come to focus on certain key sectors: industry, banking, agriculture, trade unions, government, educational and research systems. How was the Institute to take an integrated view? Was a different approach required?
- ▸ There was a certain lack of planning in the Institute, especially in relation to research and consulting. What should be the unit of planning? Should it be the areas or the PGP executive committee or something else?

Three aspects, Matthai said, had to be balanced: accomplishment of institutional tasks; individual creativity; individual development. The matter was best discussed within a small committee and then its findings could be discussed by the larger faculty body.

Matthai proposed the setting up of a committee, the IIMA Reorganisation Committee, to look into these and other issues. The Faculty Council concurred with the idea. A six-member committee was duly constituted. It was headed by a senior faculty member, Ishwar Dayal. After a series of consultations with faculty, the committee submitted its report in month should be meationed 1972 and its recommendations were implemented in September 1972.

A key recommendation was the creation of the post of dean in order to facilitate planning of faculty and area activities. This post was not intended as a deputy to the director nor was it intended that the latter delegate any powers to the dean. In the director's absence, the senior-most faculty member officiated as director.

Over the past ten years or so, the position has changed. The dean has emerged as a second-in-command and deputises for the director in his absence. It has also become the practice for the dean to officiate when the director steps down, until a new director is appointed.

The practice of setting up a committee once in ten years or so to review the Institute's functioning has endured. It is now called the Committee on Future Directions (CFD). The last one was set up in 2008. It comprised faculty as well as board members and it submitted its report in April 2010.

Let us cut to 25 January, 1972, a day that old-timers will not easily forget. Matthai, then at the peak of his stature and in full command, walks into a Faculty Council meeting and announces that he had resigned as director. He circulates his letter of resignation, addressed to the chairman.

Matthai's letter of resignation is a classic piece of writing. It is worth quoting at some length:[8]

> While each of our education institutions needs a vision to which it may aspire, the vision must not become a sacrosanct ideology, nor should the individual in charge of the institution become the ideologically vested focal point of no change ... A new person is required with whom the vision is not a vested interest and we will have a fresh point of view from which to determine how the Institute can move.
>
> An applied institution such as ours, must relate itself to national needs. The tasks can be enormous and numerous. The temptation, to which I certainly have yielded, is to move fast in new fields of academic endeavour. With this in view, at the IIMA I have emphasised 'academic entrepreneurship' which constantly demands new activities, uncertain structures and, often, conflicting values.
>
> At each major stage of the Institute's growth, a change of style might be desirable. I think we have arrived at the end of the first phase of the Institute's growth, nine years after it started. This Institute might need to change the direction of development. For

this there will be others whose styles are more suited and whose capabilities are more appropriate than mine.

Many institutions in India have suffered either from instability due to the too-frequent changes of the 'chief executive' as decided by 'the powers that be' irrespective of institutional needs, or have suffered from stagnation as a result of the perpetuation of an individual who becomes the institutionalised image of a no-change continuity, once again irrespective of institutional needs. I hope that, after a reasonable period, the next director will step down if he feels there may be more appropriate persons to determine a new direction for the Institute...

My emotional involvement with the Institute is considerable. While I am resigning as director, if my successor and the board allow me to work here, I would like to continue as a member of the faculty.

By way of elucidation, Matthai made three points to faculty:

- ▶ In the growth of any institution, there were particular stages of development which were most amenable to change. (He implied that the Institute had reached such a stage, so the time was opportune for somebody else to take over).
- ▶ The position of director should not be used for anything other than the benefit of the Institute. He had asked for permission to step down, not step out. Though he had asked to remain, whether he finally remained was the decision of the next director and the board.
- ▶ He did not wish to participate in the selection of his successor because he did not want to perpetrate his preferences.

Matthai said he was taking the earliest opportunity to communicate his decision to the faculty. His decision was final and the board had accepted it. His successor would have to take several important decisions: whether to continue at the present rate, consolidate, give a new direction, etc.

As we mentioned in Chapter 3, Matthai had told Sarabhai and Tandon that he would not stay in the job for more than five to seven years, so he was merely conforming to a plan he had set for himself. But faculty could not have been expected to be aware of this. There was a stunned silence when Matthai announced his resignation.

Slowly, the faculty began to react. One faculty member said he would have appreciated it if Matthai had discussed his intention to resign with the faculty before announcing it. A case had to be made out for his stepping down. There were doubts as to whether the Institute culture would continue under his successor.

Another faculty member said if Matthai had left scope for reconsideration, he would have liked Matthai to stay for two or three years more. Yet another said that the board should have consulted the faculty before accepting the resignation. It was suggested that faculty send a communication to the board requesting it to reconsider Matthai's resignation.

Most of the time, when the head of an institution wants to leave, people are happy to see him go. Often, they can't wait to see his back. There are those itching to grab the position. At IIMA, jockeying for the director's post commences in the fourth year of a director's tenure or even earlier. Some directors have sought a second term or small extensions. One reason they have not succeeded is that there has been strenuous opposition from faculty, including from those impatient to succeed them.

Matthai's resignation was that rare occasion when the news of a head's stepping down was received with genuine sadness mingled with concern about the future. All understood that Matthai's shoes would not be easy to fill, such had been the quality of his leadership. Matthai stood firm. He said the board had accepted his resignation. He, however, had not consulted the board on his resignation, merely informed it.

The faculty wanted to meet again to discuss the situation that had arisen and were in no mood to take up other matters at that meeting. Matthai pleaded with them to at least consider the fellowship programme item, given the tight time-frame for its launch. The faculty refused, saying they were not in a position to give their considered opinion.

One issue that arose was whether the Reorganisation Committee could proceed with its job or await the selection of a new director. Matthai felt that it could continue its labours and the new director could join when chosen, which should happen in two or three months' time. He managed to push through one decision: naming the new library after Sarabhai.

At the next meeting, the launch of the FPM was taken up for discussion. Some faculty members wondered whether the timing was right (a good enough ground for objecting to almost any decision), whether the right admission criteria had been formulated, etc.

Matthai observed that there was lack of unanimity and the decision might be taken as the director's discretion 'after sensing the opinion of the faculty.' One last time, he asserted the director's authority on an important matter but was careful to phrase the decision correctly.

He added that the Faculty Council was not a decision-making body but he, as director, had tried to take decisions after taking the faculty's opinion into account. He was gently reminding faculty members that there was no legal requirement for the director to consult them; however, such consultation was an important aspect of the culture he had tried to foster.

The faculty drafted a communication to be sent to the board on the selection of next director. It placed on record Matthai's immense contribution and asked that he be allowed to stay on as a member of the faculty. The communication also spelt out the procedure they would like the board to take in selecting a new director.

Faculty asked that their views on the kind of leadership required at the Institute be ascertained and individual faculty members also be asked to give three preferences in writing. The board could consider faculty preferences along with those obtained from other sources and, if the board thought it appropriate, discuss the final shortlist with faculty members.

The board accepted the view of the faculty and consultation with the latter has since become an integral part of the selection of any director. Eight months after Matthai announced his resignation, Samuel Paul succeeded him as director.

Under Matthai, IIMA expanded and grew. When he assumed office, it did not have a campus. There was uncertainty as to whether it could manage to raise the funds needed to sustain itself. The formation of areas had taken place only a few months before Matthai took over as director. IIMA had just 27 faculty members, at the time.

Evaluation and promotion decisions were entirely in the hands of the director. IIMA was desperate to gain degree-granting power in order to establish the credibility of its programme. The joke was that IIMA was hardly known even in Ahmedabad, ATIRA had a bigger reputation. IIMC was widely believed to be ahead of IIMA.

By the time Matthai stepped down, IIMA had an impressive campus. Finances had ceased to be an issue. Various functional areas had been formed and a full-fledged centre for agriculture was in place. Faculty strength had doubled to 55, with a large complement having been recruited from abroad. The doctoral programme had been launched.

The agriculture group had developed into a full-fledged CMA and a two-year programme in agriculture had been launched. Executive training programmes had increased in number and diversity. A Faculty Committee had been constituted for evaluation and norms for evaluation had been spelt out.

The Institute had developed sufficient confidence in its diploma to be able to forgo degree-granting power. From an institution struggling to establish its very relevance, IIMA had gone to establish itself as the pre-eminent management institution in the country, and as a centre of excellence.

Recognition of IIMA's stature was not confined to the country. As John McArthur, dean of Harvard Business School was to say later:

> Ravi was instrumental in making IIMA the premier business school in the Far East and one of the best anywhere in the world. In a world where progress is often measured in millimeters, he was able to accomplish changes that almost anyone else would have found impossible.[9]

These were significant accomplishments of the Matthai era. But the success of a leader cannot be judged merely by what he accomplishes in his own time. IIMA had a lot going for it when Matthai took over. It had strong support from the central and state governments, the benefit of collaboration with HBS and the early success in executive training before Matthai came on board. Building on these was an achievement, of course, but not one that gives title to enduring fame.

The success of a leader must be judged by sustainability. Is the success enduring? Has the leader put in place elements of vision, structure, strategy and processes that are conducive to long-term performance?

This test would be applicable in any institution but it would be particularly true of an academic institution. In academia, infrastructure or hardware is hardly the key to success. There are private institutions with very impressive buildings and other infrastructure but they count for little in the management firmament. 'Software', a culture of freedom, creativity and innovation, is everything. Matthai's unique contribution was to get the software in an institution of higher education right.

That deserves a whole chapter for itself.

6

Getting the 'Software' Right

How do you build an institution? The basic requirements are obvious.[1] Think through the mission and objectives. Get the leadership right. Put in place the appropriate organisational structure. Establish necessary linkages with the environment in which the institution exists.

With an academic institution, matters are somewhat more complicated. That is because academic institutions are peopled overwhelmingly by 'knowledge workers,' a term coined by the famous management thinker, Peter Drucker.

Drucker wrote about knowledge workers in the context of corporations. One of the central challenges in modern corporations, Drucker wrote, is the management of knowledge workers, as distinct from manual workers. The manual worker uses his physical labour or works with machines. The knowledge worker uses information or knowledge to deliver output.

The rise of knowledge workers, Drucker emphasised, has enormous implications for the way companies are run.[2] The ways of motivating the knowledge worker and measuring his output are very different from those required for a manual worker. The knowledge worker cannot be motivated by fear – fear of economic suffering, job security, etc. Because, under fear, the knowledge worker is not productive; 'only self-motivation and self-direction can make him productive.'

Defining and measuring the productivity of the knowledge worker is difficult. In the case of a manual worker, it can be reduced to, say, the number of shoes produced per day or per hour and of a standard quality. For a design engineer, service engineer or sales forecaster, defining productivity is difficult. For the teacher, Drucker says, it is 'almost hopeless'.

Indeed. Academics are no ordinary knowledge workers. They are workers who don't just use knowledge but also create and disseminate it. Academic work involves elements of quality as well as quantity. In an academic institution, it is possible to define the quantity of work to some extent but defining quality is more difficult.

Having a concentration of such highly evolved knowledge workers has its own implications for institution-building. Excellence or quality in the institution cannot be ordered or dictated. We can define the teaching load of the faculty, that is, how many courses a faculty should teach in a given year. Quality can be measured by student feedback on courses – but only up to a point.

It is possible, for instance, to get excellent student ratings on a course by doing a great job of exposition of material that is light. Excellent ratings can be obtained without updating a course for years. They can be obtained by using entirely foreign cases and not having enough Indian content. Sometimes, high ratings can be managed by appeasing students with generous grades. The possibilities for 'gaming' the system are endless.

As for research, we have seen the difficulties in assessing research quality where faculty cannot really be expected to be published in the top international journals. In such a context, research has to be evaluated taking into account various outputs – cases, project research, working papers and publications in refereed journals. This is not easy.

Further, as a former faculty member of IIMA Sashi Kolavalli points out, important activities at IIMA that contribute to the reputation of the Institute fall in the collective domain.[3] Teaching in the first year and in executive programmes, admissions, placements, all require individuals to coordinate with others to produce outputs that result in a 'collective good', namely, reputation.

As any student of economics knows, collective goods give rise to the 'free rider' problem. It is possible for any given faculty member to enjoy the benefits of a reputation created by others without having to take the trouble to contribute himself. It may be simpler for faculty to concentrate on activities which bring strictly private benefits, such as research or consulting. (In academia, contributions to the collective good are not rewarded through means such as performance bonuses or stock options which are available in the corporate world.)

The challenge at an academic institution such as IIMA is two-fold: first, to create conditions in which the faculty is motivated to excel in their individual capacities; and, secondly, to create conditions in which the faculty focuses not just on activities that bring private benefits but also on activities that contribute to the collective good. Both these require the creation of an appropriate culture in the institution.

Any institution, whether a corporation or a regulatory authority or a non-government organisation, requires a suitable culture in order to achieve excellence, a culture that gets people to give of their best. It is fair to say that the greater the knowledge-intensity in an organisation, the more crucial is the requirement of culture. To the four requirements for institution-building listed at the outset, we can now add a fifth: the creation of a culture that brings out the best in knowledge workers.

I was once asked by the chairman and largest shareholder of one of India's well-known financial services groups whether I had any suggestions on selecting a CEO for his firm.

I said, 'You might consider somebody who has made a success of an academic institution.'

He was more than mildly surprised. 'A professor?' he asked.

'No, an academic administrator,' I said. 'Somebody who has brought about a major transformation in the quality and reputation of an academic institution. Anyone who has done this would have mastered the art of handling knowledge workers. If somebody can get the best out of academics, he would know how to get the best out of investment bankers.'

The chairman smiled appreciatively. 'Interesting, very interesting.'

To say that Matthai was a thoughtful person would be an understatement. Thinking, the act of cerebration, seemed to define his existence. He was once asked which of the philosophers he had read had influenced him the most.

'Hardly any at all,' Matthai replied. 'But there is one celebrated statement that has always had a profound impact on me.' This statement, Matthai revealed, was Descartes' *Cogito ergo sum* – I think, therefore I am. One admirer adds wryly that for Descartes thinking may have been the *proof* of existence but for Matthai it was the *justification* for it.[4]

Matthai was a man given to deep reflection. Every evening, after his work at the office was done, he retreated into the privacy of his house on the campus, eschewed socialisation with colleagues and spent long hours reflecting on the day's events and on Institute matters.

He penned his thoughts in a scrapbook. He thought deeply about the Institute's philosophy, its mission, its structure, its values and beliefs. After his death, his colleagues stumbled upon various scattered writings in the form of reports, memos, notes and speeches. Matthai was publicity-shy and did not bother to get his writings published. He wrote detailed notes entirely for his own edification.

One manuscript, relating to his educational experiments in a village and intended for publication, was published posthumously in the form of a book. (More of this in Chapter 8). IIMA felt that to get his other writings published would be unfair to Matthai as he had not been keen to publish them himself. At the same time, to let these disappear into the archives would be a great loss. By way of compromise, his assorted writings were brought together in the form of a volume published by IIMA for private circulation.[5]

The writings range over many topics – management education, institution-building, education and rural development, freedom and democracy, and personalities who had impressed Matthai. Matthai is not easy reading. His thinking is evolved but he lacks the gift of exposition. His writing is convoluted, his sentences run into several lines and can drive the reader to despair. But for those willing to endure it, the experience can be highly rewarding. (I have been told by several old-timers that Matthai's speech was of a different quality. He had a beautiful voice and his spoken English was a delight).

Going through Matthai's writings, one is struck by how deeply he thought about these matters. One is also left with the conviction that the success IIMA had achieved was no accident, that its ability to maintain its reputation as an institution of excellence is the result of a carefully thought through mission and the creation of a particular culture in the Institute.

Matthai has spelt out IIMA's mission in very clear terms. Its mission would be the application of knowledge. To be able to fulfil this mission, 'the Institute must produce knowledge that can be used, it should disseminate the knowledge to those who can use it and it should help those who have received such education to use that knowledge'.[6]

Once IIMA was clear about its mission, the strategy to fulfill this mission fell into place. It involved a number of elements.

First, the Institute would engage in three mutually reinforcing activities, namely, research, teaching and consulting-cum-extension work. We know that the Robbins report had envisaged that IIMA would be involved in these activities; Hansen's report, prepared for HBS, had reiterated this point. But it was Matthai who articulated the rationale for IIMA being involved in these activities and placed them in the context of a particular mission.

It was not enough for IIMA to be involved in research, teaching and consulting. Everyone on the faculty should have all these activities as part of his portfolio. Why? Because the Institute's 'impact would be the greatest if it were the combined result of all activities.'[7] This would happen if the three activities reinforced each other; and the reinforcement would be most effective if it happened within every faculty. So, the option of having separate divisions for research, teaching and consulting was rejected.

Next, the choice of Institute of Management as the title for the two new institutions itself was significant. IIMA decided early on that it would focus on the application of management principles to several sectors of the economy, not just business or industry. The IIMs are not business schools although the short-hand term is often used to describe them.

IIMA felt it would be better placed to fulfil its mission if it focused on five key operating sectors of the economy to start with, based on national priorities at the time: industry, agriculture, banking, government systems and trade unions. There were two sectors that supported other sectors – research and education systems. The Institute decided to focus on these as well.[8]

The decision that IIMA would focus not just on business or industry was taken in Sarabhai's time, and agriculture was chosen as an area of interest. Matthai widened the Institute's ambit to cover other sectors. This accords with a theme that runs through this book: while the foundation was laid in Sarabhai's time, Matthai's contribution was to build substantially on it.

Matthai claimed with some justification that the IIMs had emphasised the applicability of management principles beyond the realm of business earlier before schools in the US had. 'In this sense,' Matthai said in one of his speeches, 'the character of management education that has evolved is not a foreign transplant, nor is it entirely a foreign adaptation, but represents the creation of Indian minds dedicated to working on the problems of their own country.'[9] IIMA took help from HBS in the initial years but it was not content to merely emulate the American B-school model. It responded with innovations that were appropriate to the Indian situation.

A third element in the Institute's strategy was that the various sectors on which it focused should be supported by the sectors themselves. This was not just a matter of raising funds from the concerned sectors, there were other compelling reasons for working closely with them. When a sector supported an activity at the Institute, it would want a return on its investment and that created an incentive for the sector to use the knowledge produced by the Institute. This, in turn, fitted perfectly with the Institute's mission, which was the creation of knowledge that could be used.

Close relationships between the Institute and the supporting sectors were required for the development of teaching material and for carrying out research. Moreover, practitioners in a given sector would be able to absorb management concepts if those concepts related to their own sectors. Matthai gave an example. 'If an agricultural administrator knew little about management concepts, it would be futile to talk to him about the information and control problems of Hindustan Steel.'[10]

Fourth, the Institute judged that it would be easier to bring about change if it could offer its knowledge to different levels in an organisation. As we saw in Chapter 2, this was the philosophy under the 3-TP. An attempt was made to incorporate this philosophy in the design of all teaching activities.

A fifth element in the strategy was to collaborate with other educational and research institutions concerned with a particular sector. IIMA itself was quite small in relation to the needs of the Indian economy and it stood a better chance of making an impact by using other institutions as a 'multiplier' for its own research, teaching and consulting. Hence the emphasis on programmes for teachers, the doctoral programme and other extension work.

Clarity as to its basic mission and a strategy for achieving the mission has been an important factor underlying IIMA's dynamism.

The ultimate objective of IIMA, the goal that Matthai wanted it to aspire to over 20 or 30 years, was to be able to develop from its knowledge of various sectors, an integrated view of the operating system of the entire country. He was aware of the seeming contradiction between the sectoral or compartmentalised view with which the Institute was starting off and the ultimate objective. But, in a longer perspective, he felt that the two objectives could be reconciled.

By way of resolving the contradiction, Matthai drew a distinction between an organisation and an institution.[11] An organisation, he said, is the structure within which decisions are made to allocate and use resources over a given period of time. The effective use of resources might require the organisation to change from one period to another.

The vision for the institution, however, extends well beyond the time horizon of any organisation. The institution evolves towards the vision through a series of organisations. The vision is permanent; organisations that are created to help evolve towards the vision are temporary. IIMA's vision was to develop an integrated view of the Indian economy; the sectors were organisations created towards the larger vision.

Matthai illustrated the implications for institution-building by taking the case of an institute starting off by concentrating on the industrial sector and then venturing into agriculture, as IIMA had done. It would not be appropriate to simply deploy the same faculty in both the sectors. In order to gain the confidence of practitioners in agriculture, faculty members who could talk the language of agriculture would be required. So the institution would have to employ specialists in agriculture and educate them in management concepts.

Moreover, if the institution was to quickly make an impact on agriculture, faculty in the agriculture group would have to work on this sector alone. At the same time, faculty from certain functional areas, such as operations research or organisational theory, would be reluctant to commit themselves solely to agriculture. They might be willing to contribute to the agriculture area but they would certainly want to work on a broader canvas that comprised both industry and agriculture.

Thus, in the institution there would be a contradiction. Faculty from industry could work in both the sectors but faculty in agriculture would be confined to it. However, once the agricultural sector in the Institute had attained a certain scale and come to be seen as an attractive sector to work in by the Institute at large, the structural barriers between agriculture and industry in the Institute could be broken down. Faculty in the two sectors would now have an equal breadth of opportunity.

The same would apply to other sectors, such as banking, trade unions, etc. At any given point in time, a variety of sectoral structures would co-exist within the institution, all moving towards the long-term vision. In this system, there were enormous possibilities for teaching.

Courses could be offered in the traditional disciplines as well as sectors, and students could design packages in relation to the careers they wished to follow. For instance, students wanting to pursue a course in banking could take courses from the general stream as well as from the banking sector. Mission, strategy, structure – Matthai thought through all of these and that too, without having been exposed to management education.

Over the years, the sectoral approach has been one of the highlights of IIMA, more than in any other management institution in the country. Some of the older centres are no longer around; several new ones have come up. There are centres for infrastructure, telecommunications, public systems, e-governance, healthcare, retailing, to name a few.

Not all centres have dedicated faculty, most centres draw on the functional areas. The integrated vision, the transfer of knowledge across sectors that Matthai spoke of, eludes IIMA. But the Institute's ability to respond to the needs of the economy by creating centres that focus on various sectors is a huge strength.

IIMA differs from the university system in three crucial aspects: the degree of autonomy it enjoys; freedom of expression for faculty; and faculty say in decision-making. The university system is exposed to political interference. Where a system is exposed to political and other inteference, freedom of expression is bound to be circumscribed.

Important decisions, including decisions on academic matters, are often taken by an administrative authority, say the vice-chancellor or the Senate.

Thus, autonomy, academic freedom and faculty governance are interlinked concepts. All became part of the culture that Sarabhai and Matthai carefully fostered. And this culture is part of the explanation for the exceptional success IIMA has had in the Indian education system.

We have seen how the idea of autonomy was built into the very design of IIMA. It was created as a society and it chose to remain one instead of being covered by an Act of Parliament so that it could maintain a certain distance from the government. If that meant forgoing the power to grant degrees, so be it.

Creating IIMA as a partnership among the Government of India, the Government of Gujarat and Indian industry; having representatives on the board from all these constituents; and limiting the Government of India's presence on the board – all these were intended to confer a high degree of autonomy on the Institute. These were made possible in the first place because Sarabhai, Lalbhai and others were able to persuade the government to go along and also because those in government were willing to be supportive of a different kind of academic institution.

However, it is not as if autonomy for a public institution can be won merely by opting for a particular organisational form. The central and state governments have two nominees each on the board and hence the power to influence decisions. Secondly, the Memorandum of Association (MOA), which defines the relationship between the government and IIMA, gives considerable scope for the government to intervene in the affairs of the Institute.

This was in evidence in 2007 during the tenure of Arjun Singh as Minister of HRD. The ministry instructed IIMA to put its admissions on hold until the issue of quota for Other Backward Castes (OBC) was reserved. IIMA toyed briefly with the idea of defying the order. However, it thought better of it when it was advised by lawyers that the MOA has a provision that specifies that rules for admissions are to be prescribed 'in conformity with the policy' approved by the central and state governments.[12]

Most importantly, IIMA was dependent on government funding right until 2002-03 when it decided not to seek government funds. Later, IIMA decided to accept funds only for the limited purpose of expanding capacity when the Institute had to provide for a quota for Other Backward Castes (OBCs). In principle, it was always possible for the government to influence the Institute's policies and decisions, even though IIMA was not governed by an Act of Parliament.

This did not happen and IIMA was able to preserve its autonomy because of the way it conducted itself and its relationship with the government. IIMA was able to create trust in the government as to its functioning. It did so by delivering results fairly quickly in the initial years, and by showing itself responsive to the expectations of society at large.

It also had the good fortune of having at the helm men such as Lalbhai who could be counted upon to sell the Institute's policies and decisions to the political class.[13] The question of any decision of the Institute being challenged by the government's nominees on the board never arose. Care was taken to informally brief them even before any formal discussion took place. Keeping people in the government informed and taking them into confidence on various matters was crucial to preserving the autonomy of the Institute.

In a speech that he made at a felicitation function after he relinquished the directorship, Matthai explained what autonomy is all about (although he used the broader expression 'freedom'):

> It is my belief that creative individuals can develop best in an atmosphere of freedom. But freedom, to my mind, is not the

freedom won yesterday. The poet Lowell described freedom as the dead seeds of yesterday's flowers. Let us not try to preserve the freedom that we won in the past in the hope that we can `bank` freedom. To my mind, freedom is won every day, every month, every year. It is won by our accomplishments, not by assuming that we are better than anybody else, and that we should defend our freedom and build up institutional barriers against intrusions.[14]

In other words, autonomy was not something that was given on a platter. It was won by creating confidence in all stakeholders, including the government. When the world saw the Institute conducting itself with a high sense of social responsibility, when it saw that the community was measuring up to high standards of accountability on its own, it was happy to leave them alone. Sarabhai and Matthai did not take the position that autonomy was a matter of divine right and that it was not for the government to question any decision of the Institute.

It is no small irony that during the forty-odd years that IIMA accepted funds from the government, nobody at IIMA ever complained about lack of autonomy and that this talk began precisely after the Institute ceased accepting government funds in the recent past.

Autonomy or freedom from government interference is a requirement for the healthy growth of academic institutions. But autonomy cannot just be at the level of the board or the director. It must devolve to all faculty. Faculty must have a sense of freedom.

As highly developed knowledge workers, faculty will perform only when they are liberated to do so, only if they feel that what they are doing is largely on their own initiative. That is the nature of the beast. It is futile for the director to thump his table and say, 'I want these things done in the next six months – and they had better be top class.'

What is 'academic freedom' all about? Matthai provided a comprehensive definition:

It was viewed as the freedom of the faculty to express their opinions without fear of reprisal, freedom to initiate academic activities within the broad objectives of the Institute, freedom of the individual to plan his work to his satisfaction, freedom to innovate according to his creative thinking, freedom of movement to achieve his academic goals, freedom from external pressures, freedom from the pressure of excessive authority.[15]

Freedom is a subject on which the faculty can be extremely touchy, as even Matthai once discovered to his cost. Matthai introduced a travel request form whereby the director's approval was required for travel. This immediately ruffled feathers. Matthai had to clarify that the form was intended to provide him information about movements of faculty members and to book travel expenditure under particular heads of accounts. It was never his intention to question faculty travels or to put a curb on them.

Faculty need freedom of expression. The need for freedom of expression in academic work is obvious. Faculty cannot do quality research unless they can express themselves without fear of consequences from politicians, bureaucrats, businessmen and the like. And yet this is not something we can take for granted in Indian education.

Matthai saw part of his role in terms of 'insulating the internal community from what he (Matthai) believed to be external pressures which were inimical to the Institute's goals and the culture he wished to see develop.'[16] In the early years, there were instances when outsiders, including industry representatives, expressed their displeasure over some of the research produced by IIMA faculty.

Matthai was firm in standing up for the right of faculty to express themselves freely. At the same time, he emphasised that IIMA faculty would need to win acceptance by building an image of impartiality. This, in turn, required a high degree of integrity on the part of the faculty.

The subject of faculty freedom was discussed in faculty meetings. In 1968, Matthai circulated a note on the subject, had several brainstorming sessions with a committee of faculty constituted for the purpose, and sought written submissions from faculty members. He was able to report back to faculty that in the notes submitted to him, there was no hint of infringement of academic freedom.

As in so many other respects, these long and time-consuming discussions had the effect of helping to evolve norms in the community as to what was acceptable and what was not. But, sometimes, the faculty's interpretation of academic freedom could be hilarious. Just two days before the semester was to begin, one lady faculty member informed the PGP chairman of her decision to drop a course she was to teach. She sought to justify her action on grounds of 'academic freedom!' Matthai had to swiftly disabuse her of her notions.

The third and distinctive aspect of IIMA's functioning is the system of 'faculty governance', that is, the involvement of faculty in decision-making in the Institute. This was borrowed from the decentralised system of governance that is common in educational institutions in the West. It came to IIMA through its collaboration with the HBS.

Harvard has a particularly vibrant tradition of faculty governance. It manifested itself dramatically in 2006 when Lawrence Summers, a reputed economist and former US treasury secretary, tried to usher in change during his stint as president of Harvard. After several clashes with the faculty, Summers was forced to quit. The rights and wrongs of the disputes are not relevant. The salient point is that, at Harvard, not even the president can take faculty for granted.

Sarabhai was receptive to the tradition of faculty governance and Matthai nurtured it systematically at IIMA so that it became central to the Institute's culture. On most matters, they made it a point to seek the approval of the Faculty Council and to defer to faculty sentiment. One small incident in the early years is telling.

At a meeting on admission policy for the PGP, Sarabhai was insistent that the Institute only admit those with post-graduate credentials. Faculty vehemently opposed the idea saying that it was sufficient to be a graduate. Following a heated debate, Sarabhai 'pulled out his white handkerchief and waved it in the air with a smile, signalling his surrender!'[17]

The decisions taken in Faculty Council meetings are not decisions *per se*. They are only recommendations. So are all decisions taken by all committees and all areas in the Institute. The power to take decisions vests with the director and the board. It is open to the director not to take matters to the Faculty Council, to disregard the views of the Council and to overrule decisions of all areas and committees, and without assigning reasons. On paper, the IIMA system confers the director with a degree of power that is frightening.

In practice, however, for most of the past 50 years, the director and the board have chosen to be guided by the decisions of the Faculty Council. Decisions emanate from the Council and are duly ratified by the board. In recent years, though, a distinction has been made between 'academic' and 'administrative' matters.

Decisions on matters characterised as 'administrative' (such as an increase in fee for the PGP) have been taken by the board without the inputs of the Faculty Council. The director merely informs the community of the board's decision. Earlier, recommendations on the PGP fee were made by the Faculty Council and the board duly gave its approval.

Decisions related to courses to be offered in various programmes and their contents are decided by the areas. Important activities such as admissions and placement are carried out by committees entirely comprising faculty (admissions) or partly comprising faculty (placement). Recruitment decisions too, emanate from the area.

We can relate the merits of faculty governance to all we know about knowledge workers. We can see how it addresses the challenge of motivating academics to contribute to the collective good in the absence of the sort of financial incentives available in the corporate world.

Faculty governance motivates faculty to contribute by giving them a sense of ownership in the institution. By appealing to and providing scope for self-direction on the part of the academics, it gets the best out of them. There is another plus to decentralised governance. It helps insulate decisions from outside interference. It is easier to influence the head of an educational institution than to sway a whole department.

We can now understand why the decentralised governance of the autonomous university in the US has produced outstanding results, even in government universities there. And why the typical Indian university, subject to political interference and direction from the top, has sunk to abysmal levels.

As Kolavalli points out, excellence pursued at the Institute was not in response to external forces such as competition or pressure from government.[18] IIMA and IIMC were unique in terms of the financial and other support they got and had no worthwhile competition. The government's financial support, once the Institute got going, was not contingent on the Institute's attaining a particular level of performance.

Excellence could come only out of the creation of a particular culture in which faculty governance was an important element.

The decentralised structure at IIMA was, of course, an import from the West, as were the notions of autonomy, academic freedom and faculty governance. Sarabhai and Matthai, both men with considerable exposure to the culture of the Western university, could readily appreciate its merits and embraced its features whole-heartedly.

Matthai's genius was to go beyond the Western model and make adaptations that were his own. Not only were these adaptations unique to IIMA but they contributed to the astonishing vitality of the Institute in his time, its early success and its sustained commitment to excellence. Like everything Matthai did, they were products of deep reflection.

Before I highlight these adaptations, let me first state some of the underlying assumptions in Matthai's own words. They echo the topic touched upon earlier, on knowledge workers. The Institute's growth, Matthai believed, 'depended on the competence, creativity and initiative of the faculty.'[19]

Competence was best ensured through faculty selection and development. Initiative would be shown if 'academic entrepreneurship' was encouraged and if the faculty developed sufficient confidence in themselves. Unleashing the creativity of the faculty was a little trickier.

In the early years, Matthai argued, the focus had to be on individual creativity. Faculty had to find their niche, grow in confidence, develop trust in their peers. All this would take time and thereafter group work would be possible. For individual creativity to develop, freedom from authority was essential.

At the same time, the task of building the Institute, of developing new activities required faculty members to work in groups. These groups were the areas and the activity committees. How to get the balance right between the focus on individuality and the need for participation and co-operation in groups?

Here, Matthai made the first of his innovations. Administrative positions would carry responsibility without authority. To this day, the area chairmen and the chairman of the PGP, admissions, placement and other committees have to carry out the mandates assigned to them but without any powers over those in their team or even any financial powers.

This is very different from what obtains in the standard Western model, not to speak of the Indian university. The area chairman or head of department elsewhere has authority over his colleagues. He decides the allocation of work and has an important say in recruitment and promotion. The reader might well wonder how on earth any chairman was to discharge his responsibilities. I will let Matthai speak for himself:

> The chairman could not dictate decisions to his committee. He had to win over his committee. He could not in any sense give orders to faculty members involved in the activity for which he was responsible. Again, he had to win them over. His responsibility was given by the director but authority stemmed from his acceptance by his peers.[20]

Thus, the area chairman has to ensure that all courses are taught but he has to depend entirely on offers from the faculty. If there are gaps to be filled, he cannot direct any faculty to fill them up. He can only request. If it does not work, he has to look for faculty from outside.

The area chairman may feel that certain new courses need to be offered in order to respond to changes in the market. He has no power to ensure that such courses are offered. He must hope that good sense will prevail in the area, and he must use his powers of persuasion.

Furthermore, the area chairmanship does not go with seniority. There is no requirement that only a full professor or associate professor can be area chairman. The post is also open to an assistant professor. Junior faculty members with only a year's exposure to the Institute have found themselves catapulted into the role of chairman.

On top of the lack of administrative power inherent in the position, junior faculty members have the thankless job of having to deal with those senior to them in rank and stature. To top it all, the area chairmanship goes by rotation, with a term of just two years.

Other positions, such as chairman of PGP or admissions, may require faculty to have some seniority but they are also bereft of authority. For instance, the admissions chair cannot impose on his group his preferences in respect of, say, cut-off criteria for admissions.

We mentioned the rationale for rendering administrative positions toothless: to ensure that, in any group, individual faculty was not imposed upon by those in administrative positions. Fair enough. But this begs the question: why would anyone want to hold an administrative position?

There were at least two reasonably clear incentives in Matthai's time. Since institution-building was considered an important activity in the early years of the Institute, some weight was given in faculty evaluation to the performance of administrative tasks. Whether this was true and whether the weight was adequate were contested and there was some resentment on this account.

Secondly, there was the opportunity to initiate new activities, the excitement of innovating in existing ones. As several studies have shown, performance is not a function only of incentives, much less of pecuniary incentives.[21] Very often, the task is its own reward and people can rise to great heights when they are entrusted with a task that they find fulfilling. So it was, with many of the activities initiated at IIMA.

It was not as if those who undertook administrative responsibilities were without support. Matthai's general approach was to entrust a faculty member with an activity, remain in the background and ensure that the faculty got all the visibility. However, if a faculty member needed assistance, say, in persuading others of the faculty to join in an effort or in raising resources, Matthai was ready with a helping hand.[22]

In general, however, it was for the administrative head to get people to cooperate with him. The results varied widely, as Matthai himself readily acknowledges.[23] When, for instance, an area chairman was able to gain acceptability, the area provided comprehensive plans, including plans for research. When he was not, the director had to sit down with members of the area and finalise even individual plans. Over a period of time, however, members of an area learnt to submit to the wishes of the group, at least in respect of the teaching load.

Similar problems occurred in the activities. Since the activity head could not impose his views on the group and since the norm also was that issues would not be decided by vote, the result very often was an impasse. The matter would be tossed to Matthai.

Matthai initially intervened but, later, made it a habit to toss the decision back to the group, thus forcing the latter to resolve the matter. Again, over time, a certain equilibrium was reached. The larger committees learned to resolve matters by vote. The smaller committees would make the effort to reach a consensus.

This naturally slowed decision-making. Matthai was not fazed. He did not believe that efficiency meant speed of decision-making.

How the decision was reached, whether it had acceptance, were more important, as in the classical, Japanese style of management. Through the endless discussions and the give-and-take amongst faculty members, a culture of collective behaviour would evolve in which groups would function without anybody imposing his authority on the members of the group.

Matthai's second innovation was as radical. He steered clear of laying down explicit rules and regulations in the Institute. Except for the rules of service laid down by the government for all the IITs and IIMs, few rules were set down in writing. For a whole range of matters – the grant of sabbatical leave or leave without pay, consulting, faculty evaluation, grievance redressal – no written rules existed.

For a given matter, a note would arrive from the director specifying norms, say, for consulting. Not until 1999 was a handbook of rules prepared but it remained in the form of a draft. It was revised in 2004 and still remains a draft. To this day, a composite book of Institute rules does not exist.

Matthai was clear as to the rationale for this seemingly lawless regime. Administrative heads had been denied formal authority. If formal rules were prescribed, they might use the rules instead to exert authority. It was far better, again, to allow norms to evolve from within the community instead of imposing rules from above. He explained the rationale as follows:

> Authority derived from rules might tend to treat them as ends and means. It was also believed that a creative faculty would be most productive if the emphasis was on their motivation to work rather than on controlling them with rules and regulations. ...
> It was hoped that norms of behaviour would evolve from such discussions and cooperative management of activities by which

faculty would impose upon themselves the behavioural restraint necessary for the accomplishment of institutional tasks.[24]

Matthai used several expressions to describe what he was attempting to build: 'a self-regulating culture ... built upon building people;[25] 'a tradition of attitudes;' 'self-regulation based on self-discipline.'

He provided an illustration of how it worked. The PGP was one of the most important programmes in the Institute. Faculty had other commitments like consulting, executive training, research. When these came into conflict with their teaching at PGP, 'it was the faculty that laid down the norm of not tinkering with the PGP schedule.'

It was the 'weight of faculty opinion' that should govern how a faculty should behave, it was not for the director to haul up somebody for missing classes. Similarly, when it came to consulting, Matthai emphasised that it was not the rules that mattered so much as the faculty's own sense of responsibility in deciding how much time they spent on consulting.

Matthai carried his lack of conviction in rules even further. He did not believe in being bound by precedents or even being consistent in his handling of situations or people. He justified his lack of consistency by insisting that in the earliest stages of institution-building, there were bound to be errors. To be bound by precedents at such a stage was to perpetuate errors. As he put it, 'Learn from your errors; don't institutionalise them.'[26]

The institutional objective was all important; rules were secondary. As Matthai put it, with disarming candour, 'Where the rules ... hampered the accomplishment of academic tasks, they were broken with little compunction.' The absence of rules and the lack of consistency in treatment of faculty, of course, meant that the director had considerable discretion.

Matthai explained that he used three criteria in deviating from rules. How important was a particular task? Was a deviation from rule necessary for the accomplishment of the task? Did the behaviour of the faculty in the past justify permitting such a deviation?

The intention was not to favour somebody; rather, it was to foster self-discipline on the part of the faculty. Matthai would convey to the concerned faculty that a deviation was being permitted and that he had reservations about doing so.

The implicit message was that Matthai was reposing a measure of trust in the faculty and they must, in turn, show adequate responsibility. If, overall, the faculty member showed himself responsible, the strict application of rules in a given situation was not called for. In the very nature of things, this latitude could not be shown to all faculty members, though.

Not surprisingly, this approach exposed Matthai to charges of arbitrariness, to not being 'objective'. In the eyes of aggrieved faculty, he was being inconsistent; in terms of the larger institutional purpose, Matthai believed that there was a certain consistency. He did not think it necessary or appropriate to explain why he had permitted something in one case and not in another. His evaluation of different individuals and their needs he kept strictly to himself.

Some discontent was inevitable. Matthai dealt with it in several ways. He allowed it the freest expression. Sometimes, he would back off from a decision he had taken. He invited faculty members to discuss their problems with them. Eventually, in 1971, he decided that at least in one area, faculty evaluation, explicit guidelines and rules were needed and he prepared the note to which we referred in Chapter 5.

The miracle, really, is that the discontent was on a small scale and, from all accounts, people learned to appreciate the merits of this unique system.

An institution in which heads of administration lacked formal authority and in which written rules did not exist so that the director was free to using his discretion in every case. This appears to accord less with the democratic system and the rule of law than with the dispensation of the Medieval era. How did such a system find acceptance and how did it deliver results?

To take up the lack of formal authority first, we are all conditioned in our notions of how authority or power is derived. We relate power to the hierarchy in a typical organisation. As we ascend the hierarchy and acquire particular titles (general manager, executive director, etc), we get to wielding more power. We exercise this power over others, and get a terrific kick out of doing so.

There is, however, a different kind of power that individuals can exercise, that comes with self-confidence, acceptance in a group and moral authority. The late Udai Pareek, a highly regarded professor of organisational behaviour at IIMA, derived many of his ideas on institution-building from a careful study of Matthai's path-breaking initiatives. Pareek poses the issue very well in a conversation with Matthai:

> How do you develop a power which creates more influence but does not restrict others? Instead of giving power in the sense of sanctioned authority which people use to apply further sanctions downwards, how do you create power which is more liberating and helps to release an individual's energy for productive purposes?[27]

In society, there are always exalted individuals who develop this kind of power. Saints, for instance. Great writers and intellectuals such as Bernard Shaw, Bertrand Russell, Jean Paul Sartre and Noam Chomsky. Scientists such as Albert Einstein. Gandhi held no office in the Congress Party but was by far the most influential personality within it. Jayaprakash Narayan belonged to no political party, yet helped topple Indira Gandhi and install a new political formation in the late seventies.

In the modern organisation too, such individuals are to be found. The Chicago Business School was very much the creation of the famous finance guru and Nobel laureate, Merton Miller, although Miller never held the position of dean. An Indian professor at Stern School, who spent time at Chicago, told me what happened when a professor had a problem. 'You went to the area chairman. If it didn't work out, you went to the associate dean. Then to the dean. If there was still a problem, you went to Miller.'

It is not as if this sort of power can be exercised only by a very superior individual. Quite the contrary. In the modern organisation of knowledge workers, it is open to all individuals to exercise such power. Indeed, it is, perhaps, the *only sort of power* that most individuals can exercise. The scope for the hierarchical exercise of power is much less.

Drucker likened the CEO's role in a knowledge-based organisation to that of the conductor of an orchestra or the coach of a football team. Both these are utterly flat organisations. In an orchestra, the pianist is not superior to the violinist nor the violinist to the cellist. In a football team, the forward is not superior to the full-back nor the full-back to the goalkeeper.

In both cases, members of the team have to cooperate in order to produce desired outcomes. Matthai's idea that in an academic institution comprising highly evolved knowledge workers, results are best attained by people functioning as equals, is by no means outlandish.

Drucker forecast that a knowledge-based organisation would be flatter than its predecessors, and he was proved right. As organisations became more knowledge-intensive, they proceeded to eliminate levels of supervision. Matthai carried this approach to its logical extreme in an academic institution and ensured there were no levels at all between himself and the faculty (although there is nothing to suggest that Matthai was influenced by Drucker or anybody else).

The whole point of the system, as Matthai put it, was to develop the 'individual's sense of autonomy and self-confidence', so that he was able to acquire power without having the trappings of authority. Building the individual was paramount.

Box 6.1: Management 2.0

In May 2008, 35 management scholars and practitioners met in California to debate the future of management. One of the members of the group was C K Prahalad. They tried to frame answers to the question: what management ideas would equip organisations to face the future? In other words, what would Management 2.0 look like, as distinct from Management 1.0, the practices that obtain today?

The group came up with a list of 25 ideas, not all entirely novel, that they felt could make a difference. Gary Hamel, the management guru, presented the list in an article in the *Harvard Business Review*.[28] Some of these are:

- Ensure that the work of management serves a higher purpose.
- Eliminate formal hierarchies.
- Operate through trust and peer review rather than fear.
- Focus on self-discipline rather than discipline imposed from above.
- Leaders should not aspire to be heroic decision-makers, rather they should facilitate innovation and collaboration.
- Involve more people in goal-setting.
- Expand employee autonomy.

I perused the list and it occurred to me that Matthai had put many of them into practice in his time. I wrote to Prahalad asking whether this was not true. I reproduce his reply:

You are absolutely right. Ravi did practice it. For example, IIMA gave me the chance, in my first year, to build MEP (Management Education Programme) from scratch. My professors (Mote, Bhattacharyya, Pulin Garg), as part of the team on that project, reported to me. That was then. It was so energising.

It takes a very secure set of individuals to make the system work – they can't use hierarchy as a veil, can't deny contribution, and must be fair (not play favourites). This is a tall order. What we need is a set of leaders like Vikram Sarabhai and Ravi Matthai.

Self-confidence and autonomy were sought to be developed in faculty members by ensuring that they were not smothered either by a 'boss' or by detailed rules. In addition, Matthai used every opportunity to boost faculty's confidence. In executive training programmes, for instance, he made it a point to praise faculty in the presence of outsiders.

He included the faculty in important meetings in which they would not normally be included, giving them responsibilities that belonged strictly to the director.[29] In his interactions with the outside world, it was always the faculty and the institution that were sought to be projected, never the director.

At the same time, through participation in administration, faculty was thrown together with colleagues in groups. In a given group, they were heads; in others, they were members. The task defined the roles.

As faculty members learnt to work in different groups, they would become acquainted with different activities in the Institute. They would develop an organisational perspective and become more responsible. Even as they gained confidence in their own abilities, they would develop a certain regard for peers. They would understand the need for cooperation, team-work and self-restraint. That is how a self-regulating community evolved its own norms for behaviour.

The balance between individual need and the interests of the group, is something Matthai emphasised all the time. Matthai made a distinction between academic freedom and academic autonomy. Freedom is strictly at the level of the individual and may degenerate into license. Autonomy is about a balance being maintained between individual and group objectives.

It is a balance that is best achieved through self-discipline. To the extent that the system imposes discipline, the balance is less autonomous. To use Matthai's own words:

> Autonomy is not something that can be provided from outside. It is something that the individual develops the capability for. All the institution can do is to provide mechanisms which facilitate the individual's understanding of it and the individual's capability of using it, but the institution cannot create it. It is an individual creation.[30]

We mentioned Matthai's lack of consistency in dealing with individuals. He later justified with the famous quote: 'a foolish consistency is the hobgoblin of small minds.'[31] We must infer that people accepted it because they could see the effort he was making to build them. They could see that his every action was informed by an institutional purpose.

As C K Prahalad put it to me, 'He never used his authority to get anything done. He always pointed to the larger purpose.' With all the discretion at his disposal, for all the inconsistency in his decisions, Matthai was never seen as autocratic. Not one person I have spoken to has used the term to describe him.

Is this all some Utopian fantasy? A mere romanticisation of the past? Well, the test, as always, is empirical. There were quarrels and complaints, no doubt, in Matthai's time. Administrative heads grumbled about lack of authority. With all the problems and limitations, however, groups did function and deliver.

Moreover, IIMA has persisted with the system to this day. It was only in June 2010 that the committees for various activities came to be disbanded. But the functioning of the areas remains the same. If the system was unworkable, it would not have lasted that long. And it would not have created an institution that has retained its pre-eminence in the country for decades.

Matthai said his greatest strength when it came to building an institution was his 'ignorance'. [32] He had not read the standard books on management. He had had very little exposure to academia. He was forced to think through his approach to institution-building from first principles.

Drucker had coined the word 'knowledge worker' in 1959 and his exposition of the implications of the rise of knowledge workers came in the late sixties and thereafter. Matthai's principles of institution-building, which he put in practice in the mid-sixties, were entirely his own creation.

Matthai started off, he said, with some 'motherhood normatives' that were ingrained in him. Creativity and innovation were good. This required freedom of expression, which required self-discipline, which required self-confidence, which again required mutual respect, and so on. 'But I had no preconceptions as to how all this could be achieved.'[33] He had to think through not only 'what' was to be done but 'how' it was to be done.

The result was a system designed to bring out the best in that most difficult of knowledge worker, the academic. It was a system that had no parallel not only in India but, perhaps, anywhere in the world.

There is a third adaptation to the Western model that occurred in the Institute and that became part of its culture. Matthai himself did not initiate it. It emerged out of the deliberations of the Re-organisation Committee that he constituted towards the end of his tenure. As somebody who continued to preside over the Faculty Council meetings for several months after he announced his resignation, Matthai went along with this innovation.

This was the practice of the director inviting nominations for various administrative positions instead of selecting people on his own. We mentioned in the previous chapter how faculty asked that its views be taken into account in the selection of the director. This principle was extended to all appointments – the dean, area chairpersons, heads of various activities.

The underlying principle is that leadership emerges from within the ranks of faculty, that the faculty develop their own perceptions of who amongst them are best suited to carry out particular tasks. The practice continues to this day although, over the years, it has lost much of its substance. Directors' requests for nominations these days elicit a certain weariness in the faculty, if not cynicism. At least for important positions, it is understood that the director has already made his choices.

We referred earlier to the speech Matthai made when he stepped down as director. In that speech, he listed the 'pre-requisites of institution building': freedom; sensitivity to the environment; humanity; discrimination. It is interesting that none of the four requirements we mentioned at the beginning of the chapter figure in Matthai's list.

Matthai not only led IIMA to greater heights in his time, he created what we might today call a 'sustainable business model'. His model has four key elements. First, a clear sense of mission. IIMA would be not just a business school but a management institution, meaning its ambit would be wider than business and would encompass important sectors of the Indian economy. Secondly, a focus on faculty freedom as the key to unleashing creativity in an academic institution.

Thirdly, the idea of a faculty-governed institute, where decision-making rests primarily with the faculty and not with the board or even with the director. (The idea was conceived by Sarabhai but it was Matthai who gave it substance and made it an integral feature of IIMA's functioning.)

Lastly, the principle that the director is only first among equals, not some super-boss. It was in order to assert this principle that Matthai spurned attractive offers from outside and chose to stay on as professor. You are professor, you become director, then you become professor again. Hubris in anybody who is given the custodianship of the Institute for a period of five years is utterly misplaced.

These four elements, along with the committee system for managing various activities, have defined IIMA. They account for its pre-eminence in management education in India. They explain the underlying dynamism of the Institute over five decades. IIMA is a fine example of what culture can accomplish in a knowledge-based organisation.

7

Light and Shadow

One episode in Matthai's time is talked about even today. A union cabinet minister, who intended to award large research projects to the agriculture area, came down to the Institute. A faculty meeting had been scheduled where a formal announcement was to be made in the minister's presence.

At a private meeting with Matthai, the minister asked that his son be given a seat in the PGP. Matthai told him politely but firmly that the necessary procedures would have to be followed. The minister's offer of projects was promptly withdrawn. The faculty meeting with the minister was cancelled.

On another occasion, a senior member of the faculty, whose son had applied to IIMA, approached Matthai with a request that faculty wards be permitted to appear for the interview irrespective of their performance in the preceding segments, including the written test. Matthai promised to give thought to the matter. Later, Matthai took the matter to the Faculty Council where the proposal was promptly shot down, as Matthai must have judged it would.

Matthai received several requests and recommendations in favour of candidates for the PGP. He replied politely to these requests, saying that if the candidate met the requirements at various stages, he would have no difficulty getting in.[1] People gradually came to realise the futility of 'putting in a word' where admissions to IIMA were concerned.

Over the years, the admissions process has come to be designed so as to virtually render impossible any attempt at interference. The chairman of the Admissions Committee is largely independent of the director. In the past 50 years, only three children of faculty members have been selected for admission to the Institute.

Safeguarding autonomy in respect of admissions is part of a broader commitment to autonomy at IIMA. We saw how Sarabhai and Matthai ensured that IIMA had elements of the academic culture that are known to be conducive to excellence: autonomy, freedom of expression and faculty governance.

Matthai introduced his own variant to this model, namely, a culture of self-regulation marked by a general aversion to imposing rules from above. I have argued that this culture was instrumental in propelling IIMA into its position of pre-eminence. It would be appropriate to evaluate the Matthai legacy. How well has the culture stood the test of time? How relevant are his ideas today?

Let us begin with the issue of autonomy, which has proved highly contentious in recent years. Some elements of autonomy are so deeply entrenched in the IIMA system as to be non-negotiable. In academic matters, the Institute and its faculty enjoy a degree of autonomy that is comparable with that at the best Western universities. Academic autonomy devolves right down to the level of individual faculty.

Faculty is free to introduce or drop courses. The contents of courses are entirely determined by the faculty. They are also free to determine what courses they would like to teach. They enjoy the highest freedom in respect of research. They have complete freedom to disseminate their research and to express themselves on matters of public policy.

Funding is scarcely a constraint for research, and policy on travel for domestic and international conferences is liberal. Individuals have joined the Institute diffident about their teaching and research abilities. They have gone on to become great teachers and competent researchers. Faculty recruitment too has remained free from outside interference although, in recent years, some dark mutterings have been heard.

The work atmosphere itself is extremely relaxed with no insistence on working hours. The teaching slots for the first-year courses are fixed. Otherwise, the faculty is free to work by day or night, on weekdays or weekends, at home or in the office. (A lady faculty member had asked Matthai whether faculty members were required to come on time and leave on time. Matthai's response: 'This is not a factory'.) In many ways, IIMA has been the creative worker's dream organisation come true, a world without too many rules and, for everyday purposes, no boss. Exactly as Matthai had intended.

IIMA thus affords faculty the fullest opportunity for growth. There is no obstacle or limitation whatsoever to their realising their potential: the Institute's infrastructure and resources are entirely at their disposal. Since faculty is the key resource at the Institute, it follows that there is no external impediment to the Institute's growth.

And yet, complaints about lack of autonomy or interference from the government have been heard, although this has happened only in the last eight years or so. From within the IIMA system, the lament is that if only the Institute had greater autonomy, it would have been better placed to become 'world class'.

The *Financial Times* reported in 2007, 'With India's top business schools eager to establish themselves as leading global brands, government control is hugely restrictive, says Prof. Dholakia.'[2] Former IIMA director, Bakul Dholakia, who was caught up in some of the most bitter clashes with the government in IIMA's history, was quoted as saying, 'What we require is full-fledged autonomy.'

What is meant by 'full-fledged autonomy'? Dholakia makes a few points that are echoed in other documents issued by the Institute in the recent past.[3] The biggest complaint is that IIMA, being part of the government system and the Pay Commission framework, is not in a position to offer salaries that can attract quality faculty.

More pay equals better talent. This proposition may seem self-evident but it does not stand up to scrutiny. We saw in Chapter 4 how Matthai was able to recruit faculty from abroad at a time when economic prospects in India were far less attractive than they are today. The IITs are also part of the government framework, yet they complain neither about lack of autonomy nor the poor salary structure and, indeed, have done a better job of hiring faculty from abroad than the IIMs.

The average compensation at IIMA, including consulting income and excluding benefits, was ₹2.1 million before the Sixth Pay Commission award.[4] Including housing and other benefits, the cost to the Institute would amount to ₹2.5 million, hardly something an academic can complain about in India.

No doubt, many at IIMA would like the base salary itself to be higher so that the faculty is not under pressure to augment income through consulting. But that would not make a material difference to its ability to attract faculty from abroad. It would be impossible for any Indian institution to match salaries offered in the US B-school market. (The starting salary for a finance professor today is around $150,000.) There are schools in Canada, Europe, Australia and Hong Kong that have offered a premium to US salaries and yet failed to attract quality faculty – the advantages to simply being in the US system are so overwhelming.

To say that if only the IIMs are freed from government restrictions, they will be able to offer salaries that are internationally competitive is nonsense. IIMA finds even the Sixth Pay Commission award more of a burden than it had supposed and has preferred not to implement some of its provisions.

There is a huge pool of Indian doctorates and academics abroad. India's elite institutions need to focus on the small proportion of academics who are interested in returning to India for their own reasons. IIMA did so successfully in Matthai's time because it was able to create an ambience that was perceived as attractive.

There are reasonable incentives in place today at IIMA for publishing in quality journals. Improving these and providing better benefits at the margin are all that is necessary and feasible, and this is entirely possible within the government framework. Moreover, the government has made clear that it is not averse to superior faculty being employed on contract on higher salaries. The degree of autonomy that IIMA enjoys is thus perfectly consistent with attracting faculty from abroad.

Other complaints have been heard from IIMA and IIMB, for instance, the lack of freedom to buy property or venture into places outside their base. (The other IIMs have seldom voiced concerns about lack of autonomy.) Since the IIMs complain that they lack faculty to even scale up in their existing locations, one wonders why they would want to venture elsewhere. In any case, these are peripheral concerns and there are indications of late that the government has shown flexibility on these demands.

There are also suggestions that being part of the government framework impinges on quality in other ways. For instance, IIMA has voiced concerns about the policy on reservations and how these 'dilute' the quality of student intake. Dholakia makes this point in his interview to the *Financial Times*. IIMA was resistant to the move to introduce a quota for Other Backward Classes (OBCs) and settled eventually for implementation of the quota over a three-year period.

The resistance to OBC quotas from within IIMA is truly bizarre. The IIMs and the IITs have had reservations for Scheduled Castes and Tribes (SC/STs) for decades and yet their standing is superior to that of private business schools and engineering colleges that do not have quota requirements.

OBCs do much better in the entrance exam to the IIMs than SCs/STs. The cut-off for OBCs in 2010 was 94 (percentile) compared to 99 for the general category; for SC and ST, it was 85 and 80 respectively. This means that OBCs who are selected are in the top 6% of an applicant pool of around 250,000, which is a more stringent entry requirement than obtains at the top B-schools in the US.

If reservation for SCs/STs has not diluted the quality of IIMs, it is hard to see why reservation for OBCs should. And, by all indications, it hasn't. We are now into the third and final year of the implementation of the OBC quota. Placement at IIMA remains unaffected. IIMA retains its No.1 position in all rankings. So much for 'dilution' of quality on account of quotas.

As many commentators have pointed out, the push for an OBC quota, which the government sought to implement through an increase in capacity, has brought about a significant scaling up in the Indian education system – of 54%; this is true of the IIMs as well.

Through the nineties, IIMA ran three sections of the PGP with a total strength of around 350-400. After continuous prodding from government, a fourth section came to be added in 2003-04, which raised the strength of the two-year programme to around 500 in 2004-05, an increase of just 25% in capacity over two decades. It remained at that level until 2007-08.

The addition of a fifth section in 2010-11 (along with the additions to seats in the existing four sections that have happened in previous years) will have resulted in a 54% increase in capacity by 2011-12. Thus, the introduction of the OBC quota, entirely a government initiative, has led to a greater addition to capacity in four years than what IIMA has achieved on its own over nearly two decades. It is a sorry reflection on the IIMs that it required a government initiative to produce a meaningful scaling-up within the IIM system.

Seats at the IIMs are too few in relation to aspirants or the needs of the economy. Around 250,000 candidates took the admission test in 2009, for a total of 1,400 seats in seven IIMs. Successive governments have been willing to provide resources to fund expansion at the IIMs.

Yet, the IIMs have been reluctant to increase their intake on grounds of 'faculty shortage'. As a result, the government has decided that capacity in the IIM system is best expanded by the creation of new IIMs. The government plans to add seven new IIMs to the existing seven, making for a total of 14 IIMs by 2012.

Some in the IIM system promptly denounced the setting up of new IIMs as 'diluting the IIM brand!' They will not scale up and they do not want the government to augment capacity either. (Again, there is no indication at all that the brand value of IIMA has in any way been impaired by the arrival of IIM Kozhikode or that the brand value of IIT Bombay has suffered on account of the creation of IIT Guwahati.)

The report of the Committee on Future Directions (CFD 2008), which was released in April 2010, estimates that IIMA faculty taught an average of 80 sessions in lucrative in-company training programmes and another 25 sessions on long-distance and management development programmes.[5] The total of 105 sessions on these two counts is equivalent to the faculty work load of 100 sessions for the academic programmes. This would mean that if IIMA faculty were to allocate to academic programmes the time they spend on executive training, the intake at IIMA could be doubled at one stroke!

This is not to make a case for faculty to do more teaching; a balance between teaching and other activities such as research is the hallmark of an institution of excellence. But the world at large would be entitled to ask: if there is no 'faculty shortage' when it comes to teaching in corporate training programmes, how is it that there is a shortage when it comes to increasing the intake for the long-duration programmes?

The Institute needs to rethink its preoccupation with in-company training which flows from a flawed business model. IIMA's management believes that revenues from in-company training will ensure that the Institute does not have to depend on government funds. It thus sees such revenues as crucial to its autonomy. This approach ignores a basic fact about quality institutions of higher learning: nowhere in the world are such institutions sustained by income from teaching and consulting alone.

There is always an outside contribution, either private philanthropy, as in the US, or government funding, as in Europe. Institutions that rely entirely on internally generated revenues end up as teaching shops. There is thus a contradiction between IIMA's avowed objective of upgrading itself as an academic institution and the business model it is following, which, in turn, rests on the false notion that autonomy means complete independence from government.

IIMA and indeed all the IIMs need to scale up by hiring more faculty, not by getting existing faculty to teach more, and by financing expansion either through government funds or by raising funds from private donors. Trying to cover costs mainly through revenue-generating programmes is the road to perdition.

Matthai mentioned 'sensitivity' as one of the pre-requisites for institution-building. By this, he meant responsiveness to the environment, to national needs. IIMA has shown such sensitivity in academic matters by coming up with programmes and centres that address the needs of the Indian market. A similar sensitivity in respect of inclusiveness, which is a national priority, has been somewhat wanting.

Complaints about lack of autonomy apart, one discerns a certain yearning in the IIMA community to exit the government framework. As one faculty member once put it, 'Why can't we get the government off our backs?' This quaint interpretation of autonomy as independence from government has been noticed by government committees.

In 2004, the NDA government asked V K Shunglu, a former CAG, to prepare a report on the finances of the IIMs. In his report, Shunglu remarks caustically:

> IIMA continues to implicitly assume authority it arguably does not possess and explicitly seeks autonomy and ownership which does not emerge from the Articles of Association.[6]

In 2008, the IIM Review Committee, headed by R C Bhargava, was constrained to observe:

> IIMs have been established by the government with public funds, are perceived as public institutions and thus IIMs cannot expect to become fully independent of government.[7]

The yearning to be free from government supervision or monitoring manifests itself in many ways. The suggestion is sometimes made that since IIMA has ceased to accept revenue grants from the government, it should not be subject to the government framework in any manner. This is a strange contention.

Let us leave aside, for the moment, the colossal investment the government has made in IIMA over more than four decades. Several leading public sector enterprises have not only ceased to depend on budgetary funds from the government but actually make large dividend payments to it. Going by the above logic, SBI, ONGC, BHEL and other enterprises should no longer fall within the purview of the government.

IIMA has taken the position that it is not subject to the writ jurisdiction of high courts because it is not a 'state' institution as defined in the statutes. In the recent past, it has even explored the possibility of getting itself exempted from the scope of the RTI Act, one of the most progressive pieces of legislation in the nation's post-Independence history. Mercifully, this attempt did not go very far. The IITs, it is worth mentioning, do not have a problem either with being regarded as a state institution or with the RTI Act.

In his convocation address of 2008, the chairman of the IIMA Board of Governors, Vijaypat Singhania, himself an appointee of the Government of India, went so far as to claim that IIMA was a 'private institution!'[8] Which, of course, left unexplained why IIMA subjects itself to quotas for disadvantaged groups, the Pay Commission award, the CAG Audit, the RTI Act, etc. And why its director, also chosen by the Government of India, is required to present his plans to the Ministry of HRD. The chairman's understanding of the Institute's status is not shared by the IIMA community. The report of CFD (2008), which included some members of the board, affirms in more than one place that IIMA is a 'public institution.'[9]

The only instance of government interference in the recent past was in 2004 when Murli Manohar Joshi was the minister of HRD. The ministry asked the IIMs to reduce their fee to a uniform

₹30,000. Joshi offered to make good on any subsidy that might be involved. The government's point was that a high fee came in the way of access to higher education for large numbers of people. IIMA and one or two of the other IIMs objected to the directive from the government.

Dholakia convened a Faculty Council meeting to discuss the matter. At the meeting, I argued that the government's directive should not be taken literally but should be seen as a plea for subsidising needy students. The government's concerns could be addressed through a two-tier fee structure: a subsidised fee for those coming from families with an income below, say, ₹200,000, and a full fee for the rest. The subsidy could be borne by the government. The Faculty Council chose to go along with Dholakia's proposal to reject the government's directive.

The NDA government soon fell and the UPA government assumed office in the summer of 2004 with Arjun Singh as the minister of HRD. Singh did not insist on an across-the-board fee cut but he did make a 'suggestion' to the IIM directors that they consider generous aid for those coming from families with an income of less than ₹200,000 (by a curious coincidence, the very figure I had mentioned at the Faculty Council meeting).

The directors, by now fearful of escalating the confrontation with the new government, accepted the 'suggestion' with alacrity. Referring to the fee issue at the IIMs, the annual report for 2004-05 of the Ministry of HRD noted with satisfaction, 'It has been decided that all admitted students whose annual gross family income is ₹2 lakh and below, will be eligible for receiving financial assistance amounting up to full tuition fee waiver.'[10]

Singh also did not relent on two other points Joshi had made and that the older IIMs, including IIMA, had been reluctant to concede earlier. One was that all IIMs submit to a separate CAG audit in addition to the statutory audit. Until then, IIMA had been subject only to 'superimposed' audit by CAG, that is, the CAG would merely go through the audit done by the statutory auditor.

The second point was that the IIMs use any excess of their corpus funds over ₹500 million for infrastructure development instead of keeping it merely to generate interest income. Again, the IIMs did not have the stomach to resist Singh. Thus, contrary to the general perception, the IIMs ended up conceding the substance of Joshi's demands. It is striking that the basic stance of the government vis-à-vis the IIMs did not change under two very different coalitions.

Since 2008, the IIMs have raised their fee very substantially with IIMA leading the way. The fixing of the fee, another aspect of autonomy that IIMA has been vocal about, is no longer an issue. In 2008, when IIMA raised the fee for the PGP sharply from ₹4.5 lakh to ₹11.5 lakh, it thought it appropriate to introduce a scheme of graded subsidy for students from families with an annual income of less than ₹600,000.

In Joshi's scheme, poorer students would have been subsidised by the government. In IIMA's scheme, the subsidy burden is passed on to students who are relatively well off. Which is preferable can be debated. But one thing is evident: IIMA's decision to raise its fee sharply has led to a secular increase in fee among B-schools all over the country.

Students at IIMA may be able to pay off their education loans without much difficulty on the strength of the salaries they are offered. But this would not be true for other students in the B-school fraternity. For many, the steep increase in fee triggered by IIMA's fee hike has undoubtedly become a burden.

Another bone of contention between IIMA and the government has been the change in the process adopted for the selection of the director.

The director used to be selected by a committee appointed by the board. Since 2002, the selection is done by a committee appointed by the Ministry of HRD, with IIMA being represented by its chairman. Many at IIMA view this as an infringement of its autonomy.

In the two rounds of selection that have happened since, the chairman has followed the same process as in the past. He consults IIMA faculty, arrives at a short-list and conveys his preferences to the selection committee. The chairman's preferences have prevailed and the outcomes have been identical to the ones in the past: the job has gone to an insider. Why the change in the selection process should occasion any resentment is a mystery.

There is certainly room for improvement in the process for selection of the director that obtains today but that does not mean reverting to the earlier process of leaving it to the board to appoint a search committee, as the CFD (2008) report suggests.[11] Both processes are susceptible to lobbying by internal candidates, within the community as well as in New Delhi. A board-appointed search committee would be especially prone to capture by the community.

The search committee forwards to the government a shortlist of three names in descending order of preference. To make it to the shortlist, a faculty member at IIMA needs no more than six to ten faculty endorsements, out of a total faculty strength of over 80. In recent years, there has been a perception in the IIMA community that internal candidates and their backers amongst faculty have used their political and other connections to influence the selection, even while whining about government interference in the affairs of the Institute. As a result, the community is now resigned to the fact that the directorship of IIMA is a semi-political appointment, as in any public sector enterprise.

Matthai's selection itself was the product of the board's insistence on looking beyond the community for a suitable person, and it was entirely free from political influence. In the subsequent decades in which the director was selected by IIMA's own board-appointed committee, it was open to the community to have insisted on a truly transparent and competitive search for the post of director.

It could have asked for the constitution of an independent search committee comprising eminent persons. Some of the most prestigious academic institutions in the world authorise their search committees to carry out a global search and also advertise the dean's position in *The Economist* and other journals. I G Patel, who had distinguished himself in policy-making in government, came to be appointed director of the *London School of Economics* following a global search for the position.

IIMA could have gone down this route. That would have created confidence in the government and in the world at large, as to the rigour and commitment to quality of the search process. The community failed to do so and instead developed a closed-shop mentality.

After Matthai, IIMA has had only one outsider as director, I G Patel. The remaining seven directors have all belonged to the IIMA faculty. The community lost sight of the Matthai dictum that autonomy is won by unilaterally setting for oneself the highest standards. IIMA certainly cannot claim that the present selection process (whereby the ministry constitutes a selection committee) is inferior to the one it had followed since Matthai's exit (when the board constituted a selection committee).

People associated with eminent public institutions in the field of education have told me that they do not find the institutions lacking in autonomy. I once asked Ajit Balakrishnan, chairman of the Board of Governors of IIMC, whether he had experienced any sort of political interference or infringement of autonomy during his tenure. 'Not at all,' he said emphatically. 'I keep asking my people: where are the shadows?' R Seshasayee, managing director of Ashok Leyland Ltd and chairman of NIT, Tiruchirapally, also told me that in no way had the government tried to influence its functioning during his tenure.

Our analysis above suggests that the position is no different at IIMA. The contention that there is a government devil out there that has smothered autonomy and that, absent this devil, IIMA would have become truly world class, lacks substance. Over the first four decades, starting from the days of Sarabhai and Matthai, no director at IIMA had any serious complaint about lack of autonomy.

I G Patel, who was director of IIMA in 1982-84, has noted:

> By and large the government, despite its generous finance, did not interfere. In this respect, it observed strictly the principle of academic and managerial autonomy.[12]

Another former director of IIMA, N R Sheth, writing in 1993, is effusive about the government's role in relation to the Institute:

> Institutions like IIMA with elite programmes should offer special temptation to the government to interfere. Yet, while dealing with IIMA, these people explicitly and implicitly endorsed autonomy in matters of internal administration, structure and design of programmes, management and accounting of funds and interface with students and industry. Neither the central nor the local government attempted unhealthy interference in the Institute's academic activities. **Such a noble though silent contribution by the government to IIMA's culture should be noted with great appreciation and gratitude** (emphasis mine).[13]

IIMA was dependent on government funds when Sheth penned his observations and yet Sheth, like Patel, found no cause for complaint. IIMA ceased to be so dependent in 2002-03. The shrill clamour for greater autonomy has arisen only thereafter. It arises from elements in the IIMA establishment that are uncomfortable with the scrutiny that goes with being part of the government framework.

The clamour for autonomy in recent years must be seen for what it is: a thinly-disguised attempt to escape the checks and balances inherent in the government system and enter a lawless paradise made possible by a dysfunctional and ineffectual board. It has nothing to do with any constraints on growth imposed by the government. The limitations and constraints to growth are internal to the Institute and are entirely self-inflicted. The devil, as always, is within.

IIMA today lacks neither autonomy nor freedom of expression. What of the third element in the culture, faculty governance? Faculty governance was something of an article of faith with both Sarabhai and Matthai. It was not a matter of going along with faculty sentiment on every issue. It was more a matter of giving the faculty a sense of active participation in decision-making.

Faculty governance requires a willingness on the part of the director to respect the wishes of the faculty. At the same time, it cannot happen only by the grace of the director. It also depends on how conscious faculty is of its rights and obligations, and how willing it is to ensure that its voice is heard.

Over the years, there has been a weakening on both counts. Directors have been less willing to defer to the wishes of the faculty, and the faculty has been less willing to assert itself. The processes relating to faculty governance continue to be followed. Faculty meetings are held, various matters are discussed. But there is a sense that the form, rather than the substance of faculty governance, remains.

Kolavalli, writing in the mid-nineties, picked up signs of a fraying of the culture of faculty governance:

The faculty feel that their participation counts for little. Frequent overruling of faculty decisions and the director's contention that many of these decisions are administrative and not academic and, therefore, outside the purview of the faculty, have given clear message to the faculty that their views do not matter. ... The organisation of collective products has been further weakened because the faculty do not have faith in the coordinators appointed by the directors in recent years; they are perceived as being the director's stooges.[14]

A little over a third of the faculty shows up for Faculty Council meetings. Many of those who attend are relatively new recruits. A large proportion of senior faculty members tends to be absent. Moreover, proposals at Faculty Council meetings are not voted on, so it is possible for the director to interpret the discussions in any way he pleases. Meandering and inconclusive discussions on proposals can easily be recorded as approvals. It is worth examining why faculty governance has tended to weaken over the years.

Faculty governance and the non-hierarchical culture, which Sarabhai and Matthai introduced into the country through the IIM system, were something of a Western implant on an essentially authoritarian soil. The culture and processes that they put in place rested on certain assumptions about the quality of leadership as well as the quality of the faculty.

As we noted earlier, both leaders came from an aristocratic background and were exposed to Western education and the best of Western influences. In giving importance to faculty governance, they showed a patrician regard for the common good as well as an appreciation of much that is worth emulating in the culture of the West.

A high proportion of faculty members recruited in the early years also had international exposure, whether through the ITP or by obtaining doctorates abroad, and they shared the values espoused by

Sarabhai and Matthai. Thus, the leadership and the faculty reinforced each other. The Institute was small in size. There was the idealism that goes with creating a new and different kind of institution. It is no surprise that, under this set of favourable conditions, faculty governance worked so well in the early years.

It follows, however, that where the underlying assumptions or conditions do not hold, faculty governance will not be as effective. Many of the directors who succeeded Matthai lacked comparable exposure to the culture of the Western university. Recruitment of faculty from abroad dwindled; most of the recruitment happened within the country, with a large number coming from the IIM system itself. The Institute grew bigger. It ceased to be a young institution. Under these changed circumstances, it was natural for a more authoritarian or hierarchical culture to surface.

Several other factors have contributed to faculty's unwillingness to assert itself and a waning of faculty governance. In the early years, there were only two levels of faculty: assistant professor and professor, and promotions happened in reasonably quick time, say, three or four years. The minutes of the early years are testimony to vigorous faculty participation in decision-making.

The position has changed since. A member of the faculty typically joins as assistant professor and there are two levels of progression now: associate professor and professor. Faculty promotion from one level to another takes a minimum of five years. The wait to become a full professor lasts at least ten years. The director has a decisive say in promotions.

Directors had the discretion earlier to provide extensions from the age of 62 to 65 to faculty members close to retirement. Now, the director has the discretion to provide an extension from the age of 65 to 70. This does give the director a certain power over senior faculty as well.

There has been another significant change in the Institute in the past decade or so. The 'India Shining' years brought about an exponential increase in consulting opportunities, mostly in the form of in-company training programmes, as we noted in Chapter 5. The director now has another powerful tool at his disposal that he can deploy at all levels of faculty.

Faculty members are permitted a maximum of 53 days of consulting in any given year, which translates into approximately ₹5.3 million in extra income. These opportunities come overwhelmingly to the Institute and are routed to the faculty by the director. There are no norms or processes for the allocation of consulting to faculty by the director, it is entirely for him to determine a faculty member's involvement (or, for that matter, his own involvement) in Institute consulting.

This has proved corrosive of faculty governance. It is harmful to the culture of the Institute in other ways as well. For instance, it accentuates incentives for groups of faculty to annex the commanding heights, so to speak, by installing their candidate as director and then to use the heights to appropriate the spoils.

Other carrots at the director's disposal include opportunities for international travel and exposure, involvement in high profile activities and committees, and nominations of faculty to corporate boards in response to requests. All these have cumulatively changed the equation between the director and the faculty. By general reckoning, faculty governance is a pale shadow of what it used to be.

Autonomy implies a certain distance from the government. Matthai's model of a self-regulating community meant a certain distance from the board as well. Combine the two and you have a community that is accountable to nobody.

The board had been active in the initial years. It set the direction for the Institute, played an important role in choosing HBS as the collaborator, formulated policies for faculty development and was closely involved in the selection of the first full-time director.

Matthai's charismatic leadership and the Institute's early success saw the board fading into the background. Matthai once joked, 'In this Institute, the board decides the sale of old chairs and tables.'[15] Many at the Institute are of the view that the position has not changed much since.[16]

Since the board did not have much of a role to play, attendance at board meetings tended to be poor. The Bhargava Committee noted this fact; it had other unflattering observations to make about the functioning of IIM Boards, too:

> Board agendas are filled with routine administrative approval requests, partly because many decisions of the director need board approval and also because officers within IIMs use board approvals as a legitimisation of their actions and a defence against government audits. This crowds out strategic debates which leads to increased disinterest on the part of talented and busy board members.
>
> Only rarely do boards discuss strategy and prepare any long-term plans. The low attendance of board members appears to be partly the result of their feeling that they cannot add value, and are thus wasting time in attending Board meetings. ... The government itself has not fixed any targets or goals for the boards, and there is no mechanism to hold the boards responsible for results.[17]

Thus, in the opinion of the committee, the IIM Boards were dysfunctional and ineffective. A colleague, who served as faculty nominee on the IIMA board, gave me an account of what transpired at a typical board meeting:

The director would brief the board about his foreign travels, which places he had visited, who he had met, etc. Then, the chairman would talk airily about whatever came to his mind. After that, people would look at their watches and decide it was time for lunch.[18]

It should be obvious that power, in this scheme of things, devolves entirely to the director. Whether it devolves further to the faculty too, depends on how strong faculty governance is. In Matthai's time and for some years thereafter, power devolved further, by design, to the faculty. The weakening of faculty governance in recent years means that there is an unhealthy concentration of power in the office of the director. In effect, we have a situation where the director is accountable neither to the government nor to the board nor to the faculty.

The absence of written rules, which was also part of the culture created by Matthai, makes matters even worse. The fulfillment of workload norms by faculty; confirmation and promotion; the allocation of consulting – on these and other matters, there is room for considerable discretion in the hands of the director. Such vast discretion, combined with a complete lack of accountability, has serious implications for institution-building.

The question arises: did Matthai carry his beliefs in self-regulation and the absence of rules a trifle too far? Bernard Shaw once famously wrote, 'Every profession is a conspiracy against the laity.' Every professional group would like to be left to its own devices but experience shows that it is not wise to permit this. Self-regulation just does not work. It has not worked for stock exchanges, merchant bankers, lawyers, doctors, auditors, the judiciary, and the media.

Box 7.1: The Bhargava Reports

In 2008, a committee headed by R C Bhargava, chairman, Maruti Suzuki India Ltd, submitted a report on changes in governance required in the IIM system. Ajit Balakrishnan, chairman, Board of Governors, IIMC, was a member. The committee said that responsibility for governance was divided amongst the government, the board and the director. As a result, none of them had been able to play an effective role.

It recommended the creation of a pan-IIM board which would assist the government in monitoring the performance of IIMs. It also made other recommendations, including a reduction in the size of IIM boards to 11.

The proposal for a pan-IIM board was opposed by the IIMs and the Ministry of HRD decided not to implement it. Instead, it constituted another committee, again headed by Bhargava (Bhargava II). This committee included the directors of IIMs. It submitted its report sometime around September 2010.

Bhargava II recommended that ownership should vest in the society of IIM and the board should be accountable to the society. While this may have been the position on paper even in the past, the societies had been largely moribund. It was the government that exercised a check on the board. Bhargava II recommended that the society be made more active by offering memberships at a price – ₹20 crore to a corporate, ₹5 crore for individual memberships.

If this proposal is implemented, it should be possible for any business group to acquire three or four memberships in the corporate or individual names and thus gain a dominant, if not controlling, position in the society. This would amount to backdoor privatisation of the IIMs. (The first Bhargava Committee had been categorical in declaring IIMs as 'public institutions'.) It is surprising that this proposal has not evoked any response in the IIM community or the public at large.

Bhargava II also suggests that the director be re-named president-cum-dean 'in line with designations prevailing in leading business schools.' In the US, 'dean' is a title used for the head of a school; 'president' is the title given to the head of a university. There is no call to mix the two titles. But, leaving that aside, it is hard to see how the re-designation of the director is critical at all.

In the meantime, there has been an interesting development in the relationship between the IIMs and the government that has attracted surprisingly little attention. The ministry has taken to reviewing the functioning of the IIMs at six-monthly meetings presided over by the minister himself. The directors are expected to outline their vision, objectives and strategies.

This is happening, perhaps, for the first time in the annals of the IIMs. Instead of a pan-IIM board reviewing the functioning of the IIMs, the ministry is doing the job by itself. In my view, this is entirely appropriate view given the infirmities in the functioning of the IIM boards. But it is strange that the votaries of autonomy, who protested vociferously against the slightest sign of any encroachment of their turf, have now fallen silent.

We have learnt that when it comes to governance, a simple tenet holds true: somebody performs, somebody else monitors and evaluates. Academics, no less than any other group of professionals, have to be accountable to some authority. In the case of IIMA, this authority should have been a compact and pro-active board.

With the benefit of hindsight, it is possible to fault Matthai on this account. A system should not be predicated on a certain quality of leadership or faculty. Matthai might have left an overseeing role for the board. The Institute would have been better served had he worked towards the formation of an effective board, with adequate representation of academics of stature.

The absence of written rules too, is not something that an organisation can afford as it grows in size. For Matthai, values were primary and eternal, rules were secondary and transient. He judged situations and people not by rules but in relation to his own moral compass. Rules could be broken if they came in the way of a larger institutional purpose, and of that higher purpose, Matthai himself was the arbiter.

However, institutions must be designed for ordinary mortals, not elevated souls. History teaches us that unbridled discretion and unfettered power, arising from the absence of rules, can play havoc with institutions. That is why we have such a thing as the rule of law.

We must be fair to Matthai. It is not as if every element in the culture or processes he put in place was intended for all time. The basic elements of the Western model, such as autonomy, faculty freedom and faculty governance, undoubtedly were.

The variants to the model that Matthai introduced like self-regulation, the absence of rules and, perhaps, even the lack of formal authority for administrative heads, were appropriate to the Institute at that particular point in its evolution. They fitted a style of leadership with which Matthai himself was comfortable. But Matthai would certainly have been open to the idea of changes in these and other aspects, as the Institute evolved.

Matthai was far from being doctrinaire in his approach to institution-building. Flexibility and improvisation were his watchwords. We must not forget his immortal dictum, 'Do not institutionalise what is organisational.'[19] When it came to structure and processes, he refused to accept any presumption as to what might be good or bad. It all depended on the context:

There are certain implied normatives in management which normatives are assumed (to be) good things. Are they really so? Eg. decentralisation and autonomy are assumed to be good things but they are not so and there are no normatives. There may be conditions in which complete centralisation and total lack of autonomy may be a pre-condition to building autonomy. There is nothing good or bad.[20]

In the early stages of the Institute, when he assumed office, Matthai felt that the overriding priorities were building people and getting them committed to institution-building tasks. The absence of rules and formal authority was a means to this end.

Once the Institute had acquired a certain stature and momentum, Matthai chose to step down as director because he felt that the time had come for changes in the structure and processes of the Institute, as well as the style of leadership. If the necessary changes did not come about thereafter, we can hardly blame Matthai for that.

As the Institute grew bigger and once its programmes had stabilised, it would have been appropriate to formalise or codify at least some norms. 'The mechanisms and systems of Matthai's time may not be appropriate for a larger institution,' C Rangarajan told me. 'They required close contact between the director and the faculty.' And yet the formalisation of norms did not happen. Partly because of the inertia in the system and partly because successive directors found it expedient not to disturb the status quo.

Faculty governance was primarily about giving the faculty a say in decision-making. It came to mean faculty participation in routine administrative chores. As activities in the Institute proliferated, so did committees and meetings. As chairman of the finance area, I once tried to find a room for a meeting at short notice. I drew a blank. Every single meeting room in every corner of the campus had been reserved! The principle of involving all of the faculty in administration ceased to be followed. The same set of 10-12 faculty members came to sit on most committees.

As I mentioned above, directors now have various tools at their disposal for undermining faculty governance. With neither the board nor the Faculty Council living up to their responsibilities, there is virtually no accountability of the director.

To the Institute's stakeholders, including the government, this manifests itself as a certain lack of accountability of the system as a whole. Lack of accountability of the director is the principal governance issue in the IIM system today, not the supposed lack of autonomy.

Much of the friction in recent years between the IIMs and the government has arisen on this account. The Bhargava Committee recommended the constitution of a pan-IIM board that would, among other things, set objectives for the IIMs, require the IIMs to prepare business plans and monitor performance against the plans. The idea was to inject a measure of accountability into the system by comparing performance against approved targets.

This proposal was fiercely opposed by the IIMs as infringing on their autonomy and was shelved. But the recommendation had arisen in the first place because the IIM boards had failed to discharge the most basic function of any board, namely, monitoring and evaluating the performance of the CEO, in this case, the director. Over all these decades, it does not seem to have occurred to successive boards at the nation's premier management institutions to put in place adequate norms for accountability of the director.

After Kapil Sibal took over as Minister of HRD, the ministry began hammering away at this issue with its representatives raising it at board meetings. At a meeting that Sibal had with IIM directors on

October 13, 2010, it was decided to evolve performance indicators for directors and not just the faculty.[21] If this does happen, it will be the first step towards making directors accountable.

It is often asked why the government cannot exit the boards of IIMs and leave things entirely to eminent professionals as happens in the corporate world. Well, that has been the position, *de facto*, all these years since government nominees rarely attend board meetings. Unfortunately, nor do the professionals from the private sector.

Having eminent professionals on the board is hardly a guarantee of its effectiveness. As we saw above, fifty years after the IIMs were set up, it required the Ministry of HRD to ask the boards to put in place performance norms for directors! This bears out a broader point: boards are effective where there is market discipline and where stakeholders demand performance.

Companies are subject to market discipline. So are top schools in the US where competition in higher education is fierce. At any good school in the US, the departure of high-profile faculty or even a failure to improve the quality of faculty, lack of improvement in research output, a decline in MBA rankings – these and other failures could easily cost the dean his job.

The director of an IIM need fear no such consequences. It is possible for him to sleep through his five-year tenure without evoking any response from the system. The leading IIMs face virtually no competition for the PGP and are hardly subject to market discipline.

Corporate boards are accountable to dominant institutional shareholders. At the IIMs, the government is the dominant stakeholder. If the government were to abjure its monitoring role, who would IIM boards be accountable to? Members of the board come and go and have no stake whatsoever in the IIMs. Any government withdrawal would create a dangerous governance vacuum with adverse implications for the very character of the IIMs.

In a number of areas, such as the scaling up of capacity, reservation for disadvantaged groups, the impact on management practice, the selection of the director, and accountability of the director, the government sees in the IIM system, either a lack of responsiveness to social need or a failure to set appropriate standards. At IIMA itself, the self-regulatory system that Matthai put in place does not inspire the same confidence in the outside world it once did.

Elite institutions are easily cocooned from the expectations of society at large. It is a tribute to the majesty of Indian democracy that it does not allow its elected representatives to be so cocooned. Parliament and the government find themselves obliged to respond to popular expectations. Proposals from the government that IIMA sees as infringing its autonomy are often no more than attempts to bring about a measure of responsiveness and accountability in the system.

As the IIMs prepare for an era of greater competition, including competition from foreign schools, the issues of governance and accountability can no longer be dodged. The starting point for any meaningful reform must be a clear recognition that the existing mechanisms have not worked.

The ministry is not in a position to exercise close monitoring through its representatives on the board. The faculty bodies at the IIMs are ineffective. A tradition of pro-active boards will take time to evolve, assuming this happens at all. Given these realities, what can we do to make the IIMs more accountable?

The answer may well be to provide for parliamentary overseeing of the IIMs. Framing an Act to bring the IIMs under the purview of Parliament (as the IITs are) would be too cumbersome. The government should seek to have *de facto* rather than *de jure* accountability to Parliament.

Let the government commission comprehensive management audits of the IIMs, say, once every five years. The audits should be commissioned by the proposed National Commission for Higher Education and Research. Over a period of time, a permanent secretariat for management audits of all institutions of higher education – say, an Office of Management Audit – along the lines of the CAG, could be created under the auspices of the Commission.

The audits must be wide-ranging in scope. They must evaluate the performance of the boards as well as directors of IIMs; the teaching and research output of the faculty; whether there has been any improvement in the faculty profile; the outputs of various activity centres at the IIMs; the appointment of chair professors; involvement of directors and faculty in consulting activities and the nature of such consulting activities, etc.

The audits must require extensive interactions with faculty, students, alumni, recruiters and others. These audits may be placed before Parliament and in the public domain. Exposing the IIMs, and institutions of national importance, in general, to parliamentary and public scrutiny could be the answer to the current lack of accountability in the system. Such accountability is in no way inconsistent with autonomy. India's leading public sector enterprises, the Navaratnas, enjoy a high degree of operational autonomy while being accountable to Parliament.

Fortunately for IIMA, Matthai left in place an important mechanism of accountability, which must rank among his greatest contributions to the Institute. This arose from his decision to step down as director at a time when there was no requirement for him to do so. A single term of five years for the director became the norm at IIMA and, in general, in the IIM system.

We saw that there are few checks in the IIM system on the office of director. It is the knowledge that a director's actions can be looked into once he has reverted to a faculty role, the certainty that he will be cut dead in the corridors by colleagues whom he has mistreated, that acts as a check, however inadequate, on the incumbent.

Limiting the director's tenure to one term has turned out to be the one potent mechanism for accountability at IIMA. Codifying and converting into an iron-clad rule what has thus far been merely a convention should be a priority for the government and the Institute. If there is one thing of which I am certain, it is this: the day the Institute departs from its convention of a single term for the director, it will be the end of IIMA as we have known it all these decades.

8

At the Grassroots

When Matthai stepped down as director, most people were certain that he would move on to greener pastures before long. Matthai was to disappoint them. He remained on the faculty of IIMA until the very end.

Matthai's restless and enquiring mind cast about for work that he would find fulfilling. Teaching in the PGP, or in any other programme, for that matter, was not really his forte. He had tried his hand a few times at teaching a course in Marketing. I have heard from alumni that he did a good job of it but it appears he did not find it satisfying enough.

Matthai decided that he would work in the field of education. He set up the Education Systems Group. He wanted the group to be part of IIMA's mission to professionalise under-managed sectors of Indian society. Two other faculty members joined him, Udai Pareek and T V Rao.

Education was then, as it still is, an area that needed vast improvement. The Education Systems Group decided that if it could focus on one state department of education, one university, one college and one school, and bring about changes at all three levels in a given state, that would be a significant contribution.

The Group got its first assignment from the newly-created Agricultural University of Gujarat which covered three colleges in three different locations, Navsari, Junagadh and Anand. Matthai and his team worked on governance issues at the University and produced a report which formed the basis for a book on the management of universities that was published later.

The next assignments came from Maharashtra. One was a report on granting autonomy for St Xavier's college in Mumbai (something that happened only in 2010!). Another was from Mahatma Phule Krishi Vishwavidyalaya on organisational health and decision-making strategies.

By 1975, the Education Systems Group had acquired some experience. The project that was to occupy Matthai for the rest of his life, came in that year and it was in the field of rural education. It came about through the confluence of several events.

Matthai had become the chairman of the Social Work Research Group founded by Aruna and Bunker Roy. The Group was involved in ushering in change in Tilonia block in the Ajmer district of Rajasthan. This gave Matthai a certain exposure to rural India. Matthai resigned as chairman following differences with the Roys over ways of bringing about change in the rural areas.

Another rural connection had been established through Matthai's friendship with Shome Das, principal of Lawrence School at Sanawar in Rajasthan. The Education Systems Group worked with Das on a programme for self-renewal at the school. Das championed the idea that public schools should be involved in rural development and he too, was involved with the Tilonia block.

A third and important connection was initiated by a good friend of Matthai's, J P Naik, the well-known educationist who was then member-secretary of the Indian Council of Social Science Research. Naik informed him that an initiative to improve rural education was under way in Rajasthan. A committee had submitted a report on the subject and there was much work to be done.

Matthai's exposure to rural India kindled in him an interest in rural education. He was quick to respond to Naik's suggestion. Matthai and his colleagues then went over to Rajasthan where they met Anil Bordia, education secretary, and Naik's wife, Chitra, who was education commissioner. They were briefed about the recommendations made by the committee on education, and the government's determination to increase the enrollment ratio and also extend education to poor families; the enrollment-in-school record for the latter was particularly low.

Following the meeting, a 'high-powered' committee was constituted that included Bordia, Matthai, Chitra Naik, T V Rao, Udai Pareek and Inderjit Khanna (Director of Education in Rajasthan) to find ways to achieve the goals laid out by the earlier committee. After much discussion, the group chose to focus on problems in rural education in the Jawaja block of Ajmer district, a block that comprised about 200 villages with a population of 80,000. Matthai has provided a comprehensive account of this experiment in a book that was published posthumously.[1]

Jawaja village itself is located within the block. The largest and only town in the block, Beawar, is 30 kms away from Jawaja village on National Highway No 8. It is 70 kms south of Ajmer and 500 kms north of Ahmedabad. The land in the block was arid and the block consisted of scattered settlements around arable land. Arable land was only one-third of the total cultivable land in the block.[2]

The problems the group came face-to-face with in Jawaja are ones that we are still struggling to address: low enrollment in schools; high dropout rate amongst students; poor learning during the schooling period.

In the initial meetings that Matthai and his group had with the villagers, the reasons for the villagers' lack of interest in schooling became apparent. The entire curriculum was intended to make the students suitable for jobs in the cities. Those jobs were, for all practical purposes, out of the reach of the students in the villages. At the same time, education did not help the villagers with the activities they were engaged in.

Matthai concluded that the problems of primary education could be addressed only by relating it to the economic activities of the villagers. The curriculum and the content would have to be built around activities that provided sustenance to the villages. For instance, if mathematics was being taught, it must include computations of yield-per-acre, consumption of fertilisers and other inputs for production of crops, etc. Similarly, costing, marketing and other relevant concepts must form part of the curriculum.

The Indian Council of Social Science Research (ICSSR) had a Rural Development Group. At their meetings, the point was made that while much effort was going into rural development, the link between these efforts and academic institutions was weak. It would be worthwhile for academic institutions to look at what was happening in rural India. This was characterised as 'action research', the systematic study of various initiatives and changes happening in rural India.

With his flair for creative thinking, Matthai expanded this idea. It would not suffice, he said, for academics to study actions initiated by others. They must actively initiate actions themselves. This would contribute to two-way learning: learning for the villagers and learning for the academics, as well. Matthai explained the rationale for 'action research' as follows:

> Management educationalists and researchers will have something to learn from the variety (of organisations working on rural development), but I suspect that the management scientist will have the most to learn from the managerially most innocent. They

will, I think, be an extremely rich source of concepts and materials on motivation, group dynamics, leadership, responsibility and authority, decentralisation, resource levels and a great deal else.[3]

Thus was the idea of the Rural University born. The ICSSR agreed to grant ₹50,000 towards the initiative.

In mooting this idea, Matthai had to wrestle with several issues. How could academic institutions justify the involvement of their faculty in rural development activities? Would such activities not make demands on scarce resources? What could academic institutions contribute in an area in which government and various non-government organisations were already involved?

Matthai argued that 'action research' was one way to make research meaningful and to address the perception that much of the research in social sciences was sterile. By engaging in action in the rural areas, social scientists might be stimulated to ask the right questions and see things from a different perspective.

Much of the research on rural development was based on the analysis of questionnaires given to rural folk. The responses that villagers gave to questionnaires were often of dubious value as the villagers lacked trust in those asking questions and wanted to play safe while providing answers. Hence, conclusions drawn from these surveys were flawed.

By being involved with villagers, Matthai argued, researchers would be able to arrive at more reliable data bases. If many academic institutions could be involved in action research, they could pool the data sets each had compiled and arrive at a database that was far more reliable than one assembled from questionnaires.

The Rural University itself was far removed conceptually from the traditional university. It was more about informal learning and sharing of ideas than the structured learning that happens in classrooms. Matthai described his concept of the Rural University in rousing terms:

> The Rural University is not an organisation in a structured sense. It is an idea. It has no campus. It does not grant degrees. Its membership is not confined to those who have passed through specified required sequences of formal education. It has no formal curriculum. It does not require the statutory recognition of an Act of Parliament. It has no organisational hierarchy and so, no office bearers. It requires no direct institutional funding either from the central or state governments. It has no overall blueprint plan nor has it a budget. It requires no rules, procedures, sanctions or controls except the self-discipline of the individual that comes with a real desire to learn.
>
> The Rural University assumes that the development of rural India will occur, not through mere target-oriented plans but through the development of people. ... This University is a locator, enabler, provider and organiser of learning wherever the opportunities for learning might exist or may be created. These spaces might be at a villager's hut, round a well, round a tanning pit, a tea shop, a school room, a roadside, a government office, a field, a mohulla, a cooperative society, a bank counter, a market place, a shop, a truck driver's 'dhaba', a village meeting place, in a vehicle, at a dak bungalow. Learning in this University can occur anywhere ... there are no teachers-and-taught as in the exclusive traditional roles of formal education. All members of the University are involved in learning and helping others learn.[4]

The basic objective of the Rural University was to link rural development with rural education. The rural education system would have to be made relevant to rural development by becoming involved with economic activities in the area. At the same time, those involved in the activities would start making demands on the education system. Such a relationship would arise from starting new economic activities in the block or improving existing ones.

The catalysts for the proposed experiment would be a team of outsiders, called Independent Volunteers (IVs). The IVs would meet villagers and help them come up with ideas for generating incomes or improving productivity. Local teachers would be involved in the implementation of ideas. The village level officials would also join and contribute. All of them, the IVs, the villagers, the teachers and the officials, were members of the Rural University. Matthai, his colleagues from IIMA and representatives from the National Institute of Design (NID), were part of the core team.

And what was the nature of learning at the Rural University? Matthai explained it as follows:

> They learn technologies, how to manage their affairs, how to create bridges of mutual help between individuals and groups. They learn about societies beyond the limits of their past experiences, of institutions and processes which will enable them to establish links with the world beyond their immediate environment. They learn about urban and metropolitan markets, about supply and demand, about products, design, and pricing. They learn to cost their activities and keep accounts. They learn about financial institutions and the banking habit. They learn about government systems, educational and research institutions, and in establishing links with them they learn from their experiences as to how these links can help them grow.[5]

These are lofty ideals; the difficulty is in making them happen. The idea of well-meaning outsiders descending on a cluster of villages and trying to help the locals may not sound very novel now, a time when non-governmental organisations (NGOs) are everywhere. Nor is the idea of an outsider group working closely with the official machinery in order to deliver results novel. But in Matthai's time, it certainly was not common in India.

In trying to effect change at the grassroots, Matthai was soon to come face-to-face with the harsh realities of rural India. Matthai tells this story in the book I have referred to earlier, and also in two volumes of letters relating to the experiment.[6]

Going through these publications is an experience. They are virtually, a saga of idealism, hope and unremitting effort. One is struck by the attention to detail, the quality of caring, the enormous effort at persuasion. The publications are a thorough compendium of what can be done by way of achieving change at the grassroots and also the limits to what can be achieved when one works within the existing structure.

One does not know if a comparable chronicle of ushering in change in rural India exists. This, however, is a book that can be read with profit even today by those engaged in rural development. I have attempted to provide a brief account of the experiment in the following paragraphs.

Matthai's experiment faced several challenges. His group had to overcome the villagers' apathy and gain their trust. There was also the inevitable opposition from vested interests in the villages. The government system had to be persuaded to co-operate without seeking to influence outcome in any way.

An important tenet of the experiment was that the villagers would have to learn to stand on their own feet. They would have to generate their own ideas on what economic activities might be useful.

To spread this message, the group organised several meetings with the villagers in 19 out of the 34 panchayats in the block.

The villagers were resistant to the suggestion. They had been used to availing benefits from government schemes; to wean them away from this pattern of dependence was no easy task. The initial meetings failed to generate any ideas. At one meeting, the visitors were told not to waste the villagers' time. The group persevered. Eventually, 26 new ideas for economic activities were generated in the meetings.

The group's elation was to prove shortlived. One of the ideas dealt with introducing new types of handlooms and handloom products in a village. The village had a handloom co-operative society that had functioned off and on. It owned a loom shed and six looms, all provided by government funds ten years ago. The president of the co-operative society was an eager backer of the idea. He got 19 people at the meeting to put their names down for new looms and sought financial support for enlarging the loom shed. He wanted new looms to be given free of cost to the co-operative.

The group felt that the cost of the loans should be met by a bank loan, not by grants but the local bank was willing to giving loans to individuals, not to the co-operative. The group went along with the bank's proposal. It was decided that everybody would assemble the next day and the list of people who would get looms and the loans to finance them would be finalised.

The next morning, the group, the bankers and the officials and other support groups arrived for the meeting. But not a single villager was present! The VLW (village level worker) was sent to round up the villagers and the president but no one was available. The meeting was adjourned to later the afternoon. Again, no villager showed up.

The group, chastened by the experience, visited the village at night and went from hut to hut, escorted by the VLW. They wanted to find out what had gone wrong. They soon understood. The president ran the looms and the shed as though they were his personal property. Villagers were allowed to work on the looms on a daily wage.

The president was a major trader and money-lender in the area. When he realised that the new looms would go to the villagers and not to the co-operative, he decided not to let the scheme go ahead. He warned the villagers that if they participated in the scheme, no money-lender would deal with them. He also scared them saying that if they dealt with the bank, they would soon lose possession of their houses and fields, and might even be jailed.

After some persuasion by the group, five villagers agreed to go buy their own looms even if it meant incurring the wrath of the money-lender. Two villagers agreed to start right away. They quit the mill the next day, signed the loan applications and were seen being trained in the designs of new products in their own looms. Bhomaram and Ganesh, in Matthai's words, 'were the first villagers to be members of the Rural University.'[7]

The idea gradually spread to other villages. The group used the same approach when it came to the introduction of leather products. To start with, about 20 households from six villages were brought together. Products were also designed that would combine handloom cloth and leather, so that these could be used to bring together two different craft groups. In the process, all kinds of links were established, with the banker, with new sources of technology (such as the National Institute of Design (NID) and Central Leather Research Institute (CLRI)), with market systems for the sale of new products, with government officials at various levels.

Matthai wanted the links with technology sources to be established only with the first level of villagers. The subsequent dissemination of technology to other villages would be the responsibility of the first learners themselves. The outsiders would be called in again only when any further change in technology was required. Only in this way would the villagers quickly learn to be self-reliant.

In other respects, it was not easy to foster self-reliance. The group decided on products for the urban market rather than the local market. The intention was to bypass the local moneylender-merchant intermediaries who had a stranglehold on the local market but were not conversant with the urban market. But this meant that the group had to take responsibility for marketing the products – the villagers would not be able to do it by themselves at the outset. Only gradually would the villagers learn to do the marketing.

Over a period of time, the weavers were persuaded to form the Jawaja Weavers' Association (JWA). The word 'cooperative' was deliberately avoided given the bitter memories the villagers had of their experiences with cooperatives. The weavers were brought round to the idea of an association by organising fortnightly purchases of their products. The weavers showed up for these meetings readily because of the prospect of the immediate sale of their products.

Once the weavers were brought together, ideas such as joint procurement of materials, joint bank accounts for working capital, joint marketing of products, quality control norms, training and mutual assistance, new product development, and the like, could be discussed. Gradually, the weavers began to see the merits of co-operation and collaboration, and the idea of the JWA evolved. Similarly the Jawaja Leather Assocation came to be formed.

Integrating economic activities with rural education was one of the key objectives of the project. That is how education was to be made more relevant; moreover, this was a significant departure from the limited initiatives taken until then. One initiative was what was called 'non-formal education'. This was nothing more than offering in a condensed form, after school hours, what was offered during the day. It would ensure that the family was not deprived of the child's labour during the day. The other was 'vocationalisation' which meant training children in vocations such as sewing.

However, whether the children opted for formal or non-formal education, the problem they faced was the same: an acute lack of jobs when they finished their education. Every family in the village has an opportunity cost of sending a child to school, namely, the contribution the child would make to the family's economic activity. If the investment in education had low probability of resulting in a job, it was natural that a high proportion of children would drop out. This explained the drop-out rates.

Vocationalisation did not go very far, either. A sewing machine installed in a school would not be available when it was required. It would be unusable because there were no funds for repairs. The school teacher would not be competent enough to teach sewing. A tailor would have been better suited but the rules required a teacher to be a matriculate.

There was a host of other problems in the rural education system: the teacher was typically somebody who could not find a better job; political interference in transfers of teachers was rampant; there was not enough initiative the teacher could take; any experiment that was attempted came into conflict with objectives by which teachers were measured, such as the conduct of examinations, dropouts, etc. The system, it was clear to Matthai, was mired in 'apathy and indifference.'[8]

Matthai concluded that instead of attempting to change the school system directly, it would be better to bring about changes in the village community which, in turn, might bring about transformation in the school system. So, introducing new economic activities in the village was the key to changing the school system. Teachers and headmasters would be the link between the school and the community. For teachers, the incentive would be the status they could gain in the community by playing an important role in new economic activities.

Integrating economic activities with rural education had the potential to give new meaning altogether to rural education. Education would be provided not just in vocational skills but in the entire gamut of activities related to the running of a business, such as accounting, costing, pricing, etc. The group realised that this objective required at least two conditions to be met. First, the teachers' involvement in work of this nature had to be legitimised, that is, it had to be accepted by the authorities as part of the teacher's responsibilities. Secondly, teachers had to be motivated to take an interest in economic activities in the area.

The group began by organising a three-day workshop for teachers and headmasters of the Beawar Khas panchayat. The workshop did increase the awareness of the teachers but it did not appear to motivate them into taking on the new roles envisaged. A few days later when one of the group members, T V Rao, visited the teachers, he was struck by their lack of interest in the experiment.

Matthai and his colleagues would not be disheartened. They made a second attempt at involving teachers in another block, Delvada. They decided not to hold another workshop but to simply tell the teachers what the group had done at Beawar Khas. The teachers would be asked to make the same efforts themselves – getting the villagers interested in new activities, getting them to form an association, helping them to get loans and to procure materials, etc.

The headmaster and the teachers at Delvada appeared interested. The deputy inspector of schools assured them that they would have the necessary freedom to make changes in their curriculum. The teachers would not have to drop the subjects they were already teaching. It was only a matter of accommodating an extra session for vocational training.

Since there were eight classes, perhaps one class could be substituted with what was proposed. The teachers agreed to contribute ₹100 each towards a co-operative. The Delvada teachers then visited Beawar Khas. They went to the loom shed and talked to two successful weavers there. Next, they visited the school. The Beawas Khas teachers told them what they had learnt from the workshop but made their own lack of enthusiasm for the project evident.

It appeared the Delvada teachers were still keen to go ahead with the project but they wanted to be assured that bank finance would be available. After further discussions and persuasion, the two weavers from Beawar Khas were persuaded to install their looms at the Delvada school. The idea was that teachers and students would be able to find time to acquaint themselves with weaving and the economics of it through contact with the two weavers.

However, this attempt did not go very far. The weavers did not feel at home in the school precincts nor did they see any advantage to working out of their school. They removed their looms after a while. Then three other weavers were persuaded to install their looms. This did not result in any significant interaction with the teachers or students. Soon, the three weavers too, removed their looms from the school. A third attempt at involving teachers, at Noondri village, also proved futile. It must all have been heart-breaking for the valiant experimenters.

The group had begun with weaving and leather. It then took up improved cultivation and the marketing of tomatoes. Tomato marketing was dominated by a few merchants. They would buy tomatoes from the *mandis* (local markets) and then sell them to wholesalers in Ahmedabad, Bombay and Delhi. Most of the value was appropriated by the merchants; the growers earned very little.

The group first thought of forming a tomato growers' co-operative which would set up a tomato processing plant. This would enable growers to realise a better value than by selling their crop. The idea did not take off because there were no subscribers even for the ₹100 share in the co-operative. It was then decided to organise marketing of tomato through the National Agricultural Cooperative Marketing Federation of India Ltd (NAFED). Five villages were made part of the pilot experiment.

NAFED agreed to charge a lower commission than it did usually, so that the farmers would benefit more. It offered two price schemes. The farmer could ask for full price payment on sale. Or he could take a portion of the price in cash at the point of sale, with any increment over this price being credited to his account a few days later.

The existing merchants perceived the scheme as a threat and they did not care to conceal their hostility to it. The group had to even think of seeking police protection. Most growers were reluctant to jeopardise their long-standing relationships with the local merchants as they had no means of knowing how the new marketing effort would pan out. Less than 1% of the local produce came to the group. This served to diminish the hostility of the merchants.

The tomato marketing effort did not quite take off for another reason as well. NAFED adopted a policy of paying a flat rate for tomatoes without taking into account the different grades of the crop. As a result, the better quality tomatoes were sold to the merchants and the lower grade ones came to NAFED. This defect in the scheme was later rectified.

On paper, the idea of getting growers a higher proportion of the final price appears attractive. However, as we have seen above, the difficulties in implementation are many. Matthai was left wondering whether the objective could be met only if the marketing effort was large enough to control the wholesale trade and reach out to the retail trade as well.

The farmers themselves needed a lot of education on what was the right plucking time, minimising damage on account of pests, and so on. The group turned its attentions to disseminating better practices of cultivation. It set up demonstration plots to introduce new varieties and organised bank loans for inputs.

Here too, an attempt was made to involve teachers and students but this effort met with opposition from some teachers and parents. The scheme was not targeted towards any group. The benefits were open to all. So, unlike some of the other schemes, this one did not encounter resistance from the power structure in the villages.

The group attempted other projects with modest success. It tried to introduce the cultivation of Agave, a cactus that is useful for soil conservation and rope-making. With the help of the Forest Research Institute, Dehradoon, a demonstration plot was organised in the premises of a school. Over two years, when the feasibility of Agave cultivation was established, the Forest Department distributed seeds to several schools. The group sought to involve teachers in popularising Agave cultivation.

The group also introduced the villages to dairy farming. The Ajmer Dairy was approached with a proposal to buy milk from the block. Ajmer Dairy also agreed to provide expertise to buffalo owners on the breeding and upkeep of livestock.

Box 8.1: *'Jawaja kiya woh nibhana padega ...'*

Matthai's commitment to the Jawaja project was total. On one occasion, his colleagues and he were due to reach Jawaja on a certain day, in order to begin the exercise of identifying village resources for starting economic activities. The sarpanches of ten villages had been notified. As luck would have it, there was a heavy downpour in Gujarat and Rajasthan, and road and rail connections were disrupted.

Matthai was insistent that the group somehow make it to Jawaja. 'The villagers are already feeling that several officials who visited them in the past made all kinds of promises but never returned. We must break this image.' Matthai and his colleagues borrowed a Matador van and drove slowly through the pouring rain for almost 24 hours. When they reached Jawaja, they found that nobody had showed up for the meeting. But the moment the sarpanches saw the visitors wading in with their umbrellas, they acted fast.[9]

It is easy to be dismissive of the Jawaja project, to regard it as a vain attempt on the part of a bunch of do-gooders to uplift the rural poor or transform rural education. But the project must not be judged only by the outcomes it produced in Matthai's time. It must be seen as a serious academic project, one that was intended to throw up answers to important issues in rural development.

In his book, Matthai attempts a comprehensive assessment, one that should be of interest to those working in the area even today. Here, I will touch upon some of the important issues that Matthai raises and to some of which he provides tentative answers. One broad conclusion that Matthai reaches is that collective action among the deprived is the solution to many problems. In many ways, his work anticipates many of today's Self-Help Groups, indeed, provides the conceptual basis for these.

One important issue in rural development is whether, given the power structures at the village level, it is possible for development efforts to bring better benefits to the disadvantaged. Will the benefits not be cornered by dominant groups? Matthai argues that the only way the poor can hope to better their lot, short of violent action, is by organising themselves.

This is not a matter of improving the bargaining position of the poor vis-à-vis powerful groups in the village, as most people would tend to believe. Group formation and group activities among the poor are necessary in order to achieve a better performance in their economic activities.

There are a number of functions that are required in relation to economic activities – marketing, finance, procurement of raw materials, technology, etc. It is simply not possible for individuals to acquire proficiency in all of these; however, groups can collectively acquire the necessary proficiency. Individuals can at best become self-reliant in some respects. Group functioning widens the possibilities of self-reliance. This is an important insight that remains valid today.

Once we accept the imperative of group formation, it has implications for the sort of education or learning that villagers need. Education cannot be just about imparting skills. It has to aim at influencing attitudes. Attitudes towards problem-solving and risk-taking have to be changed. Individuals must learn to work in groups and develop norms of group behaviour:

> …the experiment assumed that the sustained development of rural India would be feasible only if it was based on people learning to be self-reliant and to generate their own resources and opportunities. It is thus that we regard this as an experiment in learning, an experiment in education.[10]

How do we motivate the villager to learn, to invest in education? Since there are opportunity costs to sending a child to school, villagers will invest in learning only when they see usefulness in 'deliberate learning', which is different from learning that happens inadvertently. And the way to demonstrate usefulness is to start new economic activities that are gainful and that involve learning. Hence, Matthai's insistence on the link between education, broadly defined, and economic activity. It is a novel approach to addressing the problem of low enrollment and high drop-out rates in rural schools.

Another important principle that Matthai evolved was 'extensibility'. By this he meant the transfer of learning from one group to another. Extensibility was crucial to the success of any development effort because outsiders, who initiate economic and learning activities, can spare only limited time and resources.

Moreover, if the villagers were to become self-reliant, outsiders must make themselves dispensable as quickly as possible. Extensibility meant the outsiders would direct the learning of a few villagers, these villagers would teach other villagers, a village would help other villages and so on.

This is not simple as it sounds, as Matthai and his colleagues found out. Villagers taught by outsiders would want to teach other villagers only if it was in their interest to do so. For certain products for which the village itself did not provide a large market, the marketing effort would have be directed outside the village. Such an effort would be viable only if there was a large enough production base, and this meant that more people would have been taught the necessary skills.

It followed, however, that if the marketing effort was not successful, the learning would not spread. This happened in the case of both the leather and weaving products. Marketing was not successful, so the leather workers and weavers were not inclined to admit other villagers into their fold.

Extensibility also entails issues of trust: between the villagers and the outsiders and amongst the villagers themselves. The villagers must have faith in the abilities of outsiders. They must be able to persuade other villagers that they have something to offer. Creating trust all around is an important objective in such experiments.

Getting people to work together in groups was, as we have said earlier, central to the experiment. Group activity was necessary to render an activity viable. It was also useful in protecting members from exploitation. But this objective was not easily accomplished.

The villagers were reluctant to take the risk of moving into groups because they perceived the risk to be high. If things did not work out, they would be deprived of what they were making on their own. Caste was another obstacle.

One interesting observation the group made was that selling to a common buyer did not present problems but buying from a common supplier did. That is because members of the group were tied to suppliers on account of the debts they had run into. Suppliers were in a position to pressure members to buy from only them and not from others. This made a group approach to purchasing difficult. Matthai's book abounds in many such observations and insights.

Matthai and his colleagues faced quite a few problems with the institutions at the village level – the Panchayat Samiti, banks, cooperatives, schools. Matthai's insights as to why these institutions were not effective in fostering change are interesting and remain valid to this day.

Banks are intended to replace the money-lender in the village. Matthai was emphatic that this would not happen. For three reasons: first, the bank always tried to fit the villager into one of its schemes.

The activity for which a loan was sought must be viable or it must be part of a wider scheme in which the bank could depend on some other agency for recovering the loan; or there must be surety for the loan. Banks were averse to financing consumption or what they called 'non-productive' activity. The money-lender, in contrast, was willing to deal with all the needs of the villagers and this gave him an edge over banks.

Secondly, the money-lender is not just a financier, he could be a shop-keeper, trader, farmer and small factory owner as well. When the villager is unable to repay a loan, the money-lender is willing to add the installment to the debt and reduce the villager to a captive resource that can be used in his other activities. The banker is a pure financier and this limits his ability to deal with a villager.

Thirdly, the banker comes from a higher stratum of society than the typical village borrower. He is more comfortable with the rich merchants, government officers and politicians in the area where he is stationed. There is a distance between him and the villager that inhibits borrowing. The complexity of the schemes and procedures is also a deterrent. The banker is subject to statutory constraints as well as commercial objectives.

Matthai also makes a significant observation about the villager's tendency to borrow from different sources:

> From the villager's point of view, he does not see the bank as anything but another source of funds which can help keep his upward spiral of indebtedness in motion… He views his money requirements as an undifferentiated whole and attaches no sanctity to particular sources or purposes.[11]

We can easily relate these observations of Matthai's to the ongoing debate on microfinance institutions (MFIs). We can appreciate why it is so difficult for banks to dislodge the money-lender, why multiple borrowing is the norm where different sources of funds are available, and why MFIs have found willing clients in the rural areas.

One idea that Matthai mooted seems to have anticipated the business correspondent model for banks that is being talked about today. Matthai proposed that banks commission agents in the villages who combined the roles of banking, the post office, shop-keeping and wholesale trading. The villager might be better disposed to deal with a familiar entity who combined banking with traditional roles than with a bank *per se*.

Various other institutions at the village level suffered from infirmities when it came to bringing about rural development. The co-operatives were controlled by powerful groups in the village and took care of their interests rather than those of the poor. A villager steeped in debt would approach a co-operative for funds with which to buy fertiliser at the controlled rate. He would then sell the fertiliser to the money-lender at below the controlled rate. The difference would be used towards servicing his loan to the money-lender. 'This is just an instance of many ways in which the input and credit cooperatives act as agencies of exploitation,' Matthai writes.

The block development officers and extension officers worked hard but the politicians in the village took the credit for their work. If the government officers refused to heed the instructions of the politicians, they would be swiftly transferred out. For reasons of economy, officers in the headquarters were restricted in the travel they could do. So they left it to the local 'foci of power' to ensure attainment of targets under various schemes. The village level workers were asked to abide by the decisions of the local politicians. This meant that the benefits of various schemes would go only to groups close to the local politicians. The really poor in the villages were bypassed.

Matthai came to the dismal conclusion that '... there are inherent in the form of planning we have and in the implementational structure, factors which inhibit the execution of policies directed towards changes in the economic and social structure or which render such policies self-defeating.'[12]

Matthai devoted the last eight years of his life to the Jawaja project. Did he have enough to show for it? Some elements of the initiative have much to commend themselves and indeed they anticipated interventions that have become common today. The concept of Self-Help Groups, which is very much in vogue today, was integral to Matthai's scheme of things, as was the idea that villagers are better off coming together to pool their resources and upgrade their skills.

The role of outside agents in catalysing change has also come to be readily accepted and we have a large number of non-governmental organisations (NGOs) doing their bit in the rural areas. The idea of working within the power structure of the village, with all the limitations it imposes, and making use of government schemes to achieve better results at the grassroots, is also one that finds widespread acceptance.

It is the linkage between education and economic activity that Matthai sought to create that is suspect. The rural education system is so moribund, the teachers so lacking in motivation or incentive, that trying to change the system or involve it in introducing economic activities seems a distant dream.

What about 'action research', the idea that research on rural development becomes more meaningful when researchers base their conclusions on data drawn from direct involvement in economic activities? It is hard to see this sort of research being pursued under the aegis of a B-school or, for that matter, any other teaching institution. Faculty in such institutions is expected to teach, not just carry out research. And 'action research', with the demands it would make on a faculty member's time, would be difficult to combine with teaching. B- School faculty would, perhaps, be more comfortable writing case studies on 'action research' carried out by others!

However, there could be a role for 'action research' in pure research institutions or even agricultural universities. There could even be institutions dedicated to 'action research'. As Matthai's copious writings testify, the learning or understanding that comes out of intimate involvement in economic activity is of a high quality. Research on rural development can be enriched by 'action research'.

Matthai himself was supremely unconcerned at the lack of substantive outcomes from his dedicated labour. For him, it was an open-ended experiment from which he and his colleagues kept learning. Many such experiments would be required in order to arrive at a proper appreciation of how change could be brought about in rural India:

> At this stage, we do not consider success or failure as relevant. What is more important is that the (education) department and we learn from the problems in live situations so that concepts, strategies and tactics may be varied in further experimentation. When an experiment is started, the approach used imposes its own constraints on the extent of variations possible. It is, therefore, necessary to start a series of separate experiments in which other approaches can be tried out.[13]

Jawaja consumed Matthai. It became a labour of love for him. He drove his colleagues and himself in a five-tonne truck to Jawaja and back, covering more than 1000 kms. His habits and also his personality changed quite a bit. He took to eating potatoes with his hands. He had meals at roadside *dhabas* at all odd hours. He shared his room in a dak bungalow with four or five others. From being a very private person, he became more accessible and mingled freely with his colleagues.[14]

Of an evening, he would regale his colleagues with a rendering of *Malkauns* on his flute. He would belt out old love songs in his bass voice. He persuaded a volunteer to teach him to play the guitar and once tried to see if he could play the Raag *Bageshwari* on it![15] In the arid villages of Jawaja, away from the attractions of power, fame and wealth, in the midst of poverty and discomfort and all the disappointments he faced, Matthai seems to have found a very profound fulfillment.

9

Style and Substance

Of the ten directors in IIMA's history, only two have been honoured with memorials on the campus. Sarabhai has been officially declared the founder and the library is named after him. Matthai has two memorials to his name: the auditorium and the Centre for Educational Innovation.

In the foyer of the Ravi Matthai auditorium is a photo gallery. We see Matthai in a variety of poses: the young Matthai poring over a design with Louis Kahn; a suited Matthai in a class-room; sitting at a rather cramped table at a meeting of the Board of Governors; approaching a group of people including C Subramaniam, the Congress minister, with a cigarette sticking out of his mouth at a jaunty angle.

The photo of Matthai that I have found most striking is not in this collection. It is to be found in the underpass that connects the old campus with the new one. It shows Matthai sitting next to Indira Gandhi on the convocation dais. They are exchanging broad smiles. Both are completely relaxed. The bonhomie and warmth – the vibes, if you will – are all too apparent.

There is not a hint of deference, much less obsequiousness, in Matthai's manner. If you did not know who the lady was, you would not suspect that it was the prime minister of the country sitting next to the director of a small institution. You would think two old friends had got together.

That one photo says it all. It tells you the secret of Matthai's success as an institution-builder. This was a man utterly without edges, a man at ease with himself and the world. A man who harboured no grievances and did not believe he had anything to prove to anybody.

It was a combination of qualities that made Matthai a gifted manager. It made him superbly equipped to deal with people and get the best out of them. Thanks to his success as director at IIMA, the world proclaimed him a 'management expert' but his success as a manager had nothing to do with his using management techniques or theories; of these, he was blissfully ignorant. It was not about knowing 'Six Things That Successful Managers Do'.

It simply had to do with his being an exquisitely rounded human being. At ease with himself, he had the inner calm needed to judge people correctly. Being so sure of himself, he did not feel threatened by colleagues, did not think it necessary to play them against each other and never ran down anybody.

V S Vyas, a former director of IIMA and now member of the Prime Minister's Council of Economic Advisors, puts it aptly:

> But above all he had that rare gift, which not even all successful institution-builders possess, i.e., the capacity to be proud of one's colleagues' accomplishments rather than feel threatened by them. Whether one was talking about the Institute or about Jawaja, or any other enterprise he might have been involved with, Ravi would always come out with a string of names who, according to him, ought to be given credit for whatever worthwhile achievements one was mentioning. He was equally magnanimous in owning the failures and shortcomings. ... And the most important thing was the genuineness. Whether he was conveying appreciation or shouldering the blame there was no pose.[1]

Matthai's was a highly original and creative mind. But that in itself would not have enabled him to produce the results he did. There have been other very bright men who became director of the Institute. But they were not as effective as directors.

Matthai was successful for two reasons. One, he left every single person who came in contact with him, and many in the Institute who did not, with the overpowering conviction that here was a man who always put the institution above himself. Needless to say, this is such a rare quality that it quickly gets noticed and it confers on that rare individual a moral authority that others can never claim.

With people in high office, one assumes certain things. They are in it for the money (and not always, legitimate tender), they like to project themselves at every turn, they enjoy the power that goes with the office and, all too often, they view their current office as a launching pad for a bigger and more lucrative one.

Matthai just didn't seem to care for any of these things. His was a state of not wanting, that ordinary mortals would almost find impossible to relate to. He didn't seem to want anything for himself, he simply delighted in building the institution, in watching people grow and flower. He practised the Gita ideal of *nishkama karma* (action done without expectation of reward) without ever preaching it.

Secondly, and arising out of his deep concern for people, Matthai exuded great charm and warmth. In him, style and substance sat in happy union. People saw clearly that this was a man who cared. They were willing to give of their best for him and for the sake of a larger good.

When we look at what Matthai achieved in a short period of time, we understand what institution-building and leadership are all about. They are not about enormous resources or great ideas although these are useful. Institutions are built around values and true leadership is all about putting the institution first.

Matthai's qualities lent him an aura that one rarely associates with people at the top. It is also, I might add, a biographer's despair. In writing this book and trying to understand the man, I spoke to dozens of people – secretaries, officers, faculty, former directors. Some have retired, others are still with the Institute. I did not come across a single person who spoke ill of him. Almost everybody who had known him, had his fund of Matthai anecdotes and would burst into a recital at the merest prompting.

Initially, I found this difficult to comprehend. People at the top are bitterly reviled even when they are in power. The institution is split into people who are with him (at least as long as he is in office) and people who are against him. And yet here was a man, who had been gone for some three decades, whom people recalled with fondness. Matthai was respected and admired in his time. That is true of many successful heads of institutions. Matthai was also loved, and continues to be loved. That is unusual.

Matthai was a very private person. He did not mingle socially and had no friends in the IIMA community – except that he was everybody's friend. I thought, perhaps, that might be the reason people were not aware of his shortcomings. I decided I would talk to somebody who had known him at close quarters. So, I got in touch with one of his former secretaries, K S Venkitadri, now settled in Kerala.

I introduced myself and said, 'I have a problem writing this book. Nobody has anything unkind to say about Matthai. I thought I would call and ask you if you could tell me two or three negative things about him.'

'What can I say, Professor,' Venkitadri responded. 'He was the most exemplary human being I have ever come across. I have not met another like him.'

Venkitadri then proceeded to narrate some of his own anecdotes. On one occasion, when Matthai had to travel to several places in India, Venkitadri forgot to get him the ticket for his final leg from Delhi to Ahmedabad. On the day of his scheduled return to Ahmedabad, Matthai noticed that his ticket was missing and called Venkitadri to enquire. Venkitadri checked and confirmed the omission. Matthai managed a ticket at the last minute and returned as scheduled.

The next morning, Venkitadri was quaking with fear. He was sure he would be dismissed for his lapse. Matthai sent for him. 'I just want to know what happened, Venkitadri. This hasn't happened before.' Venkitadri explained that he was going through a small crisis. He was trying to give up smoking and had been experiencing serious withdrawal symptoms. He found it difficult to concentrate.

Matthai smiled and said, 'There is no need to go to extremes. You need not give up smoking. Moderation is okay.' He then opened his drawer, fished out two packets of his own brand and offered them to a stunned Venkitadri.

Some of the adulation I came across, I found inexplicable. An officer, who helped me with contacts and material, told me it was a pleasure to help out because Matthai had been such a wonderful man.

'How did you come in contact with him?' I asked.

He said, 'I did not have much contact with him. I was only a secretary in those days.'

'Then how do you say he was a great man?'

My colleague said, 'You didn't have to come in contact with him to see his greatness. When you saw him in the corridor, you felt a saint was walking by.'

Matthai was no saint. He was a heavy smoker until a heart attack compelled him to kick the habit. He needed his daily dose of gin. His private life occasioned some whispers. He was not above using guile in his dealings with colleagues. But these foibles, if they are all indeed, foibles, did not impinge on or take away from his commitment to the larger good of the institution he presided over.

In that one respect, he was not only without fault but set impossible standards of conduct.

It's the hottest summer in Ahmedabad in a century, the papers say. I am chatting with colleagues in the corridor outside my office. We are all cursing the weather. Hot waves of air lap against my face. I feel I am standing next to a brick kiln. How could anybody get work done, a colleague asks? I cut short the exchange and rush back to my office. The air-conditioning is turned on full blast but it is barely effective. The cool air in the room has a hot undercurrent to it.

Later in the afternoon, my colleague Shashi Nair escorts me to Dorm 12. It faces the faculty houses on one side and a lawn on another. We enter through a small door and make our way up a winding staircase. It's warm and dingy inside. We reach the mezzanine floor and continue our climb until we reach the first floor. A few steps from the landing, near a stinking toilet, we find ourselves in front of a line of rooms. Nair points to one of them.

'That was Matthai's office.'

Where we stand, it is humid and dusty. But for the large oval opening on one side of the floor that Louis Kahn has thoughtfully provided, the place would feel like a prison. I find it utterly dispiriting and want to leave.

A door opens and a student looks enquiringly at us. 'Congrats,' I tell him. 'You are occupying the room once occupied by Ravi Matthai.' He grins.

I peer into the room and am surprised at how small it is and how uninviting. I notice that the student has a jazzy air cooler.

Matthai's office had neither an air-conditioner nor a cooler. He believed his office should be no different from that of any of other faculty members. (When the main building was ready after

Matthai stepped down, a separate wing was created for the director's office.) There was no 'director's bungalow' either, as there is in most educational institutions. The director occupied, and still occupies, one of a row of faculty houses. (This is not true of the Physical Research Laboratory (PRL), another institution set up by Sarabhai. If the egalitarian culture that Sarabhai wanted to foster took root at IIMA but not at PRL, much of the credit must go to Matthai.)

To think that all those grand schemes for the Institute, all those profound writings and speeches, the endless discussions with faculty and others happened in that poky room! I recall our grumblings earlier in the day and feel crushed.

Box 9.1: A matter of foreign exchange

Matthai once had to make a foreign trip from out of Delhi. He had to leave in about a week's time. Several holidays were coming up, so there was not enough time to go through the then cumbersome procedures for obtaining foreign exchange. With his connections, Matthai could have easily called up somebody at the RBI and got things done but he was averse to using his connections for personal benefit. He asked his secretary, K S Venkitadri, to go over to Bombay and see if he could arrange for the foreign exchange.

Venkitadri went to the RBI building, parked himself outside the deputy governor's office and sent in a chit that said, 'K S Venkitadri, secretary to Ravi John Matthai.' The deputy governor immediately sent for him. Venkitadri explained that Matthai needed to go abroad and there was not enough time to comply with the foreign exchange formalities.

The deputy governor was gracious. 'There should not be any foreign exchange problem for the son of John Matthai. Don't worry.

I will issue the necessary instructions.' He called his secretary and rattled off a note. Venkitadri went straight to the authorised agent's office and procured the necessary foreign exchange. He called Matthai in Delhi and told him the job was done. Matthai suggested he take a flight to Delhi.

Venkitadri went to the Clark-Shiraz hotel in Agra where Matthai was staying. Matthai thanked him and suggested that he spend a day at the hotel before leaving for Ahmedabad.

Another anecdote – a VIP once dropped in at Matthai's office.[2] His son had not secured admission. Could Matthai do something? Matthai looked at the PGP chairman whose presence he had requested. The PGP chairman informed him that admissions for the year had closed.

Matthai turned to the VIP and said, 'I can only suggest that your son take the exam again next year.'

The VIP, not used to taking 'no' for an answer, digested this. He looked around the office mockingly and said, 'Don't you think the director of such an institute deserves a better office?'

Matthai stretched out his palms in a gesture of helplessness. 'Well, it serves the purpose.'

The VIP's face fell. He had been hoping to provoke an angry retort. He rose to go. As he neared the door, he took another swipe at Matthai. 'These buildings on the campus are an architectural monstrosity.'

Matthai remained unruffled. 'You are not the first person to say that.'

In other respects too, Matthai was austere. He dressed simply. As director, he was mostly seen in a bush-shirt, white trousers and

Rajasthani sandals. During winter, he was seen in a jacket without a lapel. He wore shoes only during the convocation or at official meetings. He changed later to white kurta pyjamas because, he said, he had outgrown his Western clothes after he quit smoking.

Matthai did not believe that one exercised power by flaunting the accoutrements of power. He never used his official car to go to office but preferred to walk to work (as most faculty members do, even today). After office hours, he drove his official car himself as using the driver would mean having to pay overtime. Often, when he wanted to have a word with the senior faculty, he would go over to their rooms.

The director's contract permitted Matthai to engage in consulting. He imposed upon himself a rule that he would not take up any consulting assignment. No doubt, he felt that the moral authority of the director would be compromised if he was seen to be taking advantage of his position to engage in consulting. During his years as director, he never claimed any payment for his travel bills. He asked for the travel allowance payable to him to be credited to a special fund of the Institute. Nor did he claim or receive any payment towards his medical bills.[3]

For most of his tenure, Matthai lived all by himself on the campus. His wife pursued her career elsewhere and came to Ahmedabad only on short visits. He had four children, three sons (including a pair of twins) and a daughter. They were mostly away at boarding schools and, later, pursued their higher studies outside Ahmedabad.

Matthai's house on the campus itself was spartan. So was the house next to his that served as a guest house. He once invited J R D Tata, an old friend, over for drinks at the guest house. A faculty member working on the history of the Tatas was asked to join. Matthai served Scotch and cheese.

J R D munched the cheese with relish and said, 'I didn't know they made such good cheese in India. What brand is it?'

'It's Amul,' Matthai told him.

Matthai was least awed by the rich and the powerful.

In the years after Matthai relinquished the directorship, offers poured in. He was only 45 when he stepped down, and by now something of a legend in the field of management. According to Venkitadri, the number of offers ran into 'hundreds'. Membership of the Planning Commission; a secretary-level position in the Government of India; chairmanship of a leading public sector company; consultant to the United Nations, whether on a full-time or part-time basis. Matthai spurned them all.

There were several offers from the private sector as well. The Tatas were keen to have him at the highest level. Even when he was director, they had tried to entice him. Sir Jehangir Ghandy of the Tatas told a faculty member when Matthai was director, 'Ravi can put on a piece of paper the position and the emolument he would like to have, fold the paper, and give it to us. We would say 'yes' to his terms before looking at the paper. But your director intends to remain a school master.'[4]

It is difficult, in this day and age, even to relate to self-abnegation of this sort. For most people, the whole point about an IIMA directorship is that it leads on to a more lucrative or prestigious assignment. Matthai believed that many educational institutions had come to grief because their heads had viewed their positions as a stepping stone to something else. In his code, this was just not done.

Matthai served on the boards of several companies: Arvind Mills, Escorts, Voltas, DCM, Air India, Indian Airlines, Nelco, to name a few. His association with some of these continued even after he ceased to be director, IIMA. He was also associated with three other educational institutions, the National Institute of Design, the

Institute for Rural Management at Anand and his alma mater, Doon School. He was a founder member of the Indian Council of Social Science Research. Matthai's talents were also sought out by various government committees: the Railway Reforms Commission, the Press Commission, the Morvi Enquiry Committee.

As a faculty member of the Institute, Matthai occupied a room in the main building complex as other faculty did. He refused to be considered for a chair professorship. He would not be drawn into discussing his successors and refrained from venturing any opinion on the Institute. His immediate successors, Samuel Paul and V S Vyas, sought his advice from time to time. Matthai responded whenever approached but never volunteered any advice.

Of Matthai's complete detachment from Institute matters after he ceased to be the director, Vyas writes:

> During my tenure of the directorship of the Institute, I do not recall a single occasion when Ravi compared or contrasted the developments during his directorship and those during the time of his successors. He was immune to the typical mother-in-law complex which some otherwise admirable elders find difficult to resist. At the same time, he was most forthcoming whenever one was in need of advice and help.[5]

Matthai's leadership involved a fine balance between centralised direction and delegation. In keeping with his general philosophy, he had no particular rules in mind as to which matters were to be delegated or how much. It all depended on the context and the individual. He described his approach as follows:

> Under my concept of delegation, I don't have to enter the kitchen to find out whether the rice is burning but I must have the sense to know if it is burning.[6]

He never left anybody in the slightest doubt that he was firmly in control. Long after his tenure was over, he joked that he had been an 'enlightened despot.' It's difficult to describe the balance he struck between control and delegation. Let me try to capture the flavour with a few examples.

At a quarterly meeting with PGP students, a student asked, 'Where does the buck stop in respect of PGP?'

Said the PGP chairman, 'It stops with me.'

'Correct,' said Matthai. 'And he will be PGP chairman as long as he enjoys my confidence.'

The PGP chairman would have a free hand – as long as he never lost sight of the fact that he was accountable to the director.

On another occasion, a faculty member, X, pointed out shortcomings in the arrangements for the convocation and suggested improvements. Matthai stood by the faculty member, Y, who had been entrusted with the arrangements and who was present when X made his point. 'These things are best left to the concerned person,' he told X firmly.

Then, when he was alone with Y, Matthai said, 'Don't you think that X was talking sense?'

Again, the point was clear. Y would get all the necessary support but the director retained the right to make suggestions.

Opposite the last line of faculty houses is a thickly wooded area. When the idea of planting trees at the spot first came up, the administrative officer opted for casuarina. A faculty member felt that it would be better to have *Aso palav*, a local favourite that would lend an ethnic touch to the surroundings. He mentioned his preference to Matthai.

'I agree,' Matthai told him. 'But if Chib (the administrative officer) wants to express himself, I think we should let him.'

In his own province, the administrative officer must be allowed to decide.

An earlier administrative officer, M K Subramaniam, once had a spat of sorts with Matthai. In a fit of pique, he instructed the staffer, who was tending the garden at Matthai's house, not to work at Matthai's place any more. He took the position that, under the rules, there was no provision for the director to avail of the services of a gardener at the Institute's expense.

When Matthai learnt about it, he accepted that Subramaniam was within his rights in acting the way he had done. He did not betray the slightest animosity towards Subramaniam. He advised his secretary that the gardener should heed the instructions of his superior and stop visiting Matthai's house during office hours. He could work at Matthai's place after office hours and would be paid for his services by Matthai himself.

In due course, at a board meeting, Matthai mentioned that there was a 'little problem'. It appeared that no provision for a gardener had been made in the director's terms. The board approved the provision without any fuss. The gardener's services were restored.[8]

Box 9.2: The human touch

Two of Matthai's most endearing qualities were his concern for the well-being of others and a willingness to put others' interests before his own, with scant regard for protocol. N R Sheth, a former director of IIMA, recalls an episode when he and a colleague were travelling with Matthai by car from Agra to Delhi.[9]
It was a hot afternoon and Sheth was directly exposed to the sun. They stopped along the way and got out for a few minutes. As they returned to the car, Matthai trotted ahead and hopped into Sheth's seat. Sheth tried to argue but to no avail. Sheth writes,

'This was my first direct exposure to the human side of the man whom I knew mainly as a suave institution-builder.'

There is no dearth of such anecdotes about Matthai. T V Rao, a former professor of IIMA, mentions an incident that touched him deeply.[10] He and Matthai were returning by train from Beawar (a town near Jawaja) to Ahmedabad. Matthai had a reservation for a berth but Rao did not, as he had decided to join Matthai at the last minute. Matthai refused to sleep despite Rao's repeated entreaties and insisted on keeping Rao company through the night.

Once the jeep in which Matthai was travelling with colleagues grazed past a scooter. Soon, they were surrounded by a group of unruly elements 'demanding compensation or a fight'.[11] Matthai conveyed to his colleagues in his Oxford accent that the locals must not know the identity of the driver; under no circumstances must it come to the concerned party's notice who the *'propeller of the vehicle'* was. He then proceeded to extricate himself and his colleagues from trouble as only he could.

Matthai led by example. His personal integrity, the quality of his intellect and commitment to the Institute were transparent. The ability to persuade was also part of the secret of his success as a leader.

Of his ability to persuade, Tripathi says, 'He could make the most banal statement and yet make you feel he was parting with pearls of wisdom.' He had a beautiful voice and his command of the English language helped. But there was more to it than mere glibness. There was the force of argument, genuine concern for the other person and an unfailing focus on the larger institutional purpose.

He also put to effective use a repertoire of responses and gestures that seemed to come to him naturally. A studied silence by way of cutting off a comment or inconvenient query; a raised, quizzical eyebrow; a crinkling of the eyes that made the other person look foolish; a hearty laugh that shook his frame; over the years, colleagues understood when it was wise not to push a point any further.

We saw how he persuaded the faculty, first, to offer the doctoral programme and, then, a programme in agriculture management. He was not in favour of IIMA offering a 'diploma in business administration.' He wanted it to be called 'diploma in management' as that had a connotation that went beyond business.

Faculty members were resistant. At a meeting, one faculty member said in some exasperation, 'What is the value of our opinion?'

Matthai replied, 'I am also responsible to the board.' He was implying that since the director was ultimately responsible for all decisions, he was entitled to the final say. However, he did not press the matter. The change in the title of the diploma eventually happened in 1976 after Matthai had demitted office. By then, the faculty had come around to accepting Matthai's point of view.

Akbar Hydari, a well-known corporate executive of that time, describes Matthai's approach:

> There were no didactic opinions, but a tempting array of intelligent choices laid before you in debate. His own selection he would often defer for further reflection and meanwhile listen carefully. Such people can lead, praise, or censure with equal grace, and my strongest impression of Ravi was this set of pre-eminent attributes without which no amount of learning or mental capacity can achieve real results.[12]

Yash Pal, former chairman of the University Grants Commission, recalls the time he moved to Ahmedabad as director of the Space Applications Centre. He sought out Matthai for advice. He was expecting, he says, to be overwhelmed by this great 'management expert.' After a three-hour exchange, he came away more confident about what he had in mind and appreciative of the fact that Matthai had fostered this self-confidence in him.

Pal highlights the point I made earlier about Matthai's managerial skills being just one aspect of his finely rounded personality:

> ... Ravi came to be for me what he really was; not a mere 'expert' but an analytic, cultured, and wise human being, who made people feel more capable than they actually were, and made them appreciate the delights of doing ... Even when he disagreed with you violently, his manner of conveying his disagreement was such that the very people whose views he rejected felt grateful and enhanced.[13]

It was typical of Matthai to couch his advice as mere suggestion. An industrial house once approached the IIMA dean with a request to be allowed to use the Institute buildings for some commercials they were shooting. The group had not been particularly helpful to the Institute, so the dean was hesitant to give them permission. He consulted Matthai who was then a faculty member.

Matthai said, 'Do what you think is right, not what they have done for you in the past.'

The dean said that, perhaps, he could meet the request halfway. He could let the group use the buildings as background but would not let them enter the premises.

Matthai said, 'The decision is yours. But, remember, a favour half-done is more harmful than none at all.'

It is not as if Matthai shrank from harsh or unpleasant decisions. Far from it. Several faculty members who had failed to perform were shown the door during his tenure. In some cases, he tried to soften the blow by finding them jobs elsewhere. In one instance, where an allegation of plagiarism had been made against a faculty member, he did not react immediately. At the time of evaluation, again he stayed his hand as the faculty member had suffered a bereavement. The individual, not having received his increment or promotion, sent Matthai a legal notice. Matthai immediately terminated him.

He could also be severe with student misbehaviour. A student who had been caught copying more than once was served an expulsion order. The student immediately obtained a stay from the lower court. The court permitted him to continue attending classes. IIMA moved the High Court for vacation of the stay.

Before hearing the matter in court, the judge thought he would have a private meeting with Matthai. The judge, a well-known Gandhian, asked Matthai whether it was not possible to show leniency. He struck a philosophical note, 'Every saint has a past; every sinner has a future.'

'I understand, sir,' Matthai said, 'but I have an institution to run.'

The judge did not vacate the stay but ordered the lower court to hear the case on a daily basis and complete the hearing within three months. The student, who had, no doubt, been hoping to drag out matters until he graduated, withdrew the case and left the Institute.

If Matthai had a blind spot, it was with respect to trade unions. He could not stomach the idea of an educational institution having a union. Throughout his tenure, he refused to meet any of the office bearers of the union although he had excellent relations with the staff on a personal basis. If the staff had problems, they were free to approach him. Some believe that Matthai's paternalistic approach and his refusal to talk to the unions were responsible for some of the staff problems his successors had to deal with.

I have tried to capture some of the facets of Matthai's personality. One element is missing and it is crucial to understanding the way he related to the world. He was deeply spiritual in his orientation without being religious in the formal sense. Long after he had stepped down as director, a faculty member complained bitterly to him about a colleague who was being difficult. Matthai heard him out and said quietly, 'You know, there's something our mother used to tell us when we were young. She used to say that we are all God's children.'

Some other colleagues, who had also heard this remark, decided to test the sincerity of his conviction. Once, when he was fast asleep in the town of Beawar after a long and hard morning's work, they sent a tea-boy into his room to wake him up and ask him (in Hindi), 'Am I also a child of God?'

They waited outside expectantly. Soon, there was a deafening roar, followed by a 'blurred vision of a streaking terror-stricken stripling'. Later, Matthai modified his homily to read, 'We are all God's children ... but there are some b ... s on the periphery.'[14]

Matthai's hectic lifestyle and his heavy smoking soon began to take a toll on his health. In 1977, while on a trip to Bombay, he had a heart attack and was admitted to Breach Candy hospital. He was treated by his friend, the well-known cardiac specialist, Farokh Udwadia. Udwadia gave him Ivan Illich's *Deschooling Society* to read. Matthai returned the compliment with Illich's *Limits to Medicine*. They had many exchanges on the two books.

During this hospitalisation, Matthai's mother passed away and he was not able to attend her funeral. After the heart attack, Matthai completely gave up smoking but he neglected his health in other ways. He continued his travels in connection with the Jawaja experiment, often driving long distances and subjecting his body to punishment during his stay in the villages. The plight of the poor and his experiments at ushering in change seemed to keep drawing him. His colleagues tried to reason with him but to no avail. 'Hard work never killed anybody,' he would say dismissively, 'only worry does.'

At other times, he would squelch the concern anybody expressed for his health with a raised eyebrow and a pitying smile.

In May 1983, while on his way to Jawaja, Matthai had to return to Jaipur as he had developed a clot in his leg. P K Sethi, the creator of the Jaipur Foot and a good friend, treated him. In late 1983, Matthai had to be operated at the Breach Candy hospital for a blockage in an artery supplying blood to the legs. Udwadia then advised Matthai to go in for cardiac bypass surgery, preferably in the UK or the US.

Matthai and his wife, Syloo, left for London on 6 December, 1983. The bypass was successfully done at a Harley Street Clinic on 10 December, 1983. Matthai was discharged on 20 December. He and Syloo returned to the apartment they had rented. On 22 December, Matthai had to be rushed back to the clinic as he had developed numbness in his leg. He was again discharged two days later.

On 26 December, he was examined by the attending physician who assured them that he would be available at any time should the need arise. That evening, Matthai developed severe abdominal pain. It was Christmas time and the physician was not available. Later that night, after several calls reporting his deteriorating condition, Matthai was again admitted to the clinic where his condition worsened.

He was then moved to Middlesex Hospital where he underwent an emergency operation on 27 December to remove a clot in an artery. Most of his intestine also had to be removed. After a brave fight for two months, Matthai passed away on 13 February, 1984. He was cremated at Golders Green cemetery in London. His sons, Vivek and Ashok, immersed his ashes in the Sabarmati in Ahmedabad.

The campus was enveloped in gloom, the likes of which had not been seen before nor has been seen since. The community assembled at the Louis Kahn Plaza to observe silence. Many wept. No speeches were made; they would have been inadequate. Later, a condolence meeting was held in the city. In May 1984, IIMA brought out a commemorative issue of its alumni magazine, IIMA Alumnus. The write-ups are deeply moving. The magical effect that Matthai had on a wide cross-section of people is in evidence.

What would prompt a man in his mid-forties to walk away from the directorship of IIMA, decline fabulous offers and opt for the relative anonymity of a professorship? Why would a heart patient ceaselessly travel to a village 500 kms away to pursue the idea of a rural university? What do we make of somebody with an aristocratic upbringing who adjusts effortlessly to the life of a college teacher and the privations of rural India?

A Ravi Matthai is a miracle that happens once in the life of an institution. Just as the nation threw up a Gandhi, a Nehru and an Ambedkar who moulded its destiny, so also IIMA was blessed by the leadership of an exceptional individual. I have dwelt on Matthai's contributions and tried to evaluate his legacy. There are certain values that he bequeathed; in particular, a bias towards freedom and creativity that are valid for all time. But there is no 'Matthai model' of governance for others to emulate. Matthai was unique; he is non-replicable.

Matthai lives on at IIMA. When faculty questions a decision taken without consulting the Faculty Council; when people talk of the integrity of the admissions process; when we see faculty members putting themselves out to excel in the classroom; when the director constitutes a committee to initiate or review some activity; when, once in a decade or so, the Institute sets out to chart its plans for the future; when we disapprove of the director's using his position to grab consulting opportunities for himself; when the community expects a director to leave gracefully on completion of his tenure; when we do any of these things, we are invoking the spirit of Matthai. He is an unseen presence that hovers around the campus, flits through its long corridors, makes itself felt at meetings.

The story of Ravi Matthai is the story of a man who worked tirelessly to build an institution, who spent himself in pursuit of a noble experiment in bringing about rural change, who built people and got the best out of them and who did all this without ever forgetting his basic humanity. He was that rare human being who lived up to the timeless adage in his beloved Bible: *For whoever wishes to save his life will lose it; but whoever loses his life for My sake will find it.*

No national honours came the way of this pioneer in management education. He lacked the instinct for self-projection and manipulation that, more often than not, is a requirement for winning such honours. Men like Matthai need none. The institution that he helped build – brick by red brick – and that is hailed as a centre of excellence, is a greater tribute to him than any award that anybody could confer.

In the initial decades after Independence, India was fortunate in having institution-builders of the highest calibre. Nehru showed the way by building the institutions of democracy. Then we had the likes of Homi Bhabha, Vikram Sarabhai, J R D Tata, V K R V Rao and R K Talwar. In that constellation of institution-builders, Ravi Matthai shines brightly.

Epilogue

It is the last Saturday of March, convocation time. The campus wears a festive look. Rows of potted plants spring up on the Harvard Steps, along the driveway from the main gate into the campus and on the parapet of every floor of the faculty and classroom wings overlooking the Louis Kahn Plaza where the convocation is held.

A day or two before the function, groups of families can be seen exploring the campus with their graduating children. They are all wearing broad smiles, chattering excitedly, taking snaps. Through the day, sweepers are at work and the campus looks neat and tidy.

On the morning of the convocation, I gaze down at the dais from the corridor of the second floor where my office is located. It is a pleasing sight. A spotless red carpet adorns the floor of the dais. In the centre is a table with three chairs that will seat the chief guest, the chairman of the Board of Governors and the director. On either side of the table, in a semi-circular arch, are five rows of blue-coloured chairs for the faculty. There is a podium and a mike alongside the table and another at the right end of the dais.

On the periphery of the dais, pans containing water have been laid out. It is a blazing hot month, the cooling effect will be useful. In the foreground is a massive board containing photographs of graduating students in the various programmes. In front of the dais and facing the faculty are two columns of chairs, separated by an aisle and stretching all the way up to the Tower lawn. One column is for the graduating students. The other is for guests, including families of students. The layout is impeccable. The staff has done a fine job as usual.

The circular spelling out the drill for the convocation had come from the dean a couple of days earlier. The boys will wear suits, the girls saris. Dark trousers, white shirt and tie for male faculty, saris for the ladies. The order for the convocation procession and the seating arrangements on the dais are spelt out in detail.

So are the timings. In the morning at 8:00 am, will be a dress rehearsal. At 4:15 pm, the faculty will meet in the KLMDC auditorium for an interaction with the chief guest. A group photograph of the faculty with graduating students at 5:30 pm. The convocation procession to begin at 6:00 pm.

The interaction with the chief guest is over, the faculty stream out of the auditorium for a quick cup of tea before they don the robes. The sashes differ in colour: dark blue for the faculty, light blue for PGP students, orange for fellowship students; and so on. We head for the lawn, just a few metres from the executive complex, where the group photograph will be taken.

A multi-storeyed structure has been temporarily erected on the lawns. There is a row of chairs at the foot of the structure. The programme coordinators, area chairpersons, the chief guest, the chairman and the director will occupy the chairs. Behind them in the first row, the faculty will stand. Behind the faculty, in multiple rows, will come the students.

The faculty and the students are ready. Friends and relatives of students are clicking away or shooting furiously. The chief guest arrives along with the chairman and the director. The visitors are shooed to a distance so that the official photographer has a clear view. The flash goes off several times, then the photographer signals that it is over. The students let out a roar. The Ahmedabad papers will carry the group photo the next morning. I will challenge Jayashree and Nandu to spot me in the sea of faces. This, too, is an annual ritual.

We move to the narrow path alongside the students' dorm to form the convocation procession. The dean and the FPM chairperson will lead the procession. The faculty will follow. Students will bring up the rear. We down cups of lime juice available at temporary stalls set up near the dorm.

I look at my watch. It's 6:10 pm. Ten minutes behind time. I am vexed. The Institute has always prided itself on the Republic Day-like precision of the convocation. Of late, we have become a little lax. The signal is finally given, the procession moves. On both sides of the procession, cameras are clicking away. I feel a surge of pride. This is the one time in the year that I am made to feel like a celebrity.

We approach the main building. Close to the Harvard Steps, large weighing scales made of iron are kept on either side of the procession route. Are they meant to symbolise our fairness? We file past the main building complex in a narrow path that leads to the Tower lawn. At regular intervals on both sides of the path are containers filled with petals. The lovely notes of a *shehnai* waft across. It's still quite bright but the lights have come on.

We enter the Louis Kahn Plaza. The guests are on their feet, turned towards us. The parents are wearing huge smiles, adoration writ large on their faces. We divide into rows facing each other, separated by three feet or so.

From the head of the procession, the dean and the FPM chairperson walk towards the chief guest, who is flanked by the chairman and the director. They bow before the chief guest, then turn and lead him towards the dais. The two rows of faculty follow, one moves to the left and another to the right. I make my way through the second row and towards the seat allotted to me. I check the name on the sticker. It's mine, all right.

We stand on the dais and wait for the students to assemble in front of their chairs. (The line flashes across my mind: they also serve who stand and wait.) The chairman then declares the convocation open. I notice that I am on the wrong side of the dais. The sun hasn't set and it's beating down on my side. I have to put up with the heat and the glare for at least half an hour.

A student goes up to the podium and opens the proceedings with an invocation song. In the sky above, a flight of birds, in perfect formation, soars past the Plaza. The metaphor of the Republic Day parade is strong.

The chairman rises to deliver his address. He welcomes the chief guest, congratulates the students and their parents and moves on to broader matters. The economy benefited in a big way from being freed from controls. Why is education still being stifled? Why can't prestigious institutions such as the IIMs be given genuine autonomy? Let the government leave the IIMs free to achieve their goals, he thunders.

The students cheer lustily. Government-bashing goes down well with our students, we have done a good job of preaching the virtues of the market to them. The applause from the faculty is tepid. I can see the headlines in the morning papers: Hands off IIMs–IIMA chairman.

The moment for which the students have waited, the proudest of moments for the assembled families has come. One by one, the names of students will be called out. The chairman will shake hands with every one of them – some 400 in number – and hand out a folder containing the precious certificate. The official photographer will capture the moment. The chairman's hands will need serious scrubbing later, I tell myself.

There is a roar or a ripple of merriment when some names are called out. As the students step off the dais, members of their families pop up from their seats, cameras at the ready. Some rush into the aisle and wait at the foot of the dais. A watchman comes up and politely asks them to get back.

I look up to my left. On the first floor of the classroom wing, I see a battery of cameras trained on us. Almost reflexively, I pat down my robe and adjust my tie. I glance to my right at the office wing. Nandu is on the first floor with his friends. The little fellow beams and waves at me. I am conscious of being on stage, so I permit myself just the faintest of smiles.

I glance over the gathering in front of me. The students' faces are shining with excitement. I have been used to wading into the ranks of the Great Unwashed in the classroom. In their suits and saris and impeccably groomed, the students present a different picture altogether. These are the finished products of two years of toil on our part, our offering, as it were, to society. I should be elated. For some reason, maybe the sense of parting or, maybe, just the sweltering heat, I am swept by an ineffable sadness.

The PGP chairman is done with the roll-call. He turns to the chairman of the board and requests the IIMA society to confer the diploma on the students. The chairman rises and asks the members of the society sitting in the front row to his right whether he has their permission to do so. There is a chorus of 'yes'.

The chairman intones solemnly, 'By the authority given to me by the Indian Institute of Management Ahmedabad Society, I confer on you the post-graduate diploma in management, and I charge you that in your life, by word and deed, you prove yourselves worthy of it.' The students take a deep bow.

The PGP chairman walks back to his seat. The students, clutching their diplomas, are still standing. I am baffled. The PGP chairman takes his seat. Now the students sit down. Realisation dawns! The students can't sit whilst their lord and master, the PGP chairman, is on his feet.

The PGP chairman gets up and walks up to the podium again. He will announce the awardees of the President of India gold medals. One by one, the three winners come up to the stage. The chief guest steps out in front of the table before him. The director stands next to him and passes on a case containing the medal. The chief guest gives away the gold medals.

There is generous applause for the gold medal winners. I join with gusto. I have been a student in the IIM system and have some idea of what it takes. In course after course, in semester after semester, the student would have got top grades, and while competing against some of the nation's best. It's not enough to have brains. You need grit and stamina. It's like running a marathon and being ahead all the time.

One by one, the chairmen of other programmes repeat the drill. Then, the chief guest delivers his address. You are graduating at a time of great opportunity, he tells the students. The Indian economy has done very well in recent years and even better things are to come. He is not an MBA and would have never made it to IIMA even if he had tried. However, he has seen something of the real world and would like to offer a little advice...

Finally, it's the director's turn. He tells the gathering that IIMA remains the nation's top business school and one of the best in Asia – there is wild clapping – and is determined to stay there. He goes on to highlight the activities of the past year.

It's nearly four hours since the interaction with the chief guest began. I am a little weary and find my attention faltering. It's cooler now and the quadrangle is bathed in mellow light. The murmur and rustle in the audience have given way to a stillness broken only by the twittering of birds. The excitement is beginning to fade, everybody is thinking of dinner and flights to catch.

Soon, the director will dispense the usual homilies. The graduating students must remain true to the values of the Institute. They must never forget that they are the Institute's brand ambassadors. They must not focus on personal gain alone, they must always be mindful of their larger obligations to society. When the director is done, the chairman will declare the convocation closed.

The faculty will alight from the dais and file past the throngs of students and guests. The procession will not be as tidy as when we came in, not as unhurried. The *shehnai* will play again. We will stop at the mango tree at the foot of the Harvard Steps and hand over our robes. We will then shuffle back to our homes, cracking jokes. In a week's time, the first of the new batches will arrive. Campus life, like life itself, is all about arrivals and departures.

The director is nearing the end of his address. I peer over the heads of the gathering and into the clumps of trees on the fringes of the Tower lawn. I am startled and have to stifle a gasp. In the opening between two trees, a face has appeared. Ravi Matthai is watching intently. It is the Matthai of the younger days, his thick mop of hair is jet black and he is wearing his trademark smile. Slowly, his gaze moves over the gathering below and then on to the stage. Do I glimpse a touch of anxiety in his eyes? It must be my imagination.

We are doing okay, Prof. We can't possibly let you down, now can we?

Notes

Chapter 1: The Grand Design

1. Sarabhai papers
2. Recommendations for an All-India Institute of Management, a report by George W Robbins, December, 1959, p 5
3. Hill, Thomas M et al (1973), p 48
4. Ibid., p 48
5. Ibid., p 50
6. Ravi Matthai, 'The underlying basis of IIMA organisation', IIMA (1993), Vol I, p1
7. S K Bhattacharyya, 'The early years of institutional development', IIMA (1993), p 6-8
8. Hill, Thomas M et al, p 67
9. Shah, Amrita (2007), p 104
10. Tandon, Prakash (1980), p 112
11. Ibid., p 114
12. Khushwant Singh in his column, This above all, *The Tribune* (14 January 2006)
13. Tandon, Prakash (1980), p 113
14. Piramal, Gita (1998), p 301
15. Ibid., p 304-305
16. Ibid., p 306
17. Tandon, Prakash (1980), p 116
18. Ibid., p 133
19. Sarabhai papers
20. Ibid.
21. Ibid.

Chapter 2: Laying the Foundation

1. Sarabhai papers
2. Ibid.
3. Ibid.
4. Ibid.
5. IIM Ahmedabad (1973), p 37
6. Ibid.
7. Ibid., p 38
8. Sarabhai papers
9. Ibid.
10. S K Bhattacharyya, 'The early years of institutional development', IIMA 1993, p 10-11
11. Alas, I could not track down the source although I clearly recall having come across it.
12. S K Bhattacharyya, 'The early years of institutional development', IIMA (1993), p 13
13. Ibid., p 12-13
14. Tandon, Prakash (1980), p 129
15. Ibid., p 131
16. Ibid., p 131

Chapter 3: The Master Builder Arrives

1. Haridasan V (1986), p 151
2. Ibid., p 136
3. Narrated to the author by Prof Dwijendra Tripathi
4. Jain, Uma , p 3-4
5. Ibid., p 4
6. Ibid., p 6
7. Michael Halse, 'To Ravi with respect and affection', IIMA (1993), p 78
8. Jain, Uma, p 12
9. Ibid.

10. Ibid., p 16
11. Ibid., p 17
12. K T Chandy, 'Tribute to a dedicated soul', IIMA Alumnus (May 1984), p. 3-4
13. Jain, Uma, p 17
14. IIMA Alumnus (May 1984), p 3-4
15. Jain, Uma, p 16-17
16. Tandon, Prakash (1980), p 131-132
17. 'Search for a director', IIMA Alumnus (May 1984), p 8
18. 'The Institution builder', IIMA Alumnus (May 1984), p 9
19. Ibid.
20. Jain, Uma, p 17
21. Ibid.
22. H N Pathak, 'As I remember', IIMA (1993), p 47
23. Michael Halse, 'To Ravi with respect and affection', IIMA (1993), p 78

Chapter 4: Erecting the Edifice

1. Michael Halse, 'To Ravi with respect and affection', IIMA (1993), p 79
2. S K Bhattacharyya, 'The early years of institutional development', IIMA (1993), p 18-19
3. Ibid., p 21
4. C Ramdoss, 'Ravi Matthai my mentor' in IIMA (1993), p 50
5. Ibid., p 53
6. S K Bhattacharyya, 'The early years of institutional development', IIMA (1993), p 12
7. Hill, Thomas M et al, p 108-109
8. Minutes of Faculty Council meeting,
9. S K Bhattacharyya, 'Remembering Ravi Matthai', Business India, (27 February–11March 1984)

Chapter 5: Towering Over the Rest

1. IIM Ahmedabad (1973), p 25
2. Ibid., p 26
3. Warren G Bennis and James O'Toole, 'How business schools lost their way', *Harvard Business Review* (May 2005)
4. D K Desai in IIMA(1993), p 63
5. Ravi Matthai, 'Learning and organisational culture', in Matthai Ravi J (1993), p 120
6. Jain, Uma, p 19
7. S K Bhattacharyya, 'The early years of institutional development', IIMA (1993) Vol I, p 17
8. IIMA Alumnus (May 1984) p 5
9. Ibid., p 24

Chapter 6: Getting the 'Software' Right

1. Raghavachari M (1979), p 7-8
2. Drucker Peter F (1973), p 176-177
3. Kolavalli, Shashi (1995), p 7
4. S Subramanian, 'A bearable saint', IIMA Alumnus (May 1984), p 38
5. Matthai Ravi J (1989)
6. Ravi Matthai, 'The underlying basis of IIMA organisation', IIMA (1993), Vol I, p 1
7. Ibid., p 2
8. Ibid.
9. Ibid., p 43
10. Ibid., p 45
11. Ibid., p 44-46
12. This was told to the author by Bakul H Dholakia, former director of IIMA
13. S K Bhattacharyya, 'The early years of institutional development', IIMA (1993), p 16
14. Ravi Matthai, 'Pre-requisites of Institution building' in IIMA (1993), p 106

15. Ravi Matthai, 'Academic administration in institution building', Matthai, Ravi J and others (1977), p 72
16. Ibid.
17. Samuel Paul, 'Building on a solid foundation', IIMA (1993), p 75
18. Kolavalli, Shashi (1995), p 14
19. Ravi Matthai, 'Academic administration in institution building', Matthai, Ravi J and others (1977), p 70
20. Ibid., p 72
21. Roberts John (2004), *The Modern Firm*, p 172-176
22. Ravi Matthai, 'Academic administration in institution building', Matthai, Ravi J and others (1977), p 83-84
23. Ibid., p 82
24. Ibid., p 77
25. Interview with Ravi Matthai, 'Self-regulation: the key to institution-building, in Pareek, Udai (1981), p 157
26. Ravi Matthai, 'Academic administration in institution building', Matthai, Ravi J and others (1977), p 78
27. Interview with Ravi Matthai, 'Self-regulation: the key to institution-building, in Pareek, Udai (1981), p 161
28. Gary Hamel, 'Moonshots for Management', *Harvard Business Review*, February, 2009
29. Interview with Ravi Matthai, 'Self-regulation: the key to institution-building, in Pareek, Udai (1981), p 161
30. Jain, Uma, p 15
31. Ibid., p 18
32. Interview with Ravi Matthai, 'Self-regulation: the key to institution-building, in Pareek, Udai (1981), p 165
33. Ibid., p 166

Chapter 7: Light and Shadow

1. KS Venkitadri, 'The healing touch', IIMA Alumnus (May 1984), p 22

2. *Financial Times*, October 14, 2007
3. Autonomy and Accountability (2005), IIMA; Report of the Committee on Future Directions, 2008 (published in 2010), IIMA
4. CFD (2008), p 121
5. Ibid.
6. Report on financial requirements and other related issues of Indian Institutes of Management, V K Shunglu (April 2004), Para 1.17, p 7
7. Report of IIM Review Committee (25 September 2008), p 5
8. Singhania said, 'In a private Institution that I believe the IIM to be, all resources need to be evaluated on market forces of demand and supply.'
9. Eg on p 67 and p 98
10. P 187-188
11. CFD (2008), p 83
12. I G Patel, 'The IIMA in 1984 – at the crossroads', IIMA (1993), Vol II, p 29
13. N R Sheth, 'In pursuit of institutional excellence', IIMA (1993), Vol II, p 34
14. Kolavalli, Shashi (1995), p 14-15
15. Told to me by D Tripathi
16. However, P N Khandwalla, a former director of IIMA, believes that the board was quite active in his time.
17. Report of IIM Review Committee (25 September 2008), p 16
18. For obvious reasons, the colleague must remain anonymous
19. IIMA Alumnus (May 1984), p 51
20. Jain, Uma, p 17-18

Chapter 8: Building at the Grassroots

1. Matthai, Ravi J (1985). This chapter draws heavily on this book and a monography by T K Moullik, 'Action research on rural development for rural poor: the Dharmapur and Jawaja projects (IIMA, WP no 320, 1980).
2. Moullik (1980), p 3-4

3.   Matthai, Ravi J p 4
4.   Ibid., 9-10
5.   Ibid., p 11
6.   Matthai, Ravi J and others, Rural University: the Jawaja letters 1975-79, Indian Institute of Management Ahmedabad
7.   Matthai, Ravi J (1985), p 18
8.   T V Rao, A practising behavioural scientist, IIMA Alumnus (May 1984), p 21
9.   Matthai, Ravi J (1985), p 35
10. Ibid., p 76
11. Matthai, Ravi J p 85
12. Ibid., p 102
13. T V Rao, 'A practising behavioural scientist,' IIMA Alumnus (May 1984), p 20
14. S Subramanaiam, 'A bearable saint', IIMA Alumnus (May 1984), p 40

Chapter 9: Style and Substance

1.   V S Vyas, 'A natural leader', IIMA Alumnus (May 1984), p 12
2.   Told to me by D Tripathi
3.   C Ramdoss, 'Ravi Matthai my mentor' in IIMA (1993), p 55
4.   'A flashback', IIMA Alumnus (May 1984), p 5
5.   V S Vyas, 'A natural leader', IIMA Alumnus (May 1984), p 12
6.   'A flashback', IIMA Alumnus (May 1984) , p 4
7.   Told to the author by D Tripathi
8.   Told to the author by K S Venkitadri
9.   The 'little giant', N R Sheth, IIMA Alumnus (May 1984), p 17
10. A practising behavioural scientist, T V Rao, IIMA Alumnus (May 1984), p 18
11. S Subramaniam, 'A bearable saint', IIMA Alumnus (May 1984), p 39
12. Akbar Hydari, 'A Raja among men', IIMA Alumnus (May 1984), p 34
13. Yash Pal, 'Not a mere expert', IIMA Alumnus (May 1984), p 28
14. S Subramaniam, 'A bearable saint', IIMA Alumnus (May 1984), p 39

List of Acronyms

3-TP	3-tier programme.
AICTE	All India Council for Technical Education.
ASCI	Administrative Staff College of India.
ATIRA	Ahmedabad Textile Industry's Research Association.
CAG	Comptroller and Auditor General.
CAT	Common Admission Test.
CLRI	Central Leather Research Institute.
CFD	Committee on Future Directions, 2008.
CMA	Centre for Management of Agriculture.
FDEC	Faculty Development and Evaluation Committee.
FPM	Fellowship Programme in Management.
HBR	Harvard Business Review.
HBS	Harvard Business School.
IIM	Indian Institute of Management.
ITP	International Teachers Programme.
KLMDC	Kasturbhai Lalbhai Management Development Complex.
MOA	Memorandum of Association.
MFI	Microfinance institution.
NAFED	National Agricultural Cooperative Marketing Federation of India Ltd.
NID	National Institute of Design.
PGP	Post Graduate Programme.
PGP-ABM	Post Graduate Programme in Agricultural Business Management.
UCLA	University of California at Los Angeles.

Bibliography

Drucker, Peter F, Management: *Tasks, Responsibilities, Practices*, Allied Publishers Ltd. 1973

Haridasan V, *Dr John Matthai: a biography*, Sunil, 1986

Hill, Thomas M et al (1973), Institution Building in India: A Study of International Collaboration in Management Education, Harvard University, Graduate School of Business Administration, Division of Research

IIMA, Vol I, Institution Building: The IIMA Experience, 1993

IIMA Alumnus, May 1984

Jain, Uma, Lifestyle of an Institution Builder: Reflections of Ravi J Matthai, Academy of Human Resources Development, date not mentioned

Kolavalli, Shashi, Role of Culture in Institution Building and Sustenance: The case of India, IIMA Working Paper no: 1273, 1995

Matthai, Ravi J, Occasional Writings and Speeches, Centre for Educational Innovation, IIMA, 1989

Matthai, Ravi J et al, Institution-Building in Education and Research: From Stagnation to Self-Renewal, All India Management Association, New Delhi, 1993

Moullik, TK, Action Research on Rural development for rural poor: the Dharmapur and Jawaja projects, IIMA, Working Paper No. 320, 1980

Pareek, Udai, *Beyond Management: Essays on the Processes of Institution Building*, Oxford and IBH Publishing Co., 1981

Piramal, Gita, *Business Legends*, Penguin/Viking, 1998

Raghavachari, M, Institution Building for Management Education in India – IIMA Experience, IIMA Working Paper No 295, 1979

Roberts, John (2004), *The Modern Firm*, Oxford University Press

Shah, Amrita, *Vikram Sarabhai: A Life*, Penguin/Viking, 2007

Tandon, Prakash, *Return to Punjab*, Vikas Publishing House Pvt Ltd.,1980

Index

www.ingramcontent.com/pod-product-compliance
Lightning Source LLC
Chambersburg PA
CBHW030900070526
44654CB00022B/310/J